Grant Winner's Toolkit

Wiley Nonprofit Law, Finance, and Management Series

Grant Winner's Toolkit

Project Management and Evaluation

JAMES AARON QUICK
CHERYL CARTER NEW

John Wiley & Sons, Inc.
New York • Chichester • Weinheim • Brisbane • Singapore • Toronto

Published by John Wiley & Sons, Inc.
Published simultaneously in Canada.

This publication is designed to provide accurate and authoritative information in regard to the subject matter covered. It is sold with the understanding that the publisher is not engaged in rendering legal, accounting, or other professional services. If legal advice or other expert assistance is required, the services of a competent professional person should be sought.

Designations used by companies to distinguish their products are often claimed as trademarks. In all instances where John Wiley & Sons, Inc. is aware of a claim, the product names appear in initial capital or all capital letters. Readers, however, should contact the appropriate companies for more complete information regarding trademarks and registration.

Library of Congress Cataloging-in-Publication Data:

Quick, James Aaron.
  Grant winner's toolkit: project management and evaluation / James
A. Quick, Cheryl C. New.
    p.   cm. — (Wiley nonprofit law, finance, and management
series)
  ISBN 0-471-33245-3 (paper/disk : alk. paper)
  1. Fund raising—Management. 2. Fund raising—Evaluation.
3. Nonprofit organizations—Finance—Management. I. New, Cheryl
Carter. II. Title. III. Title: Grant winner's toolkit.
IV. Series.
HV41.2.Q54   1999
658.15′224—dc21   99-44838

Printed in the United States of America.

10 9 8 7 6 5 4 3 2 1

To all the people from whom I've learned bits and pieces of the grants picture, who taught me about writing, and who shaped my professional and personal philosophies. To Muriel Lederer, our agent, who believed in us. To Martha Cooley, our editor, who saw what we saw and valued it enough to take a chance on us. To my family, who gave me the foundation and belief in myself to overcome the challenges. Most of all to my partner, pal, mentor, supporter, my love, my husband, Jim.

—Cheryl Carter New

This book is dedicated to grandfather Quick who taught me the dignity of real work, to grandfather Thompson who taught me about crows, to Dad who taught me not to take life too seriously, to Mom who taught me how to be serious, to my three sisters who taught me to be proud, to my two children who taught me to be humble, and to my two grandchildren who are teaching me to be proud again.

—James Aaron Quick

Acknowledgments

I'd like to acknowledge all the hard work and support from Kathryn Flick, who has been with me and Polaris since the beginning. Also, thanks to Mark Talemal, who has worn her fingers to the bone doing data entry. Also, a big thanks to Robin, Rachael, Ken, and all the folks at Wiley who work so hard to wrestle the manuscripts from us, keep us on task, and get our books out the door and marketed! We appreciate the fact that we couldn't have done anything well without all of you.

—Cheryl Carter New

First, from the depths of my soul, I thank Francis Pate, for without her this book would not have been written. Dr. B. Rhett Myers deserves a major tip-o'-the-hat for listening to and agreeing with Francis. Next, I must extend heartfelt gratitude to the thousands of people who have allowed themselves to be hectored, cajoled, prodded, and poked at in the grants workshops that I have taught over the past ten years. And finally, I acknowledge the one person without whom I would not be who I am today—the person who is the center of my life, my friend, my companion, my soul mate, and my wife, Cheryl Carter New.

—James A. Quick

Contents

Contents

Chapter 15 Evaluation: How to Create an Evaluation Report   293

Advance Work: Developing a Manageable Project

## Chapter 1

Beginning at the Beginning: Organizing Your Grant-Seeking Effort

Great is the art of beginning, . . .
Henry Wadsworth Longfellow,
"Elegiac Verse"

Introduction

To begin at the beginning will take us back to grant seeking. Most problems that occur in funded grant projects are best solved before you get the grant, and even before you apply for the grant. This takes us back to what happens before the application or proposal process. If your first thought is that nothing happens before we begin creating the proposal or grant application package, then we've come to the cause of many funded grant project problems, as well as the cause of much wasted time and effort in fruitless pursuit of grants you never had a real chance of winning in the first place.

The simplest, most effective, cheapest, and easiest way to fix problems is to avoid them. The place to start avoiding grant project problems is with the organization of your grant-seeking effort, which is our first topic. The guiding principles behind the organization of a grant-seeking effort are:

- Grant seeking is a team sport.
- Members of the grant-seeking team need certain skills.
- The grant-seeking team needs resources with which to work.
- The grant-seeking team needs training and support.
- Grant seeking is a project itself and as such must have goals, guiding principles, and action plans.
- The grant-seeking effort needs a management plan.

The Problem of Time

Over the last decade, we have spoken with thousands of people who pursue grants. Invariably the number one problem these people have is lack of time. The complaint is that there simply isn't enough time in the day to do all the things that need to be done to be an effective grant seeker. Most grant seekers work a full-time job in addition to their grant seeking. Also, there is the essential time for family and personal interests. Where exactly does the time come from to do all that needs doing? It comes from the multiplying effect of using a group of people working together as a team.

The principle is simple. If one person can afford two hours a week to dedicate to grant seeking, then five people working together can dedicate ten hours a week. Two hours a week is not sufficient for effective grant seeking, but ten hours a week may be. The idea is as old as time itself. One Stone Age hunter did not have a chance against a woolly mammoth, but a group of hunters working together toward a common goal had such good odds that the mammoths were hunted to extinction thousands of years ago.

The Grant-Seeking Team

The first and most obvious question in creating a grant-seeking team is: Who should be on the team? Different ideas may leap to mind, such as that we need people that occupy certain positions within the organization on the team, or that we need people with certain skills on the team. Both of these are valid criteria, but not the most important. We have found, over years of grant seeking, that while skills do play an important role, important enough that we discuss skills at length in the next section, and while position within the organization also plays an important part, the most important criteria for selection for the grant-seeking team is the type of person—their attitude, their outlook, their personality.

Effective grant seekers are self-motivated. Everyone loves pats on the back and acknowledgment of a job well done, but a trait we have found common to good grant seekers is that they are motivated more by an inward drive than by outward rewards. This doesn't mean that we don't reward our grant-seeking team, but it means that the members of the team must be the type of people who find their reason for working hard within themselves, not from outside sources.

Effective grant seekers must have a well-developed sense of humor. You will run across much that is odd, strange, and even downright absurd in the pursuit of grants. The best way to handle the "Through the Looking Glass" world in which grant seekers often find themselves is to find the humor and laugh. Also, working together as a team is facilitated by the team members not taking themselves too seriously. The best way to deal with the inevitable stresses and strains put on the team is to laugh, and you need a sense of humor to laugh.

Effective grant seekers have a positive, can-do attitude and outlook. To use an old truism, good grant seekers must be able to recognize the difference between those things that they can change and those that they cannot. Work to change the things that can be changed, and leave alone the things that cannot be changed. Good grant seekers focus on what can be done, not what cannot be done. Good grant seekers look on the positive side of an issue, not the negative side. It isn't that a grant seeker must be a Pollyanna, but he or she must stay relentlessly positive. Change for the good is accomplished only by those with the positive attitude that change can be made real.

Effective grant seekers are innovative. They push the envelope. They see what could be. They are dreamers in the good sense of having the ability to visualize new and better ways to do what needs to be done. Albert Einstein once said that one of the definitions of insanity was to continue to do the same thing and expect different outcomes. Innovative thinkers see that principle clearly, and they want to do things differently.

Effective grant seekers are pushers. They are doers. They get things done. Instead of sitting on the sidelines complaining, the people who make good grant seekers pitch in and do something, even if sometimes what they do is wrong. They are people who would much rather occasionally ask for forgiveness than be constantly asking permission.

It has been said that the person who never fails has never tried very much. Effective grant seekers are people who are not afraid to fail. Good grant seekers fail a lot because they try a lot. To be good at grant seeking, a person must be able to handle failure. First, there are the great project ideas that no one else thinks are worth anything. Next there are all the proposals that get turned down. Good grant seekers fail half the time. That can be hard to handle, but effective grant seekers must be able to handle it.

Effective grant seekers draw their sense of worth from inside themselves, not from external sources. This is one of the main reasons that they can handle failure. The failure is not a reflection of the person, but, perhaps, a reflection of the idea or proposal. Or, the project simply may not have been selected because there were five great projects, the grant maker could only fund four, and yours was the fifth in line. No one failed, but it still may feel that way. This internalization of worth stands grant seekers in good stead, because they face much disappointment, and if they draw what they think of themselves only from external sources, they will be in trouble as grant seekers.

In many ways, effective grant seekers may be the "difficult" employees, the ones always running ahead and chafing at the bit, challenging authority, and questioning tradition. The same traits that can make an employee difficult can make that same person a great grant seeker.

So then, our first set of criteria for members of our grant-seeking team are that the members have the following character traits:

- Self-motivation
- A well-developed sense of humor
- A positive, can-do attitude
- An innovative mind
- A pusher–doer disposition
- Lack of fear of failure
- A sense of self-worth drawn from within themselves

Grant-Seeking Team Skills

Although certain character traits (such as those listed in Exhibit 1.1) are the most important criteria for persons chosen to be members of the grant-seeking team, they are not the only criteria. A group of skills are needed on the team also. Grant seeking involves many activities such as project design, funding source research, project development, proposal writing, proposal publishing, partnership building, marketing, public relations, and others. Successful accomplishment of all these activities takes a set of skills. These skills must be held by one or more members on the grant seeking team.

Someone, or perhaps several someones, must be effective and efficient researchers. In grant seeking, three general categories are researched: funding sources, verification of the problem, and justification of the solution. Finding funding sources is a research project in and of itself. Tracking down federal, foundation, corporate, and state and local funding sources takes time and skill. Specific and detailed directions for this research can be found in *Grantseeker's Toolkit: A Comprehensive Guide to Finding Funding,* the companion volume to this book. Research is necessary to prove that the problem you intend to solve actually exists locally, regionally, and nationally, dependent on the grantor's requirements. And, at times, it becomes necessary to cite research or examples that show that your proposed solution has a reasonable chance of success.

Grant-seeking team members need the skill of project development, which is the process of moving from a problem to a problem-solving action plan (project). Some of the subset of skills necessary to accomplish

EXHIBIT 1.1

Team Skills

Team Skills

- Research
- Problem Solving
- Facilitation
- Outlining
- Organization of Ideas
- Organization of Process
- Organization of Project
- Budget Development
- Leadership
- Coordination
- Tracking Information
- Tracking Resources
- Writing Clearly and Simply

this are facilitating group sessions, outlining, creating goals and objectives, and developing project budgets.

It is absolutely necessary that someone on the team possess the skill of leading a team. And we do mean a team, not a committee. The purpose of this group of people is to get work done as a team, not talk about getting work done, as a committee almost always does. The leading attributes of a good team leader are patience and diplomacy.

Someone on the team needs the skill of coordination of effort. This person must be able to keep multiple people working on multiple tasks on track and on time to complete all the tasks in the right order and at the right time to finalize the grant application by deadline. It's much like preparing a complicated dinner. One dish takes three times as long to prepare and cook as another, so different dishes must be started at different but appropriate times so all the dishes come out together to form a pleasing and appetizing complete meal.

Someone on the team needs the skill of administration. By this we mean the ability to organize and track information and resources. Keeping archives of past projects and proposals, setting up simple but effective means of tracking funding source research, project development, and proposal creation are part of the administrative responsibilities.

And last and least, someone on the team needs to be able to write simply and logically. Writing is the least of the skills, because almost anyone who can express themselves clearly and correctly in writing can write well enough to be effective at grant seeking. What is needed is the ability to write simple, short, direct, descriptive, well-organized sentences and paragraphs. In grant-seeking workshops we tell participants that grant proposals are NOT Faulkner's *Sound and Fury,* they are NOT Tolstoy's *War and Peace,* they ARE Hemingway's *Old Man and the Sea.*

You will find the Grant-Seeking Team Member Interview Checklist from Exhibit 1.2 on the disk that accompanies this book. The file name is 0102.doc. The form is to be printed and then filled in by hand during an interview or series of interviews with potential grant-seeking team members. Note that the personal attributes carry more weight than skills, and that personal attributes and skills carry more weight than experience. Experience with grant seeking is a tricky thing. Unfortunately, many people with experience have exactly the wrong type of experience. You want people who can learn the correct way, not people who may have to unlearn a series of bad habits.

Another list of skills exists. This list is of the skills that you absolutely, positively do not want team members to have. Here is a partial list of skills that are NOT needed on a grant-seeking team. In fact, if team members are truly good at the things on this list, your team's chances of success in grant seeking will go down in proportion as these skill levels go up.

- Facility with bureaucratic writing
- Ability to write very long, complicated sentences
- Encyclopedic knowledge of jargon
- Knowledge of every acronym known to civilization
- An eagle eye for why things cannot be done
- An unerring ability to find fault with other's ideas
- Skill at drawing inside the lines and thinking inside the box
- Contempt for consistency

If we cast these concepts positively rather than negatively they will come out like the following list. More importantly, your chances of success in grant seeking will go up as your skill level with these items goes up.

EXHIBIT 1.2

0102.DOC

Grant-Seeking Team Member Interview Checklist

Name _____   Date _____

Criteria	Evidence (given by interviewee)	Rating (Done after interview)						
		-3	-2	-1	0	+1	+2	+3
Personal								
Self-Motivation								
Sense of Humor								
Positive Attitude								
Innovative								
Mentally Flexible								
A Pusher, A Doer								
Unafraid of Failure								
Inner Self-Worth								
Skills								
Research								
Project Planning								
Leadership								
Coordination								
Administration								
Writing								
Experience								
Grant Seeking								
Proposal Writing								
	Totals							
	Grand Total							

- Do not use bureaucratic language.
- Keep sentences short and simple.
- Do not use jargon.
- Do not use acronyms.
- Stay positive.
- Be open to other's ideas.
- Think innovatively.
- Be relentlessly consistent throughout a proposal.

Grant-Seeking Team Resources

For the grant-seeking team to be successful, selecting the right kind of people as members and having those team members possess the right kinds of skills is not enough. The team must be given the resources they need to get the job done. By resources we mean tools. Artists cannot create their work without the proper tools. No carpenter can build a house without the proper tools. No doctor can treat patients without resources. No organization can feed the hungry or house the homeless without resources. No grant seeker can be successful without the tools of the trade. Most tools are concrete, actual things, but the first and perhaps most important tool is an abstract idea, that of time.

Time

Team members must be given time in which to accomplish their tasks. Grant funds are not free. An organization will expend substantial time, money, and effort in the successful pursuit of grants. Perhaps the simplest, but certainly the most important resource that can be made available to the grant-seeking team is time: time to plan, meet, research, develop projects, analyze application guidelines, write proposals, and perhaps most importantly, time to think. Providing all the other needed resources and then failing to provide the time necessary to do the job and to use those resources effectively is a formula for failure. Once a person has been selected to be a grant-seeking team member, the organization must set aside part of that person's regular work time as dedicated to grant seeking. This takes a commitment on the part of the leaders of the organization, and this commitment is essential to the consistent success of a grant-seeking effort.

Space

Office space with a physically separate and dedicated desk, filing cabinet, and chair must be provided to the grant-seeking team. This desk may not be shared by or with any other organizational purposes. It is not a person's desk that serves double duty. It is grant-seeking command central. It is a place where everything associated with grants comes tangibly together. The fact that this desk exists sends a powerful message throughout the organization that grant seeking is a priority, it has value, and it will be pursued with diligence and purpose in an ongoing, consistent, and aggressive way.

Resources

As in any other field, grant seeking has its own support literature. The grant-seeking team will need a selection of this literature: directories of funding sources, books about grant seeking, periodicals about grant seeking, and numerous other miscellaneous reference materials.

Computers

The grant-seeking team needs a computer. The uses to which the team will put this tool are many and varied. It will be used as a writing tool, a research tool, an accounting or budget tool, a communication tool, a drawing tool, a storing and sorting tool, and many other purposes large and small that it is impossible to foresee. Two issues of importance with respect to any computer purchase are compatibility and performance. The computer needs to be able to read files from other computers within the organization. The computer needs to be fast enough, with enough memory and disk storage, to handle all the jobs that it is expected to perform. This probably precludes the use of someone's castoff computer. The grant-seeking team needs and deserves a computer with the capacity at least equal to the one sitting on the administrator's or the executive secretary's desk. A high-speed modem is also essential. Much research can now be done on the Internet, and you will want to make your connection as fast as possible.

A computer doesn't work by itself. It needs software. The grant-seeking team requires at a minimum the following five types:

1. A word processing package for creating documents
2. A database package for handling large amounts of information, such as funding sources
3. A spreadsheet package for manipulating numbers, such as in budget development
4. A graphics package to create and handle any drawings, pictures, charts, graphs, or other graphics that are put into the documents
5. A communications package with access to the world of online knowledge, especially the Internet

Additional application packages that might come in handy are programs for graphing and charting, publishing, contact management, and time management.

Two additional computer capabilities that are essential for effective grant seeking today are access to the Internet and an easy-to-use e-mail system. In practical terms this means that your organization must find an Internet provider, preferably one that also provides powerful e-mail capabilities. One shortcoming to look for with regard to e-mail service is a size limit on the files that you can attach and send along with an e-mail message. Once you start using e-mail, you will find it the easiest way to exchange documents. A person in another location can work on a part of the proposal and send it to you via e-mail as an attached file, that is, if your provider allows it. We have found the commercial online service of America Online (AOL) to be exemplary with regard to its e-mail. AOL has simply the best and easiest to use e-mail capabilities available on the open market. Any discussion of the Internet and e-mail is not complete without bringing up the issue of speed of communication. Money spent up front to purchase the fastest modem possible will repay substantial long-term dividends. If you scrimp in any area, don't make it this one. Buy the fastest modem you can find, not that you can afford. Whatever it is, spend the money. You will thank yourself in very short order.

Other resources are needed, for example, access to and the ability to use commercial delivery services such as Federal Express, United Parcel Service (UPS), and Airborne Express. The grant-seeking team needs a telephone on the grants command central desk. Team members must be able to make long distance calls from this telephone. It would be best to have two telephone lines, one for the computer modem, the other for the telephone. The team must be able to send and receive regular postal service mail. The team needs access to photocopying and a facsimile (fax) machine and access to office supplies such as paper, pens, staples, file folders, and other such day-to-day supplies.

The grant-seeking team needs a supply and material budget of its own from which it can purchase items that may be needed by the team but that are unavailable from normal organizational supply channels. The grant-seeking team needs a travel budget. Grantors hold meetings at which the grant maker explains how to apply for specific programs. These meetings are often known by the name "bidder's conference" even though there is no bidding involved in the grant application process. The origin of the name goes back to government contracts on which businesses and individuals did bid. Attendance at this type of meeting can greatly benefit an applicant, but you need a travel budget to allow attendance at such meetings.

In short, the grant-seeking team needs the same resources that any other important part of an organization receives. If an organization is serious and sincere about seeking grants, then similar time and material resources must be committed to the grant-seeking team as are given to such organizationally important functions as administration, marketing, sales, public relations, advertising, professional development, research, and development. The checklist found in Exhibit 1.3 (0103.doc) lists the resources needed for the grants team.

Grant-Seeking Team: A Vertical Slice

One important aspect of the makeup of the grant-seeking team is that all levels of the organization must be represented. The team should not consist of only those people who will do the work of grant seeking. The team needs membership from the highest levels possible of the organization. Two critical reasons exist for creating this vertical slice of an organization. One is to show, in a concrete organizational way, the commitment of the leadership of the organization to the grant-seeking effort. The other is so people in positions of authority and management come to understand the demands of grant seeking, and are therefore willing to commit the organization's time, money, and effort needed for success.

Once the grant-seeking team is established, equipped, and trained, it will begin to involve personnel from all parts and all levels of an organization. These other people must be involved in the overall grant-seeking effort. The details of this process are explained in Chapter 2, but for now let it suffice to say that even the multimember grant-seeking team cannot do the job alone. The team will draw on the knowledge, experience, and time of other members of the organization. To make this very important process work, the entire organization needs to know clearly and precisely that grant seeking is an important organizational priority and that all personnel are expected to participate. Without commitment from the highest levels, the grant-seeking team can expect to meet resistance to the idea that people other than team members are responsible for grant seeking.

It is only natural for the average person in an organization to feel that it is no longer his or her job to get involved in grant seeking once a grant-seeking team is established. Only direction from the highest levels can make it clear that all personnel are to be involved. By having high-ranking persons as members of the grant-seeking team, your organization's leaders will know what is needed and can offer the institutional support the grant-seeking team needs to be successful.

EXHIBIT 1.3

0103.DOC

Grant-Seeking Team Resources Checklist

Literature

Place Check	Item	Comment
	Catalog of Federal Domestic Assistance (CFDA)	Federal funding source research
		For Internet access, link from website URL below
	Federal Register	
	Foundation directories	Foundation Center publications
	Grantseeker's Toolkit	A John Wiley and Sons Publication
	Grant Seeker's Desk Reference	A Polaris Publication
	Area corporate directory	Corporate funding source research
	Assoc. newsletters	Keeping up
	\<polarisgrantscentral.net\>	Website with links to many, many grants resources
	Note: the *Grant Seeker's Desk Reference* listed above contains an extensive listing of valuable grant-seeking literature and website uniform resource locators (URLs).	

Budget

Place Check	Item	Comment
	Travel	To bidder's conferences and other conferences
	Subscriptions	Newsletter, magazines, periodicals
	Consultants	For training and technical support
	Temp help	Secretarial or administrative
	Long distance phone calls	To grantors and potential grantors
	Copying	For large quantities and backup
	Printing	

EXHIBIT 1.3 *(Continued)*

Technology

Place Check	Item	Comment
	Telephone	Long distance capable
	Fax	Could be shared with organization's
	Access to Internet	Highest speed possible
	Two phone lines	One for voice, one for modem
	Copy machine	Could be shared with organization's
	E-mail accounts	One for each team member
	Computer	Must be compatible with other computers in organization
	Fast processor	The faster the better
	Gigabyte hard drive	Several gigabytes actually
	CD-ROM Drive	High speed
	High-speed modem	As fast as possible
	High-capacity flex	This should probably be a removable but not really flex drive
	Large monitor	It would be good if you could see an entire page at once

Software

Place Check	Item	Comment
	Word processor	Compatible with others in organization
	Database	For saving, organizing, and sorting information
	Spread sheet	Compute costs for budget
	Graphics	Charts, time lines, organizational charts, drawings
	Communications	E-mail and Internet
	Graphing and charting	Create charts and graphs easily
	Publishing	Not absolutely necessary, but perhaps useful for creating docs
	Contact management	Address books, manage your contact list
	Time management	Manage time, plan proposal work

EXHIBIT 1.3 *(Continued)*

Intangibles

Place Check	Item	Comment
	Authority	Provided by visible and vocal backing and atten-
	Cooperation	tion from the highest level of the organization
	Time	Definite, scheduled, regular part of job
	Motivation	

General Office

Place Check	Item	Comment
	Desk	
	Filing Cabinet	
	Desk chair	Dedicated, quiet work space, for use only by grant-seeking team, not in a hallway or thoroughfare.
	Side chair	
	Book shelf	
	Heavy duty stapler	Ability to staple up to 100 pages
	Binding system	GBC (General Binding Company), or Velo, or glue-based

Grant-Seeking Team Training

Now, the best type of people to be team members are selected, the needed skills are present among the team members, and the necessary resources have been provided, but some organizations may take an extra step. The chances are that the team, while well-intentioned and highly motivated, lacks experience in grant seeking. An additional level of support is that the team can be trained and given support until it reaches the level of competence that would otherwise be gained through years of experience.

The basic concept is to send the team away, somewhere off site, to receive grant-seeking training. That the training is away from the office, school, hospital, or site in which the organization does its work is very important. Training conducted at a work site is always interrupted by the everyday exigencies of the job. But, if the team is not there, if they are in another city or state, the organization will get along without their presence for two or three days. And most importantly, the team will be undisturbed while learning a very complex, but not terribly difficult subject. The site could be as simple as a meeting room in a local hotel or convention complex, or a meeting room at the local library—any place that is inconvenient and difficult for fellow staff members to interrupt.

Be sure to include all members of the grant-seeking team in training, including people from all levels of the organization. It is important that the people in administrative or leadership positions in your organization take part in the training.

It is important to get people in leadership positions to training sessions because they then can understand the intricacies of the process, how much must be done, how many tasks and activities must be accomplished. Once they understand this, they will be much more likely to provide the concrete support for the grant-seeking effort that it needs. It is easy for a leader to give verbal support and fail to give the support of time, personnel, and resources to make the effort successful. Once a leader understands what is involved, it is more likely that the leader will also follow up with material and concrete support.

The best method of training is to train first in the basics, then have the team spend several months in actual grant seeking, applying what they learned. After several months have passed, during which the team must have submitted several proposals, many organizations find it useful to train in advanced grant seeking. This advanced level of training is enhanced tremendously by the intervening months of practice and experience. The participants now have a wealth of real, not hypothetical, questions to which they want answers. Again, after the training, the team goes back to work, submitting proposals and applying what it has learned.

After another few months have passed, during which several more proposals are submitted, the team gets another round of training. This training should be on special topics such as project evaluation, project budgets, continuation strategies, publishing, and other detailed and specific subjects. Again, the intervening experience of team members will sharpen their appreciation of the training and will cause them to gain a great deal more from the training than if it was provided all at once.

There are several places to look for this training. In almost every state an organization exists that supports the nonprofit sector in that state. One of the functions of such an organization is to provide professional development for the staff of nonprofits, and one of the usual offerings in that professional development is grant seeking, usually incorrectly called "grant writing." Also, in many states, the foundations in the state have banded together and formed an association that works to make life easier for the foundations. One task of such an association is to help applicants do a better job with their proposals. They do this through training sessions. Check with other grant seekers and the Internet for training resources.

Wise Guy

"I've got a really, really bad feeling about where this is all headed. I see more meetings, more paper work, more expense, more hassle. I'll just whip up a proposal when the time comes and dispense with all this organizational mumbo-jumbo nonsense, thank you very but not much."

Wise Lady

"Certainly that's a choice you can make. Most likely you'll fail because the competition is great and others won't have your attitude. But let's assume you succeed, once, and mostly by accident. Without putting in the appropriate time and consideration, you are very likely to have done a poor job with the project development. You might have committed your organization to activities it can't handle. You might even have committed certain people in your organization to tasks they don't have time to perform. You assuredly didn't take time to think things through. So, you got the award, but the 'project' can't succeed. Oops! No more funds from that grant maker. In fact, no more funds from any grant maker that finds out. Do you want to be a real grants manager or not? It's not a game."

Grant-Seeking Team Support

Along the way, the team should be provided with support in the form of a consultant's time. This consultant is a person with extensive, successful experience in grant seeking of the type that your organization is doing and in all aspects of grant seeking, not just proposal writing. It is much more important that the consultant be adept at all the aspects of project development and funding source research than it is that the consultant can write proposals. The topic of consultants brings up several important considerations. How do we find a good consultant? What determines whether a consultant is good? How does a consultant get paid and how much? What is the best way to use a consultant effectively? What should a consultant's involvement be and how should it change over time?

The best way to find a good consultant is the same way you most effectively find out about just about anything—word of mouth. Yes, you can scan the pages of the periodicals of the grant-seeking world. These periodicals contain advertisements, usually of the classified sort, in which consultants give you the opportunity to hire them. Yes, you can jump on the Internet and probably find hundreds if not thousands of people who will be glad to serve as your grant-seeking consultant. And yes, you can find an honest, experienced, conscientious, hard-working consultant using these methods, but our experience is that you will most likely find a person who has had success with one or two grant proposals and has decided to turn this success into a new career. Another caveat is that many grant consultants come from higher education, from academia. This is all well and good if your organization is higher education. But, if you are a museum, a K–12 school (public or private), a hospital, a rape crises center, a police department, a county, a city, or a United Way, the experience of the successful grant seeker from higher education may not transfer to your organization's grant seeking.

In short, the best way to find your consultant is to ask people you trust for their suggestions. This keeps it personal. Your friend will not want to stick you with a consultant who they know to be flawed. After all, it may adversely affect the relation between the two of you. Yes, you can still wind up with a dud, but the chances are less than if you pick a name out of a hat.

What determines whether a consultant is good comprises several things, including the answers to some questions. For example, one quick way to understand what a consultant has on his or her mind is to ask them how they want to be paid. The only completely ethical method is by the hour or by the job. Your potential consultant should be willing to work for an hourly rate. And the consultant should also be willing to cost out a job and give you a firm price for the work. Unless you change the scope of work in mid-project, this projected cost should not be exceeded.

A common, but unethical and indeed in some cases illegal, method for being paid that some consultants request is a percentage of grants won. It doesn't take much thought to realize that this isn't ethical. The budget of a project is for the expenses incurred during the running of the project, a project that does not start until the grant is awarded. The project budget is not for expenses incurred requesting the grant. From another angle, would you be willing to enter into the requested grant budget a line item called "grant-seeking consultant" or "proposal writer?" I suspect not. If not, then from where within the budget does the money come that you will pay the consultant? It can only come from funds meant for something else. This means that you misled the grantor when you submitted your budget. This is the biggest no-no in grant seeking. Never, under any circumstances, lie to a grantor.

There is one circumstance where paying a percentage is at least legal if not ethical. That is when you pay the percentage out of the operating funds of your organization, not from the grant. Again, it doesn't take much thought to realize that the organization probably doesn't have that kind of cash to spend. The ultimate intention of an organization is usually to replace the money spent on a consultant or writer with funds from the grant. This only makes the ethical problem once removed, but the same ethical problem nevertheless.

Another dodge by consultants is to place themselves in the grant-funded project as a well-paid consultant on some aspect of the project such as curriculum development, or research consultant, or some other equally nebulous position. If the consulting is actually performed and is truly necessary to the success of the project, then this may be just fine. If, however, the consultant position within the project is a cover-up for funneling money to the consultant, it is unethical and it may be illegal.

The one way of paying a consultant that is both legal and ethical is by the hour or by the job. A mutual agreement on rates must be obtained up front and preferably in writing. At the very least, insist that before beginning any work the consultant submit to you, in writing, over a signature, a firm commitment of an actual dollar amount that the job will cost. If the consultant cannot or will not submit such a bid, you are correct in thinking that either he or she does not have the experience to know what is involved in the job or does not want to be pinned down to an amount. Either way, you need a different consultant.

Let's assume that we have found an experienced, ethical, and willing consultant. What do we look for next? The ultimate job of the best consultants is to work themselves out of a job. Consultants should be teaching as they go along. Their job is guidance in the process, to provide support and technical assistance. Over time, the consultant will have transferred much of his knowledge to members of your organization. What this means is that at the beginning of involvement with a consultant, the involvement will be large. The consultant will do much of the work, will spend many hours working with your staff and on your projects and proposals. As time goes by, say within a year to 18 months, depending on how hard your people work at learning, the role of the consultant should shift to answering questions from time to time and taking on particularly difficult assignments that the grant-seeking team doesn't have the time or experience to handle. In several years, you will be calling on the consultant only when something completely new comes up or when you simply don't have the time to do something yourself. The consultant will have worked him- or herself out of a job. But, word of mouth will have opened up other jobs. Organizations that need a consultant will have talked to you, and you will have told them about the person who has meant so much to your success. This process is why good and ethical consultants charge fair and clear rates for what they actually do by the hour or by the job and work themselves out of a job. These consultants never want for work, and this is the consultant you want working for you.

Conclusion

Your organization has created a grant-seeking team. The team is made up of the right type of people with the right set of skills. Your organization is committed to the grant-seeking process from the very top. Resources of time, equipment, space, and material have been committed. The team is being trained and supported by a good consultant. This is a lot, but it's not enough.

The team needs direction. Effort without direction leads nowhere. If you don't care where you're going then any road will get you there. Grant seeking is a very real and very complex project that, like any project, needs direction and management. Chapter 2 discusses that direction and management.

Getting the Direction Right: Managing Your Grant-Seeking Effort

Begin at the beginning . . . and go on till you
come to the end; then stop.

Lewis Carroll, *Alice in Wonderland*

Introduction

Now your grant team is in place. It is made up of the right kinds of people with the right kinds of skills. The team has office space, equipment, materials, and supplies. The team is being given support from the highest level in your organization. It has time to pursue grants. It is ready to start. But, there is a hesitation. You know that you want the team to get grants. What you, perhaps, don't know, is how it starts. What does it do next? What are its first steps? What exactly does the grant team do? Yes, it seeks grants, but what does that mean in terms of concrete activities?

Perhaps even more important than what the grant team does is the direction in which the team should be headed and how that direction relates to your organization. Grant seeking is a project all its own and needs the organization and direction that you would apply to any project. A plan for making decisions about what grants to pursue needs to be in place. Team members need training and motivating. From time to time, the team will need to be augmented with additional specialized help. Your organization may even decide to hire a full-time grant seeker. These topics are discussed in this chapter.

What the Team Does

The grant team has a very definite set of tasks that needs to be accomplished in a very definite order. First the team must facilitate problem identification. That is, it must identify and clearly state all the problems that face your organization. Next, the team must facilitate project design. First, you identify and state a problem, a problem that affects a population that your organization serves. Next you describe the solution to the problem. We call these two steps together project design.

After you have your project design, your solution to the problem, you need a funding source. Therefore, the next step for the grant team is to research a funding source or sources for the new project. Once you have settled on a funding source, the project needs to be fully developed. Once you get the application guidelines or request for proposal from the potential grantor, you need to carefully analyze it, so you know how to put together the proposal. And finally, you need to create the proposal, which is, after all, simply a set of answers to three basic types of questions: questions about your organization, questions about your problem, and questions about your solution (your project). This then is the basic set of tasks that your grant-seeking team will perform. It should be obvious that this set of tasks is done not just once, but again and again. The process is repeated till all the problems that your organization wants to attack are defined and solutions developed. The process must be constant and ongoing. A few grant makers (smaller foundations) don't have written proposal guidelines, but even for them, a plan for the proposal must be developed. You still need to plan and organize what you are going to say and how you are going to say it.

This simple plan of action outlined in the previous two paragraphs is important enough to repeat in another form. It is, after all, the basic framework, the strategic view, of all grant seeking. Your success or failure as a grant seeker is largely determined by how well you perform the tasks associated with each of these major parts of the process. Exhibit 2.1 provides an overview of the grant-seeking process. These are also the steps that your grant team will be accomplishing, or perhaps facilitating.

There is one more important task that the grant team must perform, and that is to train the entire staff of the organization in the fundamentals of grant seeking. Although you have created a grant team to overcome the problem of too much work and too little time, there are things that the grant team simply cannot, or more correctly should not, do. These are things that members of the organization must do. We'll explain these things later in the next few pages.

It simply cannot be stressed too much that the grant team MUST NOT do all the work. Perhaps when we spent the first chapter detailing creating a grant team, you thought that the purpose of the team was to do all the work of grant-seeking. No, the purpose of the grant team is to lead the grant seeking effort. To be truly successful at grants, and this includes grant seeking and grant management, an organization must

EXHIBIT 2.1

The Grant-Seeking Process

Identify Problem

↓

Design Project

↓

Research Funding Source

↓

Develop Project

↓

Analyze Application Guidelines

↓

Create Proposal

↓

Repeat as Often as Necessary

actively involve all its personnel, not just a select few. A few must lead, but the organization as a whole must contribute, must participate, must be integrally involved in all aspects of grant seeking and grant management.

Facilitate Problem Identification

Formulation of a problem is far more essential than its solution.

Albert Einstein

The operative word is "facilitate." The grant team must absolutely not define the problems for the organization by itself. The problems must come from the grass roots. They must come from the minds and hearts of the people in the organization who are doing the work. Yes, members of the grant team probably know what the problems are, but they must not presume to speak for the entire organization. If the grant team decides to identify the organization's problems without consulting with all the other people in the organization, it will open itself up for one of the stranger things that happens within the grant business.

Let's set up a scenario. Your grant team identifies a problem. The team designs and develops a project and finds a funding source. It applies to the funding source and gets money, a lot of money, let's say, half a million dollars. When the team proudly presents the project to the people who have the responsibility of running the project, the response of the recipients of half a million dollars will amaze the team. The team expects gratitude. After all, it did all the work. It brought in half a million dollars. Shouldn't everyone in the organization be just as happy as can be? Well, they won't be. In fact, the people who now have the responsibility for spending the half a million dollars will most likely resent what the team has done. Their comments will go something like this: "This isn't what we wanted to do." "We don't have time to do all this extra work." "Why didn't you ask us what we wanted to do?" "This is not at all the approach we want to take." "We don't need that piece of equipment." "What we need is a . . . ;" and on and on.

You get the idea. The grant team will expect gratitude. It will get exactly the opposite. Everyone will be upset. The organization team members who now must implement a project in which they do not believe are upset. The grant team is upset, because their fellow workers in the organization have proved themselves to be terrible ingrates—at least that is how it seems from the viewpoint of the grant team. All this can and must be avoided. The solution is simple: Ask everyone in the organization to participate in identifying the problems and setting priorities. This is done through facilitated planning sessions. The need for involvement and for the organization to make decisions about how it will operate is also why you can't hire a consultant and say, "Get us grants; be our grants department." It won't work.

Facilitate Project Design

The same basic argument applies to the next step in the grant-seeking process, project design. Project design is the process in which we move from an identified problem to a project idea. Project development, similar sounding to project design but done later in the overall system, is the process of fleshing out the project design into a fully developed project about which we can now write a proposal. This is, of course, the heart of successful grant seeking—creating a project that is a realistic solution to a significant problem. The rest becomes relatively easy once you have a project. Nothing is more important than the project. It is basic to everything else you do in grant seeking.

The project is also what your organization will actually be doing once it gets the grant money. For this reason, you must gain buy-in within your organization. The people who will be responsible for actually implementing the project must be involved in creating it. If they are not involved in creating the project and if they do not have ownership of the project, then you will have the same problems we discussed in the previous section. When you show up with a grant, your people will not be grateful and they will resent the extra work you have imposed on them. The only way to avoid this trap is to involve them in the project design and development.

It is the responsibility of you, the manager, and the grant team to lead, to facilitate, this process. You must bring everyone along, so they feel that the project belongs to them. It must be their solution. This way, when the grant shows up, they will implement the project willingly. After all, it was their idea. You and your team don't do all the work. If you do, you will only be resented as outsiders imposing solutions on others. You overcome this by constantly getting substantive input from everyone in your organization. Concretely this means constant communication.

Facilitated planning sessions are necessary. At its simplest this is a process in which you, or a facilitator you bring in from outside your organization, leads your group through project design and through the stage in project development of setting goals and objectives for the proposed project. Once the goals and objectives are set, the usefulness of meeting in a group is probably over. At this point you will need to, as a grant team, flesh out the project, giving constant feedback to the members of your organization so they can give you feedback as the development moves along.

Create the Hit List

When your organization is serious about grant seeking and makes grant seeking a process, not an event, the facilitated problem identification process will probably identify a number of problems that your organization wants to attack. You will design a project as a solution to each of those problems. The output or product of the project design process is a document called a *project profile*. This document should be published smartly, kept to a two-page limit, and use lots of headings and lists rather than blocks of text. The following questions must be answered in a project profile. Forms to help with creation of project profiles can be found on the disk that accompanies the first book in this series, *Grantseeker's Toolkit: A Comprehensive Guide to Finding Funding*.

- What is the problem?
- What are the causes of the problem?
- What is the synopsis of the project?
- How long will it take to get the project up and running?
- How much money will it take to get the project up and running?
- What other organizations will it make sense to partner with to implement the project?

- What resources will it take to accomplish the project?
  - Personnel
  - Equipment
  - Materials and Supplies
  - Training
  - Travel
  - Services

Once you have created a number of project profiles, you have what we call a hit list. The information contained in this collection of project profiles is the data on which you base all of your funding source research. The set of project profiles in the hit list gives you the material to make the match between your organization and its projects and a grantor's agenda and needs. These documents, or more accurately the information that they contain, enable you to perform effective, time efficient funding source research.

Having a set of project profiles also solves one of the eternal problems of grant seekers. Suppose you are sitting at your desk, working away, when in walks your boss with purposeful stride. She dramatically and loudly whacks down on your desk a request for proposal (RFP) and announces, "Apply to this." Normally, as her back recedes out the door, you quietly panic as you see your carefully crafted schedule totally disrupted for the next 3 weeks. But, you have already identified all the priority problems of your organization and created projects for their solution. You simply pull down your hit list and match up the project to the RFP. You are way ahead of the game, because the "game" is totally predictable.

Funding Source Research

Research to find funding sources can start as soon as you have a project design. In our experience, funding source research takes up about one-fourth of a grant seeker's time, making it one of the more time-consuming aspects of grant seeking. It is also probably the simplest part of the process. This research is beyond the scope of this book. If you want detailed directions, please see *Grantseeker's Toolkit*. Fully one-third of that book is dedicated to step-by-step processes for finding federal, foundation, corporate, state, and local funding sources.

Project Development

Project development is partly facilitated and partly done by team members. We strongly suggest that you facilitate planning sessions at which you get the direction that the project should take from the people who have the eventual responsibility for implementing it. In concrete terms, this involves pulling out of them basic project organization to the level of goals and objectives. Team members can then continue with full project development. Be careful to continually check back with the appropriate folks about what the team is planning for its project. Remember, the project is the organization's. You and your team are simply the tool or conduit by which the organization will obtain the grant to fund its project to solve its problem. You and your team exist to enable others. You make it happen, but ownership belongs with the folks who implement the project.

Analyze Grantor's Application Guidelines

So far we have identified problems, designed projects to solve those problems, and found funding sources to which to apply for grants to fund implementation of the projects. A task that falls somewhere between identifying a funding source and creating a proposal is analysis of the grantor's application guidelines or RFP. In principle, analyzing an RFP is simple. You need to organize four types of information from the grantor's document(s): hot buttons, proposal content, publishing requirements, and questions.

By "hot buttons" we mean sales points, things that "turn on" the grantor, things about which the grantor is passionate. In our grant-seeking workshops, Cheryl often says that hot buttons are windows into the mind of the grantor. This is as good a short definition as you are likely to get. Another way to look at hot buttons is that they are often proposal killers. That is, if you fail to fully address a hot button, you will probably also fail to get funding. Something as important as a hot button is usually important enough to a grantor to be a make-or-break situation. Because of this importance, we make a separate list of hot buttons so that we can later check our proposal to see that every one has been pushed.

Proposal content is just that, a content outline of the proposal and it answers the following questions: What parts does the grantor require that you put in your proposal? What are these parts named? In what order must these parts occur? What must be contained in these parts, or what questions must be answered? Keep in mind that we are discussing the entire proposal here. Many grant seekers make the mistake of thinking of the proposal narrative as the proposal itself. It is not. The narrative is a part of a proposal. A proposal contains such things as forms, key personnel biographical sketches, information about your organization, letters of support, time lines, the project budget, the budget narrative, an appendix, and the narrative. Don't make the mistake of thinking of the narrative as the proposal.

Publishing requirements are such things as page limitations, word count limitations, page numbering, headers and footers, and numbers of copies necessary. We give publishing special importance because grantors tell us that fully 60 percent of applicants do not follow directions when applying for a grant, especially the publishing directions. It seems that applicants consider these directions suggestions rather than commandments. They are not suggestions. Grantors receive many applications for grant funds. It is not necessary for them to overlook your failure to follow directions. Plenty of other organizations do follow directions, and their proposal in which they followed directions will be considered over yours when you do not follow directions. The publishing requirement outline or list makes it perfectly clear how the proposal must be published. It is a simple, but important step.

As you compile hot buttons, the proposal content outline, and the publishing requirements, several questions will inevitably occur to you. Write them down. Make a list of questions. Do it as you go. Do not expect to remember all your questions. The whole point of this careful and written analysis of an RFP is so that you are not required to remember things. You will have all the information at your fingertips, organized once and for all. Once you have finished the analysis, call the grantor and ask your questions. The answers to the questions then go in their appropriate places in your list of hot buttons, your proposal content outline, or your publishing requirements. Now you are ready to create the proposal.

Create the Proposal

You might note that we use "create" a proposal, not "write" a proposal. The reason is simple. Usually, large parts of a proposal are not written at all. An example is the budget. Forms are something else that must be done, but filling out forms is not writing. Often putting together appendix material is not a writing job, but rather a compiling job. And then there is the publishing itself, which takes more time than you think, is critical to the success of your proposal, and has nothing to do with writing.

The two main parts of a proposal that are writing jobs are the narrative and the budget justification, along with perhaps an abstract. The size of your organization determines whether the grant team writes proposal narratives. For example, if you are on the grant team for a school district with 20 schools, it will be impossible for you to write all the proposals that these 20 schools can generate. In a case such as this, you must get the members of your organization to write the initial draft of the proposal. The grant team can then rewrite, edit, and shape the proposal. This point about not writing the initial draft is an important one. It goes mostly to the issue of time. If you want to send out a steady stream of grant proposals and you have a large organization for which you are grant seeking, you must get members of the organization integrally involved. This also helps to create buy-in and eliminate the problem of solutions imposed from "above" and the attendant problems that causes. Although proposal creation is beyond the scope of this book, we have included a proposal creation checklist on the disk (0202.doc) that can be seen in Exhibit 2.2.

EXHIBIT 2.2

Proposal Creation Checklist

Proposed Project _____

Funder _____

Note: For additional and detailed directions for each task, refer also to the *Grantseeker's Toolkit: A Comprehensive Guide to Finding Funding,* ISBN 0-471-19303-8, John Wiley & Sons, Inc., publishers, New/Quick authors.

Place Check	Planned Date	Actual Date	Task
			All key grants team members are trained in the fundamentals of grant seeking.
			All organizational staff are trained in the basics of grant seeking.
			A matching funder has been targeted (refer to the Funder Matching Worksheet).
			The guidelines from the targeted funder have been received.
			The necessary research on the funder has been completed.
			A thorough outline of the grantor's requirements for the proposal content is written.
			A thorough outline of the grantor's requirements for publishing the proposal has been written.
			A thorough outline of the potential sales points (hot buttons) has been written based on information about the funder gained from your research and from the RFP or application guidelines.
			All outlines have been reviewed and revised by a second person.
			Research to support your problem statement has been completed. (Refer to *Grantseeker's Toolkit,* Chapter 3: Designing the Project)
			Research to support your proposed methodology (approach) has been completed.
			Research to support the expected results on successful completion of your project has been completed.
			Biographical sketches of key personnel have been written.
			Appropriate letters of support have been acquired.
			Partnership arrangements have been made and documentation of involvement of partners has been acquired.

EXHIBIT 2.2 *(Continued)*

Place Check	Planned Date	Actual Date	Task
			Supplementary documentation required by the funder has been obtained (tax status letter, annual report, annual budget summary, etc.).
			The budget for the entire project has been developed including the summary figures as well as a complete itemization.
			There is a list of the items in the overall budget that are being requested from the funder, the items being supplied by your organization, and what items are being supplied by other organizations.
			The fact that all budget items are linked directly to the goals and objectives of the proposed project has been verified independently.
			The project is thoroughly developed.
			The problem statement is written.
			The project approach is written.
			Goals and objectives are written.
			The dissemination plan is written.
			The evaluation plan is written.
			The continuation plan is written.
			The management plan is written.
			Time lines are drawn.
			Key personnel biographical sketches are written.
			The budget is written.
			The budget justification is written.
			The introduction is written.
			The project summary is written.
			The executive summary is written.
			The appendix is put together.
			The title page is created.
			The cover letter is written.
			Drafts of all sections of the proposal have been reviewed for content.
			According to content review, revisions have been made.

EXHIBIT 2.2 *(Continued)*

Place Check	Planned Date	Actual Date	Task
			The proposal is formatted according to the guidelines set by the funder.
			A draft of the entire proposal is proofed for grammar, spelling, format, and "look" by at least two people.
			Corrections have been made to the proposal based on proofing suggestions.
			All forms have been completed and appropriate signature(s) obtained.
			The cover letter is written and appropriate signature(s) obtained.
			A master original of the entire proposal is printed, forms have been integrated into the proposal in appropriate places, and supplementary material included.
			The master original is checked against the grantor's requirements.
			A table of contents is developed and proofed.
			The correct number of copies of the original are made as required by the funder.
			The correct number of copies of the original are made as required by your organization and the partners.
			Each copy has been checked and is in comparable condition and exact order of the original.
			Copies for the funder are bound or not as required by the funder.
			The original is labeled as being the original.
			The copies are labeled as being copies.
			The original and copies are packaged so they are maintained in excellent condition and order.
			The original and required copies are boxed and the box is labeled appropriately to meet the delivery vendor's specifications and the grantor's specifications.
			The shipping address has been checked and double-checked.
			The box containing the proposal is shipped in time so that if the delivery is not made by the deadline, there is an opportunity to send a second box containing the required copies.

Project Directors

An important point needs to be made about who will serve as director of the projects for which the grant team is obtaining funding. Keep this in mind: If members of the grant team are selected as Project Directors, it won't take too long before they will be so loaded with project work that they will be unable to continue as a grant seeker. This may be what a team member wants. If so, fine, but remember that it is not necessary for the grant seeker to be the Project Director. That this happens so often comes, we believe, from the tendency in higher education for staff to seek grants for their own research. They are both grant seeker and Project Director. In an organization, however, these two positions are not necessarily filled by the same person.

Developing a Grant-Seeking Mission

Grant seeking is a project, and like any project, to be successful it needs direction and purpose. That direction and purpose comes from a set of clearly stated guiding principles, goals, and action plans. Therefore, your grant team must have in writing, clear statements of how it intends to conduct itself (guiding principles), what it is trying to accomplish (goals), and how it will get where it's going (action plans).

Often, an organization's guiding principles are thrashed out by the organization as a whole, but this situation is different. Much of what guides a grant team is based on knowledge of grant seeking that the average organization member probably does not possess. It is probably best if the team itself establishes the guiding principles of the grant team. The entire membership of the grant team should be assembled at this time. Remember that the total membership of the grant team includes people from the highest levels of leadership in your organization. These leaders most likely will not participate in the day-to-day operation of the team, but when the team discusses and decides issues such as guiding principles, it makes sense for the leaders to sit in. The following paragraphs contain some possible guiding principles. Your organization must create its own, but these may give you a few ideas of the direction in which to go.

Focus on the Organization's Mission

All projects for which you pursue grant funds must align with the mission and goals of the organization. It is relatively easy to let the prospect of big bucks lure you away from the primary purpose of your organization. A prize of a million dollars a year for five years from a federal source can turn your head if you don't keep it firmly in mind that the most important thing for your organization is to stay true to its mission. All projects and all grant seeking must be subservient to the stated mission and goals of your organization. If a proposed project doesn't fit, then discard it. If a possible funding source would change the direction in which your organization is headed, then don't apply. We have seen too many organizations chase grants and catch them, and only a few years down the road realize that they are no longer fulfilling their original mandate. An organization can lose its purpose and sometimes even its soul in the pursuit of dollars. Stay focused on what you do and who you are.

Maintain Ethical Standards

Always act or decline to act according to the highest ethical standards. This is a lesson we learned as little tikes, but bears repeating. Holding your organization and all its members to the highest ethical standards will never turn out badly. What appears to be gained from an ethical lapse is actually, in time, a great loss. This is an unequivocal and unavoidable law of consequence. Always do the right thing. Any short-term loss is more than made up in the long run.

We would like to repeat from the first chapter: Never lie in a proposal. Never, never, never, under any circumstance. The entire structure of grants is built on trust, trust between the grantor and the grantee. If we, as grant seekers, give grantors a hint that we cannot be trusted, the entire game will change, and we won't like the changes. Think about what happens. An organization writes a proposal and sends it to a grantor. The grantor doesn't truly know that organization from Adam's alley cat. But, if the proposal has merit, the grantor decides to give money to the applicant, usually sight unseen. Why? Because the grantor trusts that what the organization said in its proposal is the truth. If we as grant seekers ever give grantors reason to begin to disbelieve us, then we have killed the goose that lays the golden eggs, and it will all be our fault. Never, never lie to a grantor. There is never a circumstance in which telling a lie to a grantor is the right thing to do.

Go after no grants for which you do not intend to run the project as explained in the proposal to the grantor. This is a corollary to the previous principle to never lie to a grantor. That it happens is sometimes due to a misunderstanding of one of the basic concepts of grant seeking, that grant money is not for you to use any way you want, but to run the project detailed in the proposal. Administrators and people in the highest leadership positions are often the ones with the misconception that grant money can be spent any way they desire. They see a shortfall in the budget and task the grant team with making it up with grants. In most circumstances this is not how grants work. Some foundations fund general operating costs of not-for-profit organizations, but this money is rare and hard to get. Usually, grantors fund projects for specific purposes. This means that when you get the money, you have already committed to what you are going to do with it. You did that in the proposal you submitted to the grantor.

Stay Positive

Stay relentlessly positive. Grant seeking can bring out the negative in people. After all, we are dealing with problems here. The constant emphasis on identifying problems and designing solutions to them can cause people to become pessimistic. Also, there is a lot of rejection in grant seeking. Every time a carefully crafted proposal gets turned down, the negativity quotient goes sky high. To be effective, you and your fellow team members must, absolutely must, stay relentlessly positive. Dwell on what is possible, what you can control. Do not let all those problems over which you have no control get you down. Remember that, in grants, no does not really mean no. No means not now. Once turned down, a proposal is simply a work in progress, needing to be improved and resubmitted.

As mentioned in the previous paragraph, it may be a guiding principle to remember that your organization is not in business to solve all the problems of everybody in your community. Discern that there are problems over which you have no control. Let them go. Concentrate on those problems on which you can exert influence.

Go–No–Go Decision Making

Another small, but important, thing to get organized about is the decision-making process of deciding whether to pursue a particular grant. This is usually called the go-no-go point, or decision. You see, applying to every grant program for which your organization is eligible is not the thing to do. Once a potential funding source is identified, you should not plunge willy-nilly into the proposal preparation process. Thought needs to go into a conscious decision about whether to apply. Three basic items need to be addressed: (1) the fit with the mission, goals, and direction of your organization; (2) the return on investment; (3) what we call with some glee, the hassle factor.

One of the guiding principles of your grant-seeking team will probably be to pursue only grants that align with and promote the mission and purposes of your organization. The go-no-go decision is the point at which you apply that guiding principle. Once you have identified a funding source, there needs to be a formal, sit-down meeting at which all members of the grant team attend, including those members in leadership positions in the organization. The purpose of the grant program needs to be clearly defined and articulated by someone who stands for the position of "Go." It is, then, the responsibility of the group to make a careful decision whether the purpose of the grant program sufficiently aligns with one of your organization's purposes. More heads than one need to be involved in this process.

At this same meeting, the return on investment needs to be discussed. The grant money is not free. It costs your organization time, money, and resources to pursue grants. The question here is does the amount of return, the amount of the grant, justify the amount of investment in your organization's time and resources that it will take to get the grant. It will take approximately the same investment in time and resources to obtain $50,000 as it will to obtain $1 million.

The common wisdom is that the more money that is at stake, the harder the application process; the larger the budget request, the longer and more difficult the proposal. Interestingly enough, this is simply not true. It is true about very small amounts of money, such as minigrants of several hundred or just a few thousand dollars versus tens of thousands of dollars. This is where the idea comes from. Because it does take much more work to obtain $10,000 than $500, the inexperienced grant seeker will extrapolate that truth into larger amounts of funding, into the million-dollar range.

So, the go–no–go decision here is usually concerned with the smaller grants. The larger ones always have a good return on investment ratio. It is small grants that need to be looked at carefully. Another concept that might be helpful is that it takes a lot of $10,000 grants to total a million dollars. Going after the big bucks only makes good sense from a return on investment standpoint. The reluctance of some organizations to pursue the larger grants is usually due to lack of confidence, rather than any lack of skill or lack of good ideas. Most of the best ideas come from small organizations and spread to the big ones. Go ahead, be the innovator. Go for the big bucks. Someone wins; it might as well be you.

The third item to consider in any go–no–go decision-making process is what we call the hassle factor. This deals with the situation after you get the grant. Some grantors and some grant programs are simply more hassle than they are worth. Read carefully all the grantor's material and pick up on such things as visits to meetings and conferences. If you are allowed to request grant funding for such trips, then OK, but if the grantor expects you to foot the bill, you might want to reconsider your application. Consider how much reporting a grantor expects. For a million dollars you can do a lot of reporting and not feel put out, but for a few thousand dollars the same amount of reporting becomes onerous. Once you get the grant it is too late to complain. You have agreed to the grantor's terms by submitting the proposal. The only time at which you can decide not to put up with the hassle is before you apply. The worksheet seen in Exhibit 2.3 is

EXHIBIT 2.3

 0203.DOC

Go-No-Go Worksheet

Go	No-Go	Decision Point	-4	-3	-2	-1	0	+1	+2	+3	+4
		Does the project contribute to the fulfillment of our overall organization mission?									
		Does the project contribute to the fulfillment of the mission of the division or department of this organization responsible for the management & implementation of the project?									
		Does the project contribute to the fulfillment of current goals of the overall organization?									
		Does the project contribute to the fulfillment of current goals of the division or department responsible for the management & implementation of the project?									
		Do our organization's leaders have the necessary time to effectively oversee this project?									
		Do our department's leaders have the necessary time to effectively oversee this project?									

EXHIBIT 2.3 *(Continued)*

Go	No-Go	Decision Point	-4	-3	-2	-1	0	+1	+2	+3	+4
		Have our partners committed sufficient leadership time to effectively meet their project responsibilities?									
		Can our department's support staff effectively handle any additional work caused by this project?									
		Have our partners allocated sufficient support staff time to handle their part of the additional support work?									
		Does our organization have the funds necessary to support its part of the project budget?									
		Has our department been allocated sufficient funds to support its part of the project budget?									
		Have our partners made a firm commitment to the funds necessary to fulfill their budgetary pledges?									
		Do our organization's leaders have the necessary time to effectively oversee this project?									

EXHIBIT 2.3 *(Continued)*

Go	No-Go	Decision Point	-4	-3	-2	-1	0	+1	+2	+3	+4
		Do our department's leaders have the necessary time to effectively oversee this project?									
		Have our partners firmly committed the resources necessary to fulfill their responsibilities?									
		Is the project worth the effort for our organization?									
		Is the project worth the effort for our department?									
		Totals									

Deal Killers		
	No-Go	**Maybe Go**
Does the project match closely enough with the grantor's needs, agenda, and purpose to maintain the integrity of the project and your organization?	Yes	No
Is the project of sufficient value to the target population to balance the negatives of managing it (time, effort, and cost)?	Yes	No
After looking at the project thoughtfully, realistically, but optimistically, do you see no real way to continue the project after the grantor's money runs out?	Yes	No

included on the accompanying disk (0203.doc) to help quantify the go–no–go decision-making process.

Motivating the Team

By asking members of your organization to participate on the grant team, you are adding to their workload. Most people need a reason to take on additional work. This is where motivation comes in. You may consider it wonderful to spend extra time on grant seeking, but not everyone does. You must make membership on the grant team an honor, something that members of your organization want to do. One way is to position the grant team as leaders of a process, not as workers serving everyone else in the organization. The grant team must lead the process, not do all the work, both for the reasons of participant ownership that have been raised before, but also so that members of the grant team perceive their position as one of honor and prestige, not as just more drudge work piled on an already full plate.

A possible approach is to rotate members of the team. Have members of the grant team serve for a set period of time, say two years. They then rotate off the team and become eligible to be the project director of a grant-funded project. The project that they get to direct could be something special, near and dear to their heart. Service on the grant team then becomes the entry point to members of your organization being able to pursue their own pet project. Whatever means you use, motivating your team members is important. Establishing team camaraderie can be helpful. Perhaps you can create a logo, a team name, a team T-shirt, or whatever you know will work to motivate members of your grant team.

Wise Guy

"OK, I'm not nearly as upset as I was in Chapter 1. Now I see that getting on this grant team is a good deal. After all, you get on the team and tell other folks what to do. Sit back, do nothing yourself, and run everybody else around to do the work. Then I get to take credit when we succeed and I'll blame failure on all the little people who didn't do what I told them to do. Ahhh, yes, I'm beginning to like the shape of this."

Wise Lady

"That attitude would guarantee that you would definitely *not* be on my grant team. Grant team members must be doers. They're problem-solvers and good at using primary and secondary reference resources. Grants acquisition is hard work. Let no one begin a grants effort without first understanding that. Nothing comes free. Each team member must have assignments and each team member must complete those assignments on time and to the highest quality. This is where team planning is critical. Team members have to first decide what information is needed, from where, who is the 'keeper' of the information, and then must provide written guidance to make it easy for the 'keeper' to provide the data. This all needs to be done with enough lead time for the team to pull together the project details and get the proposal out the door in plenty of time to meet the deadline. Believe me, there's more than enough work for each team member to stay busy. So, if you think you can just 'coast,' as my Dad always said, 'you've got another think coming!'"

Additions to the Team

There will be times when you will need to augment your grant team. These temporary additions to the team can come from a number of sources that can be characterized into three headings: partners, volunteers, and paid help.

Partners

When your organization is partnering with another organization in a project for which you are pursuing a grant, members of the partner organization should have an active part in all aspects of the grant-seeking process. They should help with project design and development. They should help with funding source research. They should help with RFP analysis. And, they should most definitely help with creation of the proposal. So, the first place to look for additional help is a partner.

Volunteers

Volunteers make another very good source of people to augment the grant team. Where you obtain volunteers depends on your type of organization.

If you are a school, you have parents and retired educators on which to draw. If you are a hospital, you already have volunteer organizations active. What you then do is meet with the organizations and find if any of them have members with the needed skills and experience. If you are a nonprofit that provides a service, for example a family violence prevention center, then alumni of your program are potential volunteers. Often the people you have helped are looking for a way to return the favor, to pay back to some degree for the help they received.

Paid Help

Finally, you can hire help. You could obtain secretarial or office help from a temporary hiring service or you could hire a skilled consultant. Usually, your team has the expertise to do everything that needs doing, but time can be a problem. By paying someone to get something done, you trade money for time. Often this makes good sense, especially when you need special expertise that you cannot find in volunteers. You will find on the disk the worksheet seen in Exhibit 2.4 (0204.doc) to help with obtaining additional temporary help, along with worksheets to track which projects they are involved with.

Hiring a Grant Seeker

Up to now, we have assumed that all the members of the grant team take on that job as an added responsibility to their normal job within your organization. It is certainly possible, however, to hire a full-time grant seeker. In fact it makes a great deal of sense. In what other realm can an organization invest a few thousand dollars a year for salary, expenses, equipment, materials, and supplies and expect to obtain a return on investment of hundreds of thousands of dollars? In no other area is it possible to get such a return. Your organization must look at the costs of a grant seeker as an investment, however. One problem with many organizations in the not-for-profit world is that they think of expenditures only as expenses, never as investments. School systems are particularly guilty of this. Failure to look at the big picture, at what an investment in personnel and materials can produce, often prevents an organization from making the plunge into hiring a full-time grant seeker.

If you decide to give it a try and hire that grant seeker, there are two things to keep firmly in mind. One, it will take more than a year to see results. Give the experiment at least 2 years to show results. After 1 year, your grant seeker will only have had time to get the projects together, apply to a few funding sources, and get turned down. The grant seeker will not have had time to analyze what went wrong, correct the problems,

EXHIBIT 2.4

Grant Team Additions Worksheet

Partner Additions

Partner Organization	Potential Team Members	How to Contact Them

Volunteer Additions

Potential Team Member	Organization or Affiliation	How to Contact Them

Paid Assistants

Potential Team Member	Organization or Affiliation	How to Contact Them

Project Design

Task	Potential Team Member(s)	Person Responsible for Making Contact	Contact Deadline	Agreement
Meeting planning & set-up				
Catering				
Project planning				
Research & analysis				
Documentation/development of project profile				
Communications				
Administration				

EXHIBIT 2.4 *(Continued)*

Funder Research

Task	Potential Team Member(s)	Person Responsible for Making Contact	Contact Deadline	Agreement
Research potential foundation funders, documentation				
Research potential corporate funders, documentation				
Research potential state or regional funders, documentation				
Research potential local funders, documentation				
Meeting planning & set-up				
Evaluation & selection of potential funders				
Overall documentation				
Communications				
Further research/analysis of targeted funder(s) & assurance of "match"				
RFP/guideline analysis				
Administration				

Project Development

Task	Potential Team Member(s)	Person Responsible for Making Contact	Contact Deadline	Agreement
Meeting planning & set-up				
Catering				
Facilitation				
Communications				
Documentation				
Administration				

EXHIBIT 2.4 *(Continued)*

Proposal Development

Task	Potential Team Member(s)	Person Responsible for Making Contact	Contact Deadline	Agreement
Proposal administration & management (insurance of responsiveness and compliance)				
Research (validation and justification of project content)				
Proposal design, formatting, & publishing (includes creating graphics)				
Proposal writing				
Acquiring and writing key personnel biographical information				
General administrative support				
Acquisition of letters of support				
Communications				
Budget development and justification				
Reader 1				
Reader 2				
Packaging & Posting				

resubmit the proposals, and this time get funded. For this process, you need to invest at least 2 years.

Secondly, to reiterate a point, the grant seeker that you hire absolutely cannot do all the work him- or herself. The main responsibility of a grant seeker is to coordinate and lead a grant-seeking effort, not to do all the work. We have discussed the problems inherent in playing the Lone Ranger. They do not need to be repeated, but be sure that every member of your organization understands the purpose of the grant seeker, what it is she will be doing, and what is expected from every member of the organization to help her. This must come from the highest level possible in the organization. It must be made clear to all in your organization that it is now part of their job description to cooperate with the grant seeker and provide help and assistance that is requested by the grant seeker.

Conclusion

Now we have the basics of putting together, directing, and training a grant-seeking team. We know, in general, what it is that the team will do, and we have a general idea of what it will take to get the job done, to be successful, and to get grants. Why discuss such topics in a book about grants management, a book that is about what to do after you get a grant? Because most problems that happen after being awarded a grant can be avoided totally with proper actions before submitting a proposal. Success in managing grants starts with seeking grants for the right reasons and in the right way.

One of the best ways to avoid problems in managing a grant-funded project is to fully understand what a grantor means when it asks you to describe your project. It might also be called an intervention, or a program, or a solution, or an action plan. It doesn't matter what label a grantor applies. The principles remain the same and they are the subject of Chapter 3.

The Key to Success:
Your Project

The play's [project's] the thing
Wherein I'll catch the conscience of the King [grantor]

William Shakespeare, *Hamlet*

Introduction

In the first two chapters we discussed creating a grant team. During that discussion the subject of a project came up time and again. Just what is a project? The answer to that question is the topic of this chapter. Basically, the question has two answers. A project is a solution to a problem. A project is a set of activities. Both definitions are correct. Each defines a project from a different point of view. The first definition is philosophical or positional. The second is concrete and real.

The Project as Solution to a Problem

In a conceptual sense a project is a solution to a problem. We run a project to change something, change that we hope is for the better. The outcomes of projects are often expected to be changes in behavior of a target population. Note the reference to a project as a solution to a problem in the following quotation from the U.S. Department of Commerce Telecommunications and Information Infrastructure Assistance Program (TIIAP) application guidelines:

1 Project Definition

You should use the Project Definition section to describe your project, clearly discussing the problem(s) you are trying to solve, the solutions(s) you propose, and the outcomes you expect.

TIIAP, Application Kit for Fiscal Year 1999

If, then, a project is a solution to a problem, what do we mean by problem? Problems refer to something that is lacking, missing, not working properly, or happening that shouldn't be. Typical problems that organizations try to solve can be: teen pregnancy, early death due to poor diet, violence in our communities and schools, poor performance in school, unemployment due to out-of-date job skills, dropping out of school, substance abuse, poor quality of life due to health-related choices, unemployment due to lack of job skills, and on and on. The list is practically endless.

When we define a problem, there are some pitfalls to avoid. The first pitfall to avoid is to make sure that what we are calling a problem is truly a problem and not a symptom of something else. A good example of a problem that is not a problem is low test scores in our K–12 schools. Low test scores are a symptom of many things, including but not limited to poor home environment, lack of motivation, poor teachers, poor teaching techniques, insufficient teaching materials, drug use, poor reading skills, poor test-taking skills, peer pressure, and lack of role models. Nothing can be done directly about low test scores, because the low scores are a symptom of the problems just listed, and perhaps many others. To increase test scores, solve the underlying problems. Attacking a symptom instead of the underlying causes is one sure way to design a project that has no chance of success.

Be sure to attack problems not symptoms. This allows you to avoid the first major pitfall in defining problems. The second pitfall is that the word "need" is sometimes used in place of "problem." Use of "need" is falling into disfavor among grantors, because grant seekers tend to describe a need as something that their organization is lacking, such as computers, or staff, or operating funds, or facilities. When a grantor asks you for a need or a problem, the grantor means for you to define human conduct or social relations performed or not performed by a target population such that the conduct or lack of conduct is harmful, hurtful, negative, or just plain bad.

Problems are always focused on a target population. Your target population is probably defined by the mission of your organization. If you are a rape crisis center, your target population is obvious. If you are a high school, the target population might not be quite so obvious. There might seem to be a number of possibilities—teachers, parents, administrators, and students. For those readers employed in education, we define your target population: It is always the students. Even if the project is for professional development of staff, the actual target population is the students. Other readers must define your target population, and once you do, all of your problems center on it.

Another important distinction needs to be made as clearly as possible. The absence of your solution cannot be your problem. This amounts to circular reasoning. The progression is something like this. Person One says, "We need a swimming pool." "Oh," says Person Two, "Why do we need a swimming pool?" Person One responds promptly, confidently, and perhaps a bit condescendingly, "Because we don't have one." Do you see the circle? We say that our problem is that we don't have a pool. Then we make the obvious next step, which is that our solution is to build a pool. This is called circular reasoning and it simply will not fly with a grantor.

Breaking out of circular reasoning is relatively simple. Ask this question, "To what ultimate purpose will the solution I suggest be put?" Note that we are not asking the proximate purpose or use, but the ultimate purpose. That means that the answer may not be to use the solution. For example the response to this question about a swimming pool cannot be, "So people can swim." You must think of the reasons that a community might build a swimming pool. Such reasons might be to provide summer recreation or to give active adolescents something to do during the summer thereby reducing juvenile pranks and vandalism.

The foregoing discussion about recognizing circular reasoning should enable you to avoid the most common pitfall of stating problems. That pitfall is to word your problem as a negative statement of your proposed solution. It goes something like this. Problem: We need professional development for our teachers so they can integrate technology into curriculum. Think about this for just a moment. Here a solution masquerades as a problem, because the clear solution to this problem (our project) is to provide professional development on technology integration to our teachers. We now have circular reasoning. The absence of our solution has become our problem. In addition, we have stated the problem in terms of our organization, not our target population.

The simplest and most direct way to ensure that you do not use circular reasoning and state your problem as the lack of your solution is to focus on the target population. Keep the problem human. Think in terms of real people and real problems—your neighbors, your family, your fellow worshippers, your bowling buddies. You are trying to serve people. Do not think in terms of your organization. Your organization comes in as part of the solution, not as the problem, which, if you think about it, is the way you should be looking at things.

Other terms can be used also when defining problems, such as "barriers" and "obstacles." At times a grantor will ask, What are the barriers to success for your organization? What the grantor means is, What are your problems? This is just another way to get at the same thing. There is an ongoing discussion among experienced grant seekers, and it is that the grantors have not agreed on a vocabulary. What one grantor calls a problem another calls a need and a third calls a barrier to success. You need mental flexibility to deal with the situation. Just keep in mind that every grantor wants to know what problem your project intends to solve. A particular grantor may not use the word "problem," but be not deceived; somewhere in the application guidelines is a word that means the same. You just have to recognize it.

There is a difficulty with defining a project as a solution to a problem. While correct, this definition is incomplete and can leave a person with no real understanding of what a project actually is and what is involved. This is, after all, a concept, a philosophy. But there is more to a project than just mental gymnastics.

The Project as a Set of Activities

Concretely, from the viewpoint of doing rather than thinking, a project is a set of activities, a set of things that are done, accomplished, performed, or implemented. Note the following definition of a project as a set of activities quoted from the Rural Health Outreach Grant Program, U.S. Department of Health and Human Services:

> PROJECT refers to all proposed activities
>
> *Rural Health Outreach Grant Program, Program Guide FY 1999*

What exactly is an activity? *Webster's New World Dictionary* tells us that an activity is "any specific action or pursuit." The key word is action. To perform an activity is to act, to do something. If a project is a set of activities, then a project is a set of acts, a group of things that are done. What kinds of things are done in the course of a project? What kinds of activities are accomplished?

When you combine a group or set of these simple actions together in a meaningful combination with the intent to solve a problem, you have created a project. Let's look at an example. For our example project we will use the following list of activities:

Buy equipment	Fish
Buy supplies	Talk
Teach to fish	Visit
Transport people	

It should be apparent that a simple list of activities is not enough to define a project. Several questions may have occurred to you. For example, who is the target population? What organization is doing these activities?

And, why are they doing them? These are all-important questions, because they lead us to fill in the blanks and make sense out of what is just a list of activities without meaning or structure. Read through the following items that you might find in a project profile, and the project will come alive:

Problem: Many residents of rest homes in our community are lonely and have limited outside activities

Mission of Project: Provide residents of rest homes in our community with companionship and outside activities

Project Description: Our project will provide, on a regular and scheduled basis, companionship for residents of rest homes in our community on fishing trips. Each resident will have his or her companion. Equipment and supplies will be provided. Transportation will be provided. Fishing will be done in the Benton Lake Facility, a lake stocked with fish for maximum success. Companions will be trained both in how to relate to the mostly elderly project participants as well as in how to fish.

Lead Agency: Council on Aging

Partner Agencies: County Parks & Recreation, Municipal Transportation Authority, Boy Scouts, Girl Scouts, and the School District

Now that we know the target population, the lead agency, the partners, and the intent of the project, it becomes clear, or at least somewhat clearer, what the purpose behind the set of activities is. There could be much more to this project, and indeed when fully developed there would be a great deal more detail involved. In Chapters 4 and 5 we take this project profile level of information and expand it into a fully developed project. Interestingly, the same set of activities can be used to accomplish a very different project.

Determining a Project's Fundability

Comparing and contrasting the two examples leads us to realize that calling a project a set of activities that provide a solution to a problem, while correct, is incomplete. In fact, it is very difficult to give a complete and accurate definition of a project that doesn't run on for paragraphs. Perhaps what is easier and ultimately more helpful would be to define the several characteristics of a project. Then, when you begin to create your own projects, you can measure them against the yardstick that we have created. A grant project will have all of the following characteristics to some degree. The degree or amount that a project fulfills a particular characteristic may vary, but all grant projects need to conform to this set of characteristics, because grantors are expecting them to do so. This list isn't made up out of whole cloth, it is gleaned from years of successful grant seeking. This list details what grantors expect.

1. The project must solve a problem.

The problem needs to meet three criteria. First, the problem must truly be a problem. Second, the problem must be solvable. Third, the problem must be worthy of being solved. Admittedly, these criteria are subjective, nevertheless, a grantor will want you to show that your problem actually exists, that it can be solved, and that it is worth spending the grantor's money to do so.

2. The project must solve a problem shared by other localities.

Because grants are not charity, and because grants mainly fund model or demonstration projects, grantors want to know that the problem you intend to solve exists elsewhere. If you have a unique problem, a problem that no other community has, then you are not a good candidate for a grant. The essence of a model or demonstration project is that other communities can replicate your solution. They can only replicate your solution if they have the same problem. This is why you often find in the grantor's application instructions guidelines to show how your problem compares statewide, regionally, and nationally. The real point behind this request is to show that your problem is not unique, but rather is widespread. If the problem is widespread, then your solution can become widespread as well. This is the grant process at work as it is intended to work.

Another word that gets attached to this concept is significance. When a grantor talks about the significance of your project, the usual meaning is that the problem you are addressing is present in many places around the country or the world, so that when you demonstrate a solution that works, you will have contributed in a significant way to solving the problem on a large scale. This makes your solution, your project, significant. And all it truly means is that lots of other places similar to your place have the same or very similar problems. When this is true, your solution is exportable or replicable.

3. The project will be run, coordinated, or overseen by a lead agency.

One agency or organization must be in charge. From a legal standpoint, one agency is the fiscal agent. That is, one agency receives the grant funds and is responsible for all disbursements. Usually the lead agency is the organization doing the bulk of the work of the project. There are other circumstances in which the lead agency is more of a coordination agent, ensuring that everything is getting done, rather than actually doing things. Regardless, the lead agency or fiscal agent has entered into a legal agreement with a grantor once a grant has been awarded. The proposal that was submitted and funded is, in effect, the contract between the two entities. It is the responsibility of the lead agency to do what it said it would do in the proposal. This is a legal and fiduciary obligation.

4. The project will have partners to the lead agency.

It is possible to run a grant project without partners, but it is not probable that you will be allowed to do so. Today, grantors expect to see a partnership or consortium of agencies or organizations working together to solve problems. Assume that you must have partners. Always ask yourself this question. With which organizations does it make sense to partner to accomplish my ends? Grantors expect a partnership; you might as well begin all project development with the expectation that you will work with other organizations to implement your solution.

5. The project will need less money to continue than it does to start.

When you conceive a project and that project needs the same amount of money to operate each year into perpetuity, the project is probably not a good candidate for a grant. Remember that we are dealing with social projects here, not research. Grantors expect your organization to be able to continue the project after the grantor's money runs out. Realistically, how will you do this if you continue to need the same amount of money each year as has been provided by the grant? We realize that this is a hard message, but the truth is, if you cannot see a way to continue the project without the grantor's money, then you are not a viable candidate for that money. Grants are not intended to let you run your project indefinitely. A grant is to get you started. It is up to you to continue, to sustain, to institutionalize the project.

6. The project has a set of actions to be performed.

A grant project cannot be simply an intellectual exercise. The grantor expects you to do something with your target population. Of course, the planning grant is an exception. From time to time, grantors will allow you to spend money to do nothing but plan, that is, to research how to solve a problem. Usually, in this case, you have already defined the large problem but are not sure about the underlying causes or the method of overcoming the barriers to the solution to the problem. In either case, a grantor expects you to perform certain concrete actions that, taken in summary, will provide a solution to the problem that you have posed.

7. The project will have a broad purpose.

This broad purpose is often called a mission or vision. A useful way to look at the broad purpose or mission of your project is to think of it as the ultimate outcome you desire. Perhaps you want to eliminate domestic violence in your community. Or you want to eliminate drug use among school children. Or you want to eliminate underage drinking of alcoholic beverages. The broad purpose or mission of your project will flow directly from the problem that you set yourself to solve. If you say that your problem is that there are homeless in your community, then the broad purpose or mission of your project could be to eliminate homelessness in your community.

8. The project will have a few realistic, measurable, and clear major steps that, if accomplished, lead to accomplishing the broad purpose.

These few realistic, measurable, and clear major steps are often called goals or perhaps objectives. This subject is treated in detail in Chapter 5, so we will not belabor the point here.

9. The project is innovative.

The expectation of innovation is basic. Almost all grantors, almost all the time, expect that your project will be innovative. But what does it mean to be innovative, to innovate? Checking with *Webster's New World Dictionary* again, we find that innovation is "change in the way of doing things." A useful definition that we have picked up over the years is that innovation is "improvement on present practice." The key feature of innovation is change. It is not innovative to continue to do the same things that you have been doing only doing those things faster, bigger, smarter, more energetically, or more expensively. There are valid reasons for doing each of these things, but grant money is not intended to fund it. Grants fund innovation, which is changing the way you do business.

10. The project has evaluation as an integral part.

Chapters 11 through 15 are dedicated to project evaluation, so discussion of this very important part of any and every project is delayed until those chapters. Suffice it to say that every grantor expects you to be able to assess your project from both the viewpoint of its internal workings and its ultimate outcomes.

On the accompanying disk is a checklist (0301.doc) to help determine if your project is fundable. Grantors expect your project to have all the ten characteristics listed previously. The checklist seen in Exhibit 3.1 distills the information down into a simple format.

EXHIBIT 3.1   0301.DOC

Project Fundability Checklist

Place Check	Required Conformation Points for Grant Fundability
	The project solves a problem, not a symptom, but a real problem.
	The problem to be solved focuses on the population being served by our organization.
	The problem is worthy of being solved.
	The problem can be solved (at least partially).
	The problem to be solved is a problem shared by other organizations in other localities.
	The project will be run, coordinated, or overseen by a legally established lead agency.
	The project has significant support within our organization.
	The project has partners and/or significant related community support.
	The project will need less money to continue than to start.
	The project has a broad purpose (mission or vision).
	The project has a clear set of actions that will be performed.
	The project has a few realistic, measurable, and clear major steps that, if accomplished, will lead toward the achievement of the broad purpose.
	The project is innovative (for explanation, refer to *Grantseeker's Toolkit*).
	The project can be continued financially beyond the ending of the initial grant funding.
	The project can be continued operationally beyond the ending of the initial grant funding.
	The project results and benefits to the target population can be effectively evaluated.

Wise Guy

All this preaching about projects is making me nauseous. I just want the money. I know what's best for my organization. I'll decide how to spend the money. I just want the grantor to give it to me and get out of my face and out of my business.

Wise Lady

Then focus on something other than grant seeking. Just eliminate grant seeking from your strategy because you will not
succeed. Grant makers want projects. They want accountability. They
want results. There is a problem to be solved and they want to monitor
their grantee's attempts to solve it. Grant makers see that one of their
eternal problems has been to determine whether their grant funds have
actually accomplished anything. More and more stringent evaluation
requirements are being placed on grantees. I repeat, you do not get
something for nothing. Either stop seeking grants or get over it. Have a
bake sale.

Conclusion

In summary, a project is a solution to a problem. A project is a set of actions. A project has a set of characteristics. We have spent so much time
discussing the creation of projects in a book on project management because it is devilishly hard to fix project problems after you receive funding. The time to fix the problems is before you even apply. If you want
your project to run smoothly, then create it correctly. Also, you will raise
your likelihood of getting funded if your project is good to start with.

## Chapter 4

Making Sense of It All: Project Organization and Outlining

Well begun is half finished.
James A. Quick

Introduction

This chapter and the next are dedicated to detailing the process of creating and fully developing a project. The project is normally created and developed before a proposal is written. Or perhaps more correctly, the project *should be* fully developed before a proposal is written. Sadly, many applicants for grants skip this critical step. All too often, the information in the proposal is all that exists about that project. When this is true, the project director probably does not have enough direction to adequately run and manage the project. If, as often happens, you get a grant and then find that you do not really know what you are going to do with the money, apply the process in this and the next chapter. Then you will have a fully developed plan of action, a project that you can run and manage.

It is easy to see that projects are complicated, with many aspects, so you might overlook that all projects can also be thought of as rather simple—not in characteristics but in organization. This chapter explains the common underlying organizational scheme of all projects, regardless of their content or subject matter. It doesn't matter what the subjects of a group of projects are. There is an organizational scheme common to them all. Or more correctly, there could be a common organizational scheme. Projects can be organized in such helter-skelter fashion that commonalties are hidden. Careful analysis can unearth the common threads. Once you finish this chapter, you should be able to see the common threads in projects.

We can start by reiterating one of the conclusions from Chapter 3. During the implementation of a project that solves a problem, a set of activities are performed that accomplish a purpose for a target population. This is a central truth about projects, and can be used as the central piece in our organizational scheme. It can be said safely that all projects implement activities with a target population. For the sake of keeping things short and sweet, we call this simply "implementation." Use of this word is not to be confused with the use within certain disciplines of the term "implementation project."

Getting Organized

Remember that we have decided that there will always be implementation activities, implementation with the target population. With a little more thought, we realize that things need to be done before we are ready to implement activities with the target population. We can call these activities preparation for implementation. Again, to keep things simple, we call this part of our organizational scheme "preparation." A little more thought leads us to realize that there is another set of activities associated with all projects, activities that are not directly involved with working with the target population. These activities include such things as oversight of project tasks, financial responsibilities, and determining whether the project is accomplishing what we intended. We can call these activities monitoring and managing the project, or for our shorthand notation, "monitor and manage."

We now have the three basic structural parts of a project: preparation, implementation, and manage and monitor. Thinking about preparation of a project can lead us to further divide that phase into activities that are mainly physical in nature and outcome, and activities that are mainly mental or intellectual in nature and outcome. We might call the largely physical activities "setup," and we might call the largely intellectual activities "research and development." By the same token we can divide the management and monitoring of a project into two sets of activities. We can call one set of activities management, tracking, and communication and the other set of activities evaluation or perhaps assessment. This now enlarges our original three sets of activities into five sets. Summarizing, the activities performed during the accomplishment of projects can be grouped into five topics and are illustrated in Exhibit 4.1.

The obvious question then becomes, what exactly do we mean by these five categories? What are the definitions of the categories, and what are examples of activities that would fall under each of the categories? Answers to these questions and other similar ones comprise most of the rest of this chapter.

Another point on this subject is worth making. While every project will more than likely have activities that fall under each of the five topics,

EXHIBIT 4.1

Project Activities

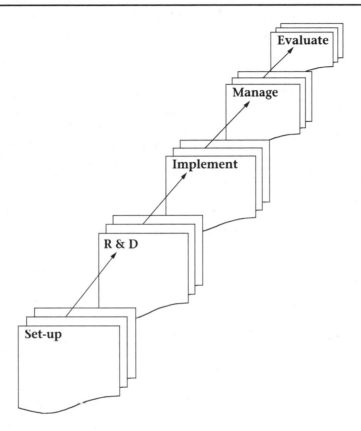

an individual project may have very few to no activities that fall under one particular topic. In other words, your project may not need all five topics for its organizational scheme. Quite frankly, this is unlikely, but it is possible. Actually, the only topic in which it is remotely possible that you will have no activities is research and development. It is basically impossible to run a project without performing activities in all the other categories.

Set-Up

The set-up phase of a project consists of activities that are largely physical and prepare or make ready for all the rest of the phases. The clearest way to understand the type of activities we mean is simply to make a list of activities that would fall into this category. Such a list of activities would include but not be limited to the following:

Hire consultants	Purchase equipment
Hire service providers	Purchase facilities
Hire staff	Purchase land
Install air conditioning	Purchase materials
Install electrical outlets	Purchase supplies
Install heating	

The list could go on virtually forever. Your project will not need all of these activities, but look at the list and you will see that it is highly unlikely that any project you run will fail to need one or more of these activities to be performed. Part of the preparation to implement any project is to get the things that are necessary—people, services, materials and supplies, equipment, and facilities. One way to look at this list of activities is that they lead to establishing the infrastructure necessary to implement your project. These activities are the largely physical activities performed during preparation. The next set of activities, also done during preparation, is largely intellectual.

Research and Development

The research and development phase of a project consists of activities that are largely intellectual and that prepare or make ready for the implementation phase. Saying that these activities are largely intellectual does not mean that only thinking takes place. For example, a set of physical activities are necessary when doing research, even though the purpose of research is largely intellectual. As in the set-up phase, the simplest way to explain the type of activities that belong in this phase is by example. Following is a list of activities that could be included in the research and development phase of a project:

Create a training curriculum	Recruit participants
Create a video	Recruit volunteers
Create a web site	Screen mentors
Create brochures	Train mentors
Create processes and procedures	Train staff on curriculum
Create written materials	Train staff on procedure
Develop software	Train staff on technology
Recruit mentors	

Implementation

Implementation activities are the easiest to define of all the activities we've reviewed so far. When an activity directly involves the target population and works toward accomplishing the purpose or mission of the project, it is an implementation activity. Notice the two characteristics of implementation activities: (1) The activity works directly with the target population and (2) the activity works toward accomplishing the desired outcome of the project. When you find these two characteristics together in one activity, that activity belongs in the implementation phase of your project.

The target population of a project cannot be, or more correctly, should not be, the staff of your organization. Yes, often projects focus on staff training or preparation, but the ultimate reason for the staff development is to better serve your target population. The grantor is interested in your organization and its staff only insofar as it impacts a target population. In and of itself, your staff has no purpose. Only by working with a target population does your organization and its staff gain meaning and purpose, within the context of grant projects. Clearly your personnel have purpose and meaning of their own and do not need a grantor to verify such.

With it kept firmly in mind that all activities in an implementation phase of a project deal directly with the target population, the following activities might be included in an implementation phase:

Administering medical procedures	Performing medical tests
Apprenticing	Providing medical screenings
Counseling	Role modeling
Exercise	Teaching
Mentoring	Training
Performing entry interviews	

It bears repeating that the activities in our lists are generic. They do not contain content or subject matter. That is provided by your organization. An example are the two activities above of teaching and training. You could be teaching anything, from bricklaying to rocket science, from basket weaving to archery, from brain surgery to turkey farming. Additional subjects about which your organization might be teaching or training a target population could be conflict resolution, dealing with diversity, life skills, hygiene, cooking, child care, and so on. It is not by accident that all the words on the list are action words. Implementation is action.

Management, Tracking, and Communication

Monitoring and managing occur throughout a project, from beginning to end. Management and communication activities fall into that category. The areas of a project that need management divide relatively easily into two large categories: finances and personnel. Managing the finances of a grant project is the subject of Chapter 10, so we defer discussion of this topic until then. Managing grant project personnel is the topic of Chapter 8, but one point can be made here. The personnel that you must manage during the running of a project can come from several sources—your organization (employees), other organizations (partners), volunteers, consultants, service providers, and project participants.

Communication activities are just that, those tasks that involve letting people know stuff. The official title for these activities is dissemination. Chapter 16 is dedicated to this topic, so we do not go into detail here. The kind of information that you will be letting people know about your project includes results, methods, problems, processes, evaluations, and lessons learned. The one additional category of activities involved in monitoring and managing a project is tracking. Tracking is usually called documentation and involves keeping track of the activities that take place during a project. Chapter 7 is dedicated to this topic.

Evaluation

Evaluation is one of the most important functions of a grant project. It's also one of the most neglected, which is a big problem to the grant maker and ultimately to the grantee when attempting to acquire more grant funding. As such it should occupy a significant amount of the time and money allocated for a project. The huge importance of the evaluation of your project is the reason that it is a topic all by itself. Evaluation is a complex and extensive subject. So extensive, that five chapters of this book are dedicated to the subject. For now we will leave the comments about evaluation to the simple observation that an evaluation involves more than simply measuring the degree to which your project attained its expected outcomes. This outcome evaluation is an important part of an overall evaluation, but it is by no means the only part. For example, it is just as important to investigate how well each of the activities involved in set-up, research and development, and implementation were performed as it is to discover the ultimate outcome.

Project Profile

We have now defined the five categories into which can be put all the activities you will perform during the running of a project. Next we are going to organize your project. When you have completed the project organization process you will have created the foundation of your project from which you can go on to create goals and objectives and then fully develop your project.

Before starting this process you need a project profile from which to work. To review quickly, a project profile is the outcome of the project design process. This process is explained in detail in *Grantseeker's Toolkit*, but we will take the time to review the steps now:

1. Identify a broad problem that affects a population that your organization serves.

2. Identify the causes of the broad problem, or identify the barriers to solving the broad problem. This we define as the "real" problem.

3. Create a project that solves the real problem. The real problem is the set of causes of the broad problem. Or, create a project that overcomes the barriers to solving the broad problem.

4. List the resources of personnel, equipment, materials, supplies, facilities, and services needed to accomplish the project.

5. Estimate the amount of money it will take to run the project.

6. Estimate how long it will take to get the project up and running.

7. List potential partners in the project.

Once you have committed all this information to paper, you have created a project profile. A project profile seen in Exhibit 4.2 and included on the disk (0402.doc), is also the jumping off point for the project organization process that follows. Once a project profile exists, you can move forward with funding source research, a topic that is beyond the scope of this book but is covered extensively in *Grantseeker's Toolkit*. Even so, we have included on the accompanying disk (0403.doc) a Funder Research Plan shown in Exhibit 4.3.

Project: From Idea to Outline

For project organization, you will need three-by-five cards, hopefully a large number. This process can be a team effort. More than one person can participate. In fact, it is often helpful to have more than one mind working on what we are about to do. Follow the steps in order, especially the first time you go through the process:

1. Pick a project profile for which you want to organize a project. If you don't have a project profile, complete the project design process and create one.

2. On a three-by-five card, write one task that needs to be accomplished during the project. Put one and only one task or idea on a card. Use no sentences. Express the idea in as few words as possible.

3. Keep putting tasks on three-by-five cards until you run out of ideas. Do not try to be organized. Just throw onto a card whatever enters into your mind. It does not matter if you jump from topic to topic. Just put the ideas on the cards, as rapidly as you can.

EXHIBIT 4.2   0402.DOC

Grant Project Profile

Description of the Broad Problem Addressed by the Project

_____

_____

Statement of the "Real" Problem Addressed by the Project

_____

_____

Project Summary

_____

_____

Potential Project Partners

_____

_____

Primary Resources Required

Facilities	List or Description	Approx. Cost

Total Cost _____

Primary Resources Required

Services	List or Description	Approx. Cost

Total Cost _____

Primary Resources Required

Equipment	List or Description	Approx. Cost

Total Cost _____

EXHIBIT 4.2 *(Continued)*

Primary Resources Required

Materials	List or Description	Approx. Cost

Total Cost _____

Primary Resources Required

Supplies	List or Description	Approx. Cost

Total Cost _____

Primary Resources Required

Personnel	List or Description	Approx. Cost

Total Cost _____

Estimated Project Budget

Facilities	
Services	
Equipment	
Materials	
Supplies	
Personnel	
Total Approximate Project Budget	_____
Approximate Percentage to Be Requested from a Grant Maker	X 0._____
Total Approximate Project Budget to Be Requested from Grant Maker	_____

Estimated Project Duration

1. Desired Start Month & Year	_____
2. Estimated Date & Year When Concrete Results Can Be Shown	_____
Number of Months Between Number 1 and Number 2 Above	

EXHIBIT 4.3

0403.DOC

Funder Research Plan

Using
1. The project you've designed
2. The information you've gathered
3. Knowledge of your local area and resources

plan a strategy to research funding sources. The strategy should cover the following areas:

I. List the pieces of information needed

Examples: We need a list of

- Foundations in close proximity to our organization
- Federal programs that apply to the project and are let between January and August of next year
- Local corporations
- State associations that might be of help
- State departments that might be interested in the project

II. List the people inside and outside your organization who can help with the research.

Person	Location	Telephone & E-mail

III. List the resources (publications and other) necessary to do the research and where they're located.

Resources Needed	Location

IV. Match people with research needs and resources, and gain commitment from them to do pieces of the research.

Name	Research Needs	Deadline

EXHIBIT 4.3 (*Continued*)

V. Design a plan to capture and catalog the information so that research doesn't have to be repeated.

Carefully think through a plan to organize and store the information you acquire from your research efforts. Except for updating information about sources, the basic information, once gathered, can save valuable time on the next project or proposal. Following are some suggestions and questions to ponder:

- What people within your extended organization will want to be involved in the grants effort? Grants acquisition should be a team effort. What team members will need the information gathered through your research?

- What resources can you acquire that will save time running back and forth to the public library? Consider asking community supporters to donate references. *Examples: A subscription to the Catalog of Federal Domestic Assistance (CFDA) is only about $60 per year; a Grantseeker's Desk Reference costs $30; a Foundation Center Directory costs around $300.*

- If you choose to set up computer databases to store information you receive about funding sources, consider setting up special files in a centralized location so others seeking grants will not have to redo research that has already been done.

- You will certainly need to set up files to maintain hard copy. Consider centralizing those files as well.

- If a large number of people in your organization are seeking grants, or if grant seekers are spread out among several locations, you might consider setting up a communications mechanism via electronic mail or memo to regularly inform people about new information.

- It's a good idea to designate a person to specialize in a given type of source research (such as for foundation or government sources). Each type of source has its own "personality" and system of research. Once someone is familiar with the peculiarities of a given source, the research goes much faster.

- Consider enlisting the aid of persons outside your organization to assist with the research efforts—retired business persons, volunteers, students, retired personnel, parents of students, and so forth.

- Partner with other grant-seeking organizations to spread out the research duties.

- Enlist the aid of local public library personnel. They can be valuable resources to help you find the best way to organize your research information.

- Use searchable databases (when cost effective) to aid you in your efforts. Plan what information is best acquired through these services.

EXHIBIT 4.4

0404.DOC

Project Outlining Worksheet

Set-Up

  I. _____

     A. _____

        1. _____

        2. _____

     B. _____

        1. _____

        2. _____

     C. _____

        1. _____

        2. _____

     D. _____

        1. _____

        2. _____

Research & Development

  II. _____

     A. _____

        1. _____

        2. _____

     B. _____

        1. _____

        2. _____

Implementation (1)

  III. _____

     A. _____

        1. _____

        2. _____

EXHIBIT 4.4 *(Continued)*

    B. _____

        1. _____

        2. _____

Implementation (2—if needed)

IV. _____

    A. _____

        1. _____

        2. _____

    B. _____

        1. _____

        2. _____

Management, Tracking, & Communication

V. _____

    A. _____

        1. _____

        2. _____

    B. _____

        1. _____

        2. _____

Evaluation

VI. _____

    A. _____

        1. _____

        2. _____

    B. _____

        1. _____

        2. _____

4. Next, sort the completed cards into the following five stacks based on the type of activity you have written on the card. You may want to create a card with each of these headings written on it to facilitate the sorting:

- Set-up
- Research and development
- Implementation
- Management, tracking, and communication
- Evaluation

5. Next, spread a stack of the cards out in front of you. Sort the cards into groups based on tasks that work together toward a common end.

6. Next, order the groups of cards within the stack in time sequence. By "time sequence" we mean the order in which the tasks will be completed during the performance of the project. If the tasks on two or more cards or groups of cards take place simultaneously, then the order doesn't matter.

7. Repeat the grouping of step 5 and the ordering of step 6 for each of the remaining stacks of cards.

8. Using a standard outline format, create a project outline. Your outline will have five Roman numerals, one for each of the five original topic stacks into which you sorted your cards in step 4. The capital letters under each Roman numeral will be assigned a topic according to the groups you made during step 5. The Arabic numerals under each capital letter will be assigned the task written on an individual card.

We have included a form on the disk (0404.doc) and in Exhibit 4.4 on which you can put your project outline. You might have more than one major section on implementation. An example could be a project that had an academic component and a mentoring component. It would probably make sense to separate the two, giving each major component of the implementation its own Roman numeral in the outline. The worksheet is set up with two implementation Roman numerals (III and IV), just in case.

Wise Guy

You know, this is all well and good. It makes sense, sure. But, I'd just as soon make it up as I go along. All this planning makes me feel trapped. I want wiggle room. I don't want to be pinned down about what I'm going to do. I need to be able to improvise on the spot.

Wise Lady

What I hear you saying is that you don't want to take the time and put forth the effort to do this right. So be it. If I were the grant maker, I'd toss your proposal in the round file or take back the grant money, whichever is appropriate. Why? Because if you're not willing to put forth the effort to appropriately design and plan the project, what guarantee do I have that you'd do what you said you'd do in the proposal—in the contract between you and me? What guarantee do I have that my money is well spent on a quality effort? What guarantee do I have that what you really want to do is better serve your target population? Grants are not about wiggling. They're not about a free ride. They're about applying serious effort to solving a problem. It sounds like I have no guarantees from you. If you want to shoot from the hip, then do it with your own money. You won't do it with mine. Wiggle your way to that bake sale I recommended before.

Conclusion

We have demonstrated a way to start organizing your project. True, you should have done this before you requested the grant, but if you didn't, it's never too late. Most project difficulties come from lack of a clear plan or scheme of action. This is also the main reason that budget problems occur. If you haven't taken into account all the activities involved in the project, then your budget probably doesn't contain enough money in the right places to actually run the project. This hurts the bottom line of your organization, and in fact can financially ruin the unwary. This is perhaps the main reason to carefully and fully develop a project before ever requesting grant funding. It is of paramount importance that you know as closely as possible how much it will cost to run the project. The question is: "Who will make up the difference if you get too little grant money?" The answer is obvious, "Your organization or agency will."

You may be questioning the amount of work involved in what is, after all, a speculative venture, submitting a grant proposal. Why, you might ask, should I spend all this time when I don't know whether I will be getting the money? That is a good question, but now you should see that when you don't plan thoroughly and effectively, the chances of success go down appreciably. We mean success in running the project, but the same is true about getting the grant. Grantors are not dummies. They read proposals all the time. They can tell when you haven't done your homework and truly figured out all the things that must be done. One of the obvious truths that come out of the realization that all projects have similar organization is that anyone familiar with this fact can tell if your project description contains all the necessary parts. They don't need to be experts on your subject matter to know that parts of the project have been neglected.

Many if not all the problems that occur during project management can be avoided if you follow this type of procedure and carefully and fully come to an understanding of all that is necessary to accomplish your proposed project. "A lot of work," you say. True, it is a lot of work, but someone or some group will do it, and they are the ones who will get funded. They are the ones who will be able to effectively run the project.

## Chapter 5

Putting in the Details: Fully Developing Your Project

"When *I* use a word," Humpty Dumpty said, in rather a
   scornful tone, "it means just what I choose it to mean—
   nothing more nor less."
"The question is," said Alice, "whether you can make words
   mean so many different things."
"The question is," said Humpty Dumpty, "which is to be the
   master—that's all."

Lewis Carroll, *Through the Looking Glass*

Introduction

The next logical step in our progress from broad problem to fully developed project is to create the goals and objectives of our project. No other single topic, except perhaps the use of jargon, inspires as much heated debate during the workshops that we conduct around the country. No other topic in grant seeking elicits as much puzzlement, as much confusion, or as much disagreement. Ten years ago, this was a mystery to us, because goals and objectives are simply statements that provide direction and information about a project's expected outcome(s), organization, implementation, and evaluation.

We have learned that the real problem is twofold. First, there are no widely accepted definitions of a goal or of an objective. Second, almost every organization or discipline has established its own definitions. Put these two facts together and you have a formula for confusion. Within our own organization, within our field of expertise, within the funding sources with which we are familiar, the definition of a goal and the definition of an objective are clear, understandable, and agreed upon by all. As long as we stay within the confines of our organization (agency), within our discipline, and within our usual funding sources, things roll along comfortably. But, what happens when we apply to a new funding source with differing definitions? What happens when we partner project development with an organization from a totally different academic background? Typical examples of this last situation are: a K–12 school partnering with a medical institution; an arts council partnering with the police department; a government health and human services agency partnering with the Salvation Army, or an institution of higher education partnering with anybody.

Confusion reigns. Partners lose confidence in each other. After all, if your partner doesn't even understand something as simple as the definition of an objective, how can it possibly be a contributing and useful part of your project? Why people invest as much emotion as they do into defending their particular definitions is beyond us, but we see it almost every day. Here are the facts. NO definitions of a goal or an objective are accepted by everybody. But, everybody does have a definition. It's just different from everybody else's. The people with the largest problem with these differences seem to be our friends in higher education. In all fairness, it is understandable. After all, they usually set standards. But to some degree, they live in a secluded world. Outside the world of academe many differing definitions can be used by your neighborhood not-for-profit, or by your local K–12 school, or health clinic, and by many grant makers.

Project Organization Concepts

The solution is to divorce yourself from set definitions and from rigid application of terms. The solution is to understand the underlying organization of any and all projects. Once you have a clear concept, you can plug in words to act as labels for your concepts at your leisure. The proper words with which to fill in the blanks come directly from the grantor to which we are applying. Don't use your definitions and your words; use the grantor's words and the grantor's definitions.

Exhibit 5.1 illustrates the model for all project organization. It doesn't matter whether your project is to make a peanut butter sandwich, take the family on vacation, or run an after school program for middle school students—from a conceptual viewpoint it is organized the same. At the top, the single box is the overall purpose of the project, the reason the project is being done in the first place. This highest level of purpose can be called several things. One of the more common names it is given is mission, but you may have experience with it being called vision, outcome, purpose, goal, or even objective.

EXHIBIT 5.1

Project Model

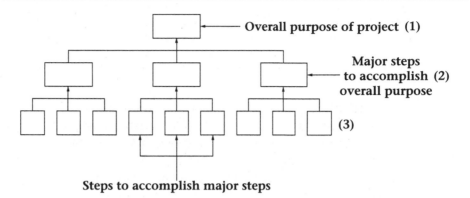

Immediately below the highest level of overall purpose is a set of boxes, perhaps three to five of them. These boxes represent the major steps it takes to accomplish the ultimate purpose recorded in the single box above them. This level of project organization is labeled variously by different agencies and organizations as goals, objectives, outcomes, or strategies.

Below the first row of boxes is another set of boxes, one set for each box in the row just above. These boxes represent the steps that must be taken to accomplish each of the statements in the boxes to which they are attached. We have seen this level of project organization called objectives, plan of action, tactics, activities, tasks, and project description.

If you are now shouting at the page that we clearly do not understand the meaning of these various words, it is you to whom we want to speak the most seriously. The rest of the world does not necessarily adhere to the definitions that you know and love. Under normal circumstances you can insist on using your definitions. But we are seeking grants. Under these circumstances, there is one and only one authority, and that authority is the grantor to which you are currently applying. Not the grantor to which you applied last year or last month or a hundred times in the past, but the one to which you are applying right now. Do not assume that the way you look at goals and objectives is the way that everybody does. It is not.

With that in mind, the following table illustrates several sets of words that we have seen used to describe the same three-level project organizational model. A fourth level of complexity can be added easily, usually with a term such as task, job, or activity to label the smallest or simplest level of complexity (see Exhibit 5.1).

(1) Mission	Vision	Purpose	Outcome	Goal	Mission
(2) Goals	Strategies	Objectives	Goals	Objectives	Objectives
(3) Objectives	Tactics	Activities	Tasks	Activities	Methods
(1) Objective	Mission	Purpose	Vision	Outcome	Goal
(2) Action Plan	Objective	Outcomes	Objectives	Objectives	Outcomes
(3) Steps	Action Plan	Activities	Tasks	Action Plan	Methods

This discussion has one purpose, to convince you to be flexible. To convince you that while the basic organizational scheme of any project is always the same, the words that describe that organization can and do differ. We also hope that by now you realize that any time an "expert" in grant seeking tells you with authority exactly what a goal or an objective is, that you will realize that they are giving you a limited view. You are not getting the whole picture. Yes, it is much simpler to give a definition. Most people feel most comfortable when given a definite answer, a definitive answer, a definition on which they can depend. The problem with that approach is that it is misleading when applied to grant seeking. To illustrate, several quotations concerning our subject from a variety of funding sources follow. After each quotation we have commented on the import of the quotation, and included a "word set" of the words used to label the three levels of organization that we defined previously.

Before we get to the quotations, we have a huge hint for you. When analyzing a grantor's instructions for project organization, the appropriate word that is singular refers to what you might usually call the mission of the project. In other words, the organizational word without an "s" on the end goes at the highest level of the our project organization model shown in Exhibit 5.1. For example, if the grantor asks you "what is the goal of your project?" then "goal," because it is singular, becomes what we may have called our project mission. You will see at least one example of this in the following quotations:

Quotation

The application package asks you for . . . specific goals and measurable objectives.

—*The Pew Charitable Trusts, Program Resource Guide 1999*

Comment

Here we have a foundation using the basic goals and objectives nomenclature. Note the implication that your goals are not required to be measurable, but you are directed to make the objectives measurable.

Word Set

Mission

Goals

Objectives

Quotation

Step 5: Develop your proposal's curriculum, instructional, and professional development goals.

Step 6: Develop action plans for each proposed goal.

Georgia's Technology Literacy Challenge Fund Grant, Application Package for Professional Development Grants, February 1998

Comment

Here the grantor tells us to use goals, but instead of objectives, the steps leading to the accomplishment of the goals are called action plans.

Word Set

Mission

Goals

Action Plans

Quotation

Will the activities achieve the goals of the project in thoughtful and creative ways?

National Endowment for the Humanities, Grant Application Instructions and Forms

Comment

Here, the National Endowment for the Humanities uses "goal" in the standard position, but uses "activities" to label the steps to take to achieve the goals.

Word Set

Mission

Goals

Activities

Quotation

Applications will be evaluated against the standard criteria listed below. . . . 2. The extent to which the applicant has . . . developed measurable goals and objectives for carrying out the project.

Program Guide FY 1998, Rural Health Outreach Grant Program, US Department of Health and Human Services

Comment

This is the basic usage of the terms goals and objectives. Also note that here the grantor expects both the goals and the objectives to be measurable, which is what we suggest you always do.

Word Set

Mission

Goals

Objectives

Mind Mapping

An additional point probably needs to be made, and here is as good a place as any. There is abroad in the land a "new" method of organizing projects. It is usually called Mind Mapping. What makes it different is that instead of starting with a rectangle at the top of the page you start

Exhibit 5.2

Example of Mind Mapping

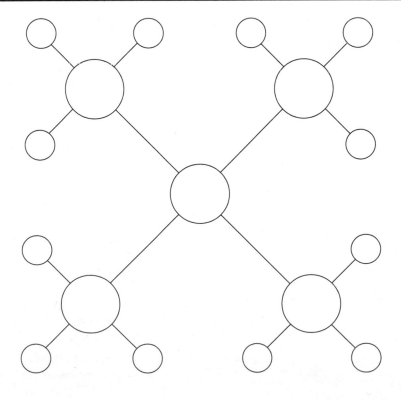

with a circle or oval in the middle of the page. Then instead of working down the page from the top, you work out from the middle in all directions. An example of Mind Mapping appears in Exhibit 5.2.

This method is excellent for original creation of project ideas and parts. Our minds often work better when allowed to jump all over the place. This "new" method does just that. But, when all is said and done, the new method is exactly the same organizational scheme as the old one. To see this, imagine taking the central circle in the Mind Map in Exhibit 5.2 and dragging it to the top of the page. Gravity affects all the attached circles and they drop down underneath the circle that is now at the top of the page, as in Exhibit 5.3. Do you see that we now have exactly the same organizational scheme as before? What is different, and this is an excellent and useful difference, is the way we arrived at the content of the circles

or boxes.

With all this uncertainty that we seem to have injected into this subject, what are we to do? How are we to know what to name the levels of complexity of our project? How are we to know what these names or labels mean? If nothing is definite, how do we arrive at any set organizational scheme for our project? The answer has two parts, because you are dealing with two audiences for your project description. One target for your project description is the personnel in your organization, those who

EXHIBIT 5.3

Looking at Mind Mapping in a New Way

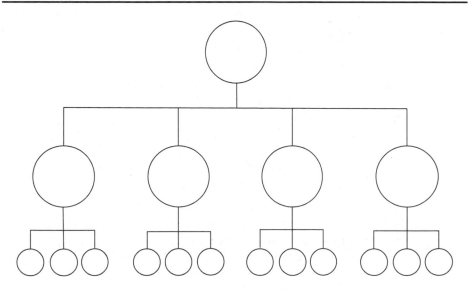

will run the project once it is funded. For this audience you use the terms and labels with which they are already familiar and comfortable. There is no reason to confuse them with new terms. The second audience for your project description is the grantor. For the grantor you use the terms that the grantor uses in the application guidelines. This is one of the more important things you can do to get funded. This entire discussion has been for the purpose of convincing you to be flexible, to allow more than one word to stand for the same thing. Here is where you apply that flexibility. You must not insist on using your own terminology when applying for a grant. You must use the terminology of the grantor. We can call a beautiful rose "that red flower," but our label doesn't change the nature of the rose. The same is basically true of your project organizational scheme. This simple fact is what takes the uncertainty out of the process. All the discussion about using different sets of words to mean the same thing doesn't leave you adrift, because you will use the grantor's words, the words that the grantor uses in the request for proposal.

From Outline to Goals

Keeping in mind that the words we choose to use are simply labels for our mutual convenience, we will use "goal" to label the first level of complexity just under the singular mission or purpose of our project. Remember, however, that the description that follows is actually for those major steps it takes to accomplish the ultimate purpose of a project, not for the word "goal" for which there is not a universally accepted definition. We use "goal" as a convenience and also because it is used more often than any other word to label this particular level of complexity in project organization.

A goal has three characteristics. First, a goal is realistic. That is, a goal is something that can be achieved or is doable. Second, a goal is measurable. There must be a means of quantifying the results. Third, a goal should be clear and easy to understand, not written in some convoluted bureaucratic language.

A goal has five parts. What are you going to do? What approach will you use? When will it happen? What is the measurement attached, how many or how much? What result or outcome will accrue after the accomplishment of the goal? The simplest way to construct goals is to use your project outline as the starting point. For example, read over the Implementation part of the project outline developed in Chapter 4 that is shown in Exhibit 5.4. Read all the activities and answer the question, "In general what are we doing?" At this stage don't get specific, stay general.

EXHIBIT 5.4

Project Outline

III. Implementation

    A. Academic Activities

        1. Hold supervised and tutored homework sessions

        2. Hold supplemental academic instruction

    B. Social Activities

        1. Hold conflict resolution training

        2. Hold antitobacco, alcohol, and drug training

    C. Cultural Activities

        1. Hold Boys Club activities

        2. Hold Girls Club activities

        3. Hold Boy Scout meetings

        4. Hold Girl Scout meetings

        5. Hold 4-H Club meetings

    D. Physical Activities

        1. Serve snack

        2. Hold outside sports

The answer might be, "Implement after school program." This statement then goes in the first box of our Goal Creation Form. Those of you who have read *Grantseeker's Toolkit* will recognize this form. If you have not seen it before, there is just one simple rule for its use. Do not use sentences. Put your ideas down in the shortest form possible using the fewest words possible. For example:

Do What?	Approach?	When?	Measure?	Result?
Implement after school program				

The next box to complete is the one labeled "Result." It will not be obvious that this is the next logical step until you have done it a few times, especially if you do it in some other order. It is difficult to explain why the Result should be next, but we'll try.

We complete the Result box next because this gives us a target for which to aim when completing the remaining topics. If we can state the result we expect from a goal (or an objective for that matter; they work the same with regard to this), then we understand much better exactly what we are trying to accomplish. It is best to establish this right up front, not wait till the last. Trying it this way is the best way to prove to yourself that it works.

A problem with stating the expected result is that it is often so obvious that it eludes us. Or, we think that it is so obvious that it is not worth stating. Another way to say the same thing as "result," and a way that some people find more helpful, is to ask yourself, "What benefit will eventuate if I accomplish this goal?" The use of the word "benefit" helps some people. The whole point of the "Result" box is to state clearly the outcome that will occur when this goal is completed. Usually, the implementation goal is directly related to solving the stated problem that the project is intended to solve. As a result, normally, the result expected from the implementation goal is all or a major part of the overall mission of the project. The "Result" of the goal on which we are working might say, "participants will not contribute to increased crime by predriving age children." Remember, this is the original problem that began the whole project design and development process.

Do What?	Using What Approach?	By When?	With What Measure?	With What Result?
Implement after school program				participants will not contribute to increased crime by predriving age children

The next item to complete is the "Approach." This item is sometimes called "methodology" and is basically how you intend to go about whatever it is you are doing. Let us digress a bit here. "Approach" is a word that causes a lot of confusion, especially to educators at all levels, because that word means something specific filled with import and complication to an educator. It's associated with the word methodology and we took whole courses in methods. Grant makers use the word regularly and have no idea what commotion is wrought with the use of it. All the grant maker means by the word "approach" or "methodology" is how are you going to do the "Do What." They want the "how to" part described here.

Let's look at our example. We have the "Do What" completed, the "Result" completed, and now we're working on the "Approach" box. How were we planning to connect the "Do What" to the "Result?" We could say that we are going to "provide supervised academic, social, cultural, and physical activities." It's as simple as that. This is how we intend to assist and educate community young people.

Do What?	Using What Approach?	By When?	With What Measure?	With What Result?
Implement after school program	*academic, social, cultural, and physical activities*			*participants will not contribute to increased crime by predriving age children*

The penultimate box we will complete is the "When" box. That should be fairly easy to complete after we've worked on the other three boxes. The question is: "When do you expect start-up of all the activities you've mentioned to be underway?" It's usually best to express this time frame in project months rather than calendar months. An example would be "project month eleven till end of project." This is shorthand notation for the complete idea that this goal will begin implementation during project month eleven and continue through till the end of the project. You could also express the "When" in calendar time—"September, 2004 till end of project." The project month approach is preferred, unless the grant maker has a specified method to use. Using project months or project quarters, or project years divorces you from the calendar and removes the uncertainty that always creeps into time frames. After all, you usually don't know exactly when the grant money is going to show up. But using the project month approach, it doesn't matter when the money shows up. Whenever it does, that begins project month one.

Do What?	Using What Approach?	By When?	With What Measure?	With What Result?
Implement after school program	academic, social, cultural, and physical activities	in PY One, start in PM two till end of school yr in other PYs, start when school starts		participants will not contribute to increased crime by predriving age children

Now, on to the remaining unfilled box, "Measure?" Measurement is a subject about which we can get truly frightened. We want to wiggle and weasel and not promise anything concrete. But, wiggling and squirming does not appeal to a grant maker and does not help when it comes to the all-important evaluation. We discuss evaluation in Chapters 11 through 15. Remember this step and come back to it after you've read those chapters. Suffice it to say, measurement is critically important to the success of your project. In fact, how do you know you've succeeded if you have nothing against which to measure progress? The answer is that you won't.

In our example, we have completed the "What?" the "Result?" the "How?" and the "When?" boxes. The question now is, how do we measure what we're doing? How do we tell if we've gotten results? Look at what we have planned carefully and the measurement is easy to establish. We're having supervised academic and training sessions, making presentations, supervising sports activities with all desired participants involved. What parts of this statement are measurable? The number of participants, the number of sessions/presentations/discussions, the number of training sessions, and the number of sports activities. So, what we have to know is how many participants we desire and how many of the various activities it's our goal to hold. That's it. It's not complicated or magic, just logical. Don't pick a low number "just to be safe." There's no point to the goal if you set the bar so low that anyone can jump it.

When establishing measurement (how many or how much) at the goal level, it is important to remember that we have another level of organization just under this one, what we call objectives. Each objective has its own measurement. The result is that we don't have to jam in all the things we are going to measure here at the goal level. Keep this measure general, and then be more specific in the objectives. Indeed, you might even go one level below objectives. Let's call that level tasks. These tasks will have measurement built in, so you are not necessarily required, even at the objective level, to put in all the measurement that will take place.

Do What?	Using What Approach?	By When?	With What Measure?	With What Result?
Implement after school program	academic, social, cultural, and physical activities	in PY One, start in PM two till end of school yr in other PYs, start when school starts	400 participants	participants will not contribute to increased crime by predriving age children

From Goals to Objectives

Creating objectives for the goals is fairly easy now. Our goal is descriptive and measurable. Objectives are just the steps for accomplishing a specific goal. We're moving from overview (goal) to more specific detail (objective), but we're still talking about the same topic, the same set of activities. What actions would we have to take to successfully accomplish the goal we've just completed? Objectives are realistic and measurable, just like goals, and objectives should be clear and easy to understand.

An objective has five parts. What are you going to do? What approach will you use? What is the measurement? What result or outcome will accrue after the accomplishment of the goal? Who is going to do it? Notice there is one difference in the parts of a goal and objective. We've substituted a Who? for the When? With objectives, it's important to specify "who" is responsible for the actions. "When" has already been specified in the goal statement.

Let's do what we just did with goals, only apply the process to objectives. We return to the Implementation part of our outline, seen in Exhibit 5.4. That is where we are getting all the information on which we are basing our project plan. Note that we have four main headings under Implementation: Academic Activities, Social Activities, Cultural Activities, and Physical Activities. This will guide us into realizing that we most likely need four objectives under our Implementation goal.

The format with which we capture the information for objectives looks almost exactly the same as the one we used for goals and it is shown here. By the way, this form is not on the disk that comes with this book. It is, however, on the disk that comes with *Grantseeker's Toolkit*.

Do What?	Using What Approach?	By Who?	With What Measure?	With What Result?

First we determine the "Do What?" We've already decided that we have four categories of activities: academic, social, cultural, and physical. So we could develop a formula and use it for each of the four sets of activities. The formula statement could look like this: "hold _____ activities." Now all we do is plug in our four categories of activities and we have our "Do What? for all four objectives. Using only one of the objectives as an example, what we have now looks like this:

Goal Three—Objective One

Do What?	Using What Approach?	By Who?	With What Measure?	With What Result?
hold academic activities				

Next, we determine the logical desired result. What do we want to happen? Why are we doing this objective anyway? What benefit will accrue to the target population and/or the community if we accomplish this objective. The answer to these questions will become the content of the "With What Result?" box. This information isn't in our outline. We need to know why we are doing these particular activities in the first place. Action without purpose may appear to be accomplishing things, because a lot may be getting done. But, the real question is, "Why do things if we don't understand what outcome we expect after we have done them?" This is the purpose of the content that goes into the "With What Result?" box.

For this particular project, our ultimate purpose for providing the after school program is to drive down the incidence of juvenile crime between 3:00 P.M. and 6:00 P.M. on school weekdays. In addition, however, we have a set of subsidiary purposes, one of which is to help students improve their academic performance. This improvement in academic performance is what we are after with this objective. It might look like this:

Goal Three—Objective One

Do What?	Using What Approach?	By Who?	With What Measure?	With What Result?
hold academic activities				*Improve academic performance*

Third, we look at our approach—remember this is just the "how to" part of the objective. It's time to look at our outline again. When we do, we see that under the academic activities category we plan to do two main things: hold supervised and tutored homework sessions and hold supplemental academic instruction. Therefore, our approach to academic activities is to hold these two types of sessions. The result will look something like this:

Goal Three—Objective One

Do What?	Using What Approach?	By Who?	With What Measure?	With What Result?
hold academic activities	*supervised and tutored homework sessions & supplemental academic instruction*			*improve academic performance*

Next to last, we list who will do the things we've committed to do in this objective. For project development and proposal completion, a job function or title is the right thing to use to fill in this blank. However, if you're writing a working management plan, we suggest you list the name of the person who will actually be doing the work. In our case the overall responsibility for this objective lies with the Project Director. That person will oversee high school student monitors and tutors of the homework sessions as well as certified teachers for the supplemental academic instruction. Our objective might look like this now:

Goal Three—Objective One

Do What?	Using What Approach?	By Who?	With What Measure?	With What Result?
hold academic activities	supervised and tutored homework sessions & supplemental academic instruction	supervised by Project Director high school student tutors and monitors for homework sessions & certified teachers for supplemental academic instruction		improve academic performance

Finally, we come to measurement. What can we measure? How about the number of participants in homework sessions, the number of tutoring sessions, the number of participants in each of the supplemental academic instruction, and the number of sessions held. Here we have to do a little educated guesswork. We don't know how many participants will need tutoring and we want everyone who does need it to have access to it. Look at the numbers you expect to participate and make a good, logical assumption about how many will need tutoring. Then use your expertise to guesstimate how many sessions per participant will be necessary. No one is going to shoot you if you aren't exactly right. The grant maker and anyone who is evaluating the project will both know you couldn't have known exactly what the numbers would be at this stage of the game. You are just setting a benchmark, a guideline, a yardstick. This is where your expertise comes in. You are an expert in your field and you know about what to expect, so your judgment is as good or better than anyone's when it comes to establishing preliminary measurement.

Also note that we said we wanted our result to be improved academic performance. We need to be sure we address that with a measurement also. What you decide to measure is up to you and open to discussion. We will pick "improvement" as our measure. We expect participants to improve their academic performance from the beginning of a school year to the end.

Goal Three—Objective One

Do What?	Using What Approach?	By Who?	With What Measure?	With What Result?
hold academic activities	supervised and tutored homework sessions & supplemental academic instruction	supervised by project director high school student tutors and monitors for homework sessions & certified teachers for supplemental academic instruction (SAI)	300 participants completing homework each day 50 participants tutored each day SAI in math and language arts for 100 participants daily All participants have statistically significant academic improvement	improve academic performance

Now we need to continue the process for the other objectives. Note that the "Who?" in the objectives is where project partners begin to be mentioned. After you have done this project development process several times, you will note that this consistently happens. A problem with many project organization schemes is that they try to say everything at once. This confuses readers who can't keep all the detail straight when it's fed to them all at once. Begin with one broad purpose and work down to major steps. Next describe how each major step will be accomplished. If you are patient and let the project description process work its way out, an amazing amount of detail will emerge. The great benefit is that the detail will emerge in such a way that it is logical and easy to understand. You will be stepping any reader, including yourself, through the process in simple, easy-to-understand steps, with each step getting progressively more detailed. But, as we go down in levels, the number of individual steps multiplies greatly, so that while a level can contain huge amounts of information, each individual piece contains only a manageable amount. A proposal reviewer will reward you with high grades, and your project director will reward you with well-run projects. After all, the project director has a clear road map to follow. If we continue the process through the remaining objectives the result might look like this:

Goal Three

Do What?	Using What Approach?	By When?	With What Measure?	With What Result?
Implement after school program	academic, social, cultural, and physical activities	in PY One, start in PM two till end of school yr in other PYs, start when school starts	400 participants	participants will not contribute to increased crime by predriving age children

Goal Three—Objective One

Do What?	Using What Approach?	By Who?	With What Measure?	With What Result?
hold academic activities	supervised and tutored homework sessions & supplemental academic instruction	supervised by project director (PD) high school student tutors and monitors for homework sessions & certified teachers for supplemental academic instruction (SAI)	300 participants completing homework each day 50 participants tutored each day SAI in math and language arts for 100 participants daily All participants have statistically significant academic improvement	participant homework is getting done and participant academic achievement increases

Goal Three—Objective Two

Do What?	Using What Approach?	By Who?	With What Measure?	With What Result?
hold social activities	Conflict resolution training and tobacco, alcohol, and drug prevention training	PD Supervised Police Dept staff & School District counseling staff	All participants complete both training curriculums	Participants have fewer incidents of reported conflicts and use of alcohol, drug, and tobacco use than nonparticipants

Goal Four—Objective Three

Do What?	Using What Approach?	By Who?	With What Measure?	With What Result?
hold cultural activities	Boys Club Girls Club Boy Scouts Girl Scouts 4-H recruit others	PD supervised Respective leaders of these groups	All participants provided with a weekly cultural activity of their choice & five additional choices by end of PM four	Participants previously unable to participate due to travel and money problems will now have opportunity

Goal Five—Objective Four

Do What?	Using What Approach?	By Who?	With What Measure?	With What Result?
hold physical activities	individual and team sports and serve snack	PD supervised Parks and Recreation staff & School District Cafeteria staff	All participants participate in a daily physical activity & receive nutritious snack	contribute to wellness of participants and let kids be kids & keep from getting hungry till evening meal

As you look over the contents of the boxes just above, you might decide that you would have put different information in some of the boxes than we put there. If this is your position, you will get no argument from us. The purpose of this example is not to suggest that this is the correct and most elegant way to put together such a project. What we are trying to illustrate is a process, a method of getting a project organized and down on paper. The exact composition of your organization will most certainly be different from ours, but the principles will remain the same. The principles are truly simple to state. The prime principle is to work from the general to the specific. Start with broad statements and work your way down to very detailed and specific statements. Do this in a logical sequence with an easy-to-understand physical layout, and you will have been successful in developing a project.

Task Level Analysis

What happens after you create Goals and Objectives? Well, that's up to you. In a management plan, you might ask each of the "Who's" you listed with each objective to analyze the tasks necessary to complete each of their jobs. You might use boxes just like you did under Goals and Objectives. It's critical to effective management and measurement to carry your planning to this level. What you call this level isn't particularly important. It could be task, activity, job, or simply step. If you do create a format for another level of specificity (we're calling it the task level), then the boxes you need are:

Do What?

With What Result? (what end product are you looking for?)

Who Will Do It? (here's where delegation is important)

By When? (this question represents a deadline for those performing various tasks)

Measurement (important when the tasks are dependent on each other for completion)

Task Analysis

Do What?	With What Result?	Who Will Do It?	By When?	Measurement?

There's another way to plan and capture the task level of project management, and we've created a tool to use for this purpose. Called the Task Analysis Worksheet, it can be found on the disk (0505.doc) and in Exhibit 5.5. Print the number of copies of file 0505.doc that you need for your Task Analysis, one for each objective. You will see how to label each page to make a long series. Exhibit 5.5 documents the same information as the task boxes, but in a chart format. Whatever tool you use to record your plan, it's important that the plan is written down and followed. We don't believe in planning just as an exercise. Plans should be dog-eared with use and covered in notes and scribbles. That's why we call the planning we teach Action Planning. To be effective, planning has to lead to action.

Completion of Project Development

There's one last step to complete project development. We're not going to discuss this step to any depth here because it's covered fairly extensively in the *Grantseeker's Toolkit*, but there's still information that you need to know to have a completely developed project. What is missing? A list of resources needed for everybody to do their jobs. Every task requires

EXHIBIT 5.5 0505.DOC

Task Analysis Worksheet

Goal #: _____ _____

Objective #: _____ _____

Task List	Resources Needed				Project Month
	People	Materials/ Supplies	Facilities/ Contracts	Funds	

Exhibit 5.6 0506.DOC

Expanded Project Outline

Goal #: _____

Objectives & Tasks	When?	Who?	Where?	Resources?	Cost?
Obj. 1					
Tasks					
Obj. 2					
Tasks					
Obj. 3					
Tasks					
Obj. 4					
Tasks					
Obj. 5					
Tasks					
Obj. 6					
Tasks					

"things," materials and equipment. The facilities required have not been determined. Every job must be done somewhere. Finally, but very importantly, how much is it going to cost to do each task, objective, and goal? Goal is listed last here, because it's really the total of the funds allocated to tasks and objectives. Seldom are there costs involved directly at the goal level. The costs are incurred further down in the organizational process. In the budget process, it's best to work backward, from tasks to objectives to a goal. Determine the cost of each task in personnel, resources, and facilities. Add up all the tasks for a total for each objective. Add up all the objectives for a total for the goal.

We capture this part of the planning process on what we call the Extended Project Outline. We expand our project outline as described in Chapter 4 to include resources, facilities, and the cost of each level of activity. An example of an Expanded Project Outline is included in Exhibit 5.6. This form can be found on the disk that comes with *Grantwinner's Toolkit* (0506.doc). The worksheet is two pages and designed to handle one goal on those two pages. Therefore, you need to print the appropriate number for your particular project.

Conclusion

It is impossible in one chapter to describe fully a process to which we have dedicated an entire third of a previous book. For more detail, more forms, and more examples, please see *Grantseeker's Toolkit*. This chapter is intended to be an introduction to the topic of project development, not a full explication of the topic. It is very important to note, however, the central importance of a fully developed project to successful grantseeking. One of the major and constant complaints that we hear about many if not most proposals that grantors receive is that the project is "little more than a good idea, without the form or substance to let us know if the applicant really understands what is involved." You will not fall into this common trap if you fully develop your project so that when you are answering the grantor's questions you answer responsively, completely, and in detail.

The proof that you "understand[s] what is involved" is in the details. When you add sufficient detail to your project description, it is clear to the grantor that you have thought through carefully the project and its ramifications with respect to personnel, time, resources, and money (both the grantor's and others'). When faced with a decision between funding two equally valid, innovative, and significant solutions (projects), grantors invariably choose the project that is more fully developed, that shows the most careful planning and attention to detail. Make sure that the project that fits that description is always yours.

## PART II

Managing the Funded Project

## Chapter 6

The Basics of Managing a Funded Project

"The time has come," the Walrus said,
"To talk of many things:
Of shoes—and ships—and sealing wax—
Of cabbages—and kings . . .
And whether pigs have wings."

Lewis Carroll,
Alice's Adventures in Wonderland

Introduction

What is management? What does it mean to manage a project? We know what "management" means in the sense of "the boss." As in, "Management is at it again. The 'suits' are cutting staff, increasing workload, and demanding that morale had better, by golly, go up." This, of course, is not the type of management in which we are interested. Still, we need some entry point into understanding what is meant when we are asked to manage a project. We use baseball as an analogy.

A professional baseball team has a number of coaches, a hitting coach, a pitching coach, a bullpen coach, a first base coach, a third base coach, and others. None of these coaches, however, is responsible for strategy on the field, for changing pitchers, for calling a pitch-out, for calling for a runner to steal a base, for telling the pitcher to issue an intentional walk. The manager makes decisions such as these. In baseball, the person in charge of directing the actions of the team on the field is called a manager. Thinking about all the decisions and directions given during the course of a baseball game will bring into focus what a manager does. The manager decides who will hit and in what order, who will pitch and for how long, whether to call for a hit and run play, and whether to pinch run for someone. The manager directs the flow of a game. Now, as we all know, the manager does not play the game (yes, there have been player-managers, but let's leave them out of the discussion). The manager does not go to bat and get hits. The manager does not take the mound and pitch to opposing batters. The manager directs who will do so. As the director, the manager has a great deal of control over what happens, but, and this is an important but, the manager does not have absolute control. His batters can fail to get hits. His pitchers can fail to throw strikes. His fielders can fail to catch the ball. The most skilled manager in the world can only direct, he cannot play the game for his players. The same is true in business, in education, in the nonprofit sector, in health care, in fact in any field, area, or discipline you choose.

Leaving our baseball analogy and moving to a concrete definition, *Webster's New World Dictionary* tells us that "manage" means "to have charge of; direct; conduct; administer." So, in the most general sense, managing a project is to direct the activities of the project, to be in charge, to have responsibility for seeing that things get done, and to have the authority to see that things get done. The last two points are worth repeating and thinking about. If a person is given the responsibility for managing a project, then that person should also be given the necessary authority to manage the project. The two work together; one without the other is a recipe for disaster. Giving a person the authority to act but not the responsibility to do so leads to inaction. Giving a person the responsibility to act without the authority also leads to inaction, for different reasons, but inaction nevertheless.

What the Grantor Expects

Now that we have a very general definition and understanding of what it means to manage a project, let's move to the specifics of what a grantor expects. To set the stage we will quote the grantor. After all, the grantor is the only real authority, the only source of truly knowing what we should do. The fact is, the grantor is the only source of ultimate truth in the field of grant seeking and grants management.

Management Plan

Evidence that the project activities will be effectively completed, that the applicant is capable of carrying out the project to its successful conclusion through the deployment and management of resources including money, personnel, facilities, equipment, and supplies, and that financial management will be sound.

Grant Application and Guidelines, 1999 National Leadership Grants,
Institute of Museum and Library Services

"(d) Quality of the management plan (10 points)

 (i) The adequacy of the management plan to achieve the objectives of the proposed project on time and within budget, including defined responsibilities, timelines, and milestones for accomplishing project tasks;

 (ii) The adequacy of procedures for ensuring feedback and continuous improvement in the operation of the proposed project;

 (iii) The adequacy of mechanisms for ensuring high-quality products and services from the proposed project;

 (iv) The extent to which the time commitments of the project director and principal investigator and other key personnel are appropriate and adequate to meet the objectives of the proposed project;"

> *Application for New Grants under the Individuals with Disabilities Education Act (IDEA), Fiscal Year 1999, Office of Special Education & Rehabilitative Services, US Department of Education*

"Management—provides project management information that can be used to strengthen a project. Such formative information could document delivery strategies, implementation methods, barriers to implementation, and achievement of milestones and objectives."

> *Program Announcement and Guidelines, Advanced Technology Education, National Science Foundation*

"In developing this section, you have an opportunity to provide evidence that the applicant team has the ability to effectively deal with both the technical complexity and the organizational challenges associated with managing the project.

> *Application Kit for Fiscal Year 1999, Telecommunications and Information Infrastructure Assistance Program (TIIAP), US Department of Commerce*

"3) 20 points Demonstrated capability, experience and knowledge (i.e. managerial, technical, and clinical) of the applicant and other network members to implement the project and to disseminate information about the project."

> *Program Guide 1999, Rural Telemedicine Grant Program, Office of Rural Health Policy, US Department of Health and Human Services*

We learn from these five quotations that the management of a grant project includes several varied and distinct topics. Points made in the quotations above deal with the management, oversight, and direction of: personnel, money, time, performance, record keeping, feedback, evaluation and assessment, information dissemination, and continuous improvement.

Putting these points into an organizational scheme, we can arrive at the following topics. It should come as no surprise that each of these topics is the subject of one or more entire chapters in this book:

- Documentation of project activities
- Management of project personnel
- Management of project finances
- Evaluation of the project
- Dissemination of information about the project
- Replication activities
- Continuation activities

This chapter, however, only introduces the general topic of management. We begin by answering a series of questions. What exactly is this thing that people call management? Who does this management? Who manages the manager? What does a manager manage? By this time you might be ready to say, with some amount of frustration, "Look, all that stuff is interesting, but very general. What I want to know is how, specifically and in concrete terms, does a project manager know what to do?" That is an important topic also. How does the project director know what to do? Are there outside regulations by which a project manager must abide? And finally, we discuss miscellaneous topics that could go any-where or nowhere, but which we put in this chapter.

What Managers Do

We need a good practical working definition of what is meant by the term "management." As good a short definition as you are likely to get is that management means "allocate resources to accomplish things." "Where," you might ask, "does leadership come into the picture? Isn't leadership much like management?" The answer is yes and no, but mostly no. A leader provides vision and direction. A manager sees that tasks are per-formed on time and correctly.

If we think about a couple of recent presidents of the United States (while leaving aside politics), we can illustrate the point. Jimmy Carter is universally acknowledged to be a really nice guy, honest, moral, and with integrity that most everyone feels they can trust. Why, then, was Jimmy Carter pilloried by many as a poor president? Because he was/is a manager. He is interested in the minutia of things; after all, his education was as an engineer. We expect a president to be a leader. Turning to another recent president, Ronald Reagan is universally acknowledged, by those who have met him, to be one of the nicest guys around. He is consistently upbeat and positive, confident in his and the country's ability to do anything to which they set their mind. Why, then, was Ronald Reagan pilloried by many as a poor president? Because he was a leader. He was interested in the broad sweep of things, the vision. After all, he started life as an actor, selling ideas and emotions to audiences. We expect our president to be a manager.

Does this seem schizophrenic? Well the truth is, we expect a president to be both a leader and a manager. A president is supposed to lead the nation with passion and vision but is also supposed to manage the nation with diligence and attention to detail. The best leaders have good management skills. And conversely, the best managers have good leadership skills. So what is the wrap-up to this little discussion? It is that to be a good project director, you will absolutely need management skills. Having a few leadership skills will not hurt, however they are not absolutely necessary.

Managers Allocate Resources

We started by saying that the simplest definition of management is to allocate resources to accomplish tasks. There are two parts to that definition, the allocation of resources and the accomplishment of tasks. We will leave the discussion of what tasks will be accomplished to later. Now, we want to ask the question, "What are these resources that a manager allocates?" Resources can be divided arbitrarily into three categories: time, money, and things. There is a great deal of interrelationship between the three categories. They are not mutually exclusive. After all, money can buy time and things, but we need a simple starting point. Breaking the three categories of resources down further, we come up with the following list of resources that a manager might allocate to a task:

- Time
  - Managers
  - Staff
  - Volunteers
  - Partners
  - Participants
  - Consultants
  - Service Providers
- Money
  - Purchases
  - Leases
  - Rents
  - Salaries

- Stipends
- Service Fees
- Travel
- Things
  - Equipment
  - Materials and Supplies
  - Facilities

Managers Need Skills

Allocating resources is the most basic way of looking at management, but it only takes us a short way down a long road. To be able to allocate resources effectively a manager will need a number of skills. Any list of these skills would include communication, coordination, organization, and planning. Just as with the last list, these items are not mutually exclusive. There is a lot of interaction. After all, skill in communicating clearly is a prime requisite for being able to coordinate activities between different people or organizations.

Managers Must Have Responsibility and Authority

In addition to skills, a manger must be given responsibility and authority. Having responsibility for a thing means that a person has been delegated some duty or obligation for which that person is accountable, the accountability being the key point. Having authority, on the other hand, means that a person has the power or right to take action, to give commands, and to make final decisions. Authority without responsibility means that a person can take action and not be held accountable for those actions. This is not good. Responsibility without authority means that a person can be held accountable for something without having the power or right to influence the performance or outcome. This is not good. The two go together in a careful balance. When a person has authority over a thing, that person must also be given the responsibility for it, be held accountable for it. The reverse is also true. If a person is to be held accountable, given responsibility, then that person must have also the authority to influence the performance and outcome.

Who Does Management? Who Manages the Manager?

Usually the person who manages a project is called a Project Director. Other titles are often used, however, titles such as Principal Investigator, Project Coordinator, Project Leader, Team Leader, or Project Administrator.

This last title, Administrator, brings us back to a discussion of labels, of words and their meanings. We must be very, very careful that we don't let our personal experience dictate what we expect with respect to titles. In education, "administration" means one thing. In other fields it may well mean something very different. For example, the people that head up a school are often called "the administration" or "the administrators." In other settings this set of people might be called the "management team" or "managers," or "management."

You may have heard the saying that "You manage people, but you administer things and money." In the context of your field this may well be absolutely correct. Just don't assume that it is true in every other field. When working in the field of grants, we always take our lead from the grantor. So, the only definitions that matter are those that the grantor holds. If you can tell what the grantor thinks, then take that lead. If the grantor doesn't give you any guidance, use your own terms. Just be sure to explain clearly what you mean by them. Do not assume that the grantor uses or knows your own management terms.

The three terms that give the most trouble are management, coordination, and administration. Do these three terms have different definitions? Yes, they do. Does that matter, within the context of most grant projects? No, it doesn't. Coordination and administration are subsets of skills that fall under the overall mantle of management. That some organizations and some grantors break them out separately doesn't change the fact that coordination and administration are part of a manager's responsibilities. This discussion is here because throughout the rest of this book we refer to the person in immediate charge of a grant funded project as a Project Director. Keep in mind that when you see the term "Project Director" we mean manager, coordinator, and administrator, all rolled up into one. Might you divide some of those responsibilities out and place them under another person? Of course you could. So, the answer to our lead question, "Who does this Management?", is the person named as the Project Director. A person with authority and responsibility.

The Organization Chart

In Exhibit 6.1 is a diagram known as an organization chart. All you need to know to be able to understand organization charts are a few simple rules. The lone box at the top indicates the person and position in charge of all people and positions in boxes connected with solid lines in levels below. Boxes on the same horizontal plane (side by side) are at the same level within an organization. For example, in a museum, the Director's box would stand alone at the top; the three Assistant Directors would each

EXHIBIT 6.1

Organization Chart

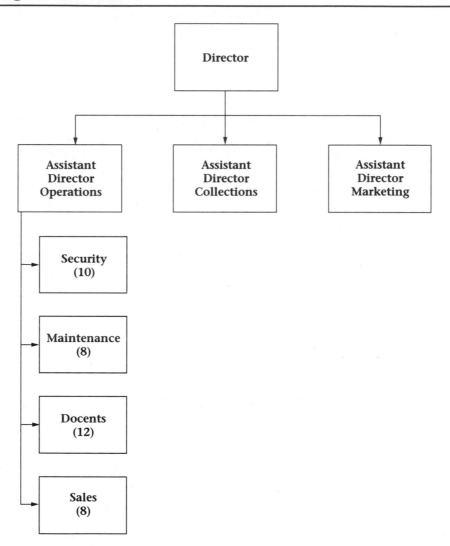

have a box on the same row (side by side) just under the Director. Another obvious rule is that all people and positions indicated by boxes below any other box and connected with solid lines report to or work for the person or position indicated by the uppermost box in the group. To continue with our museum example, one of the Assistant Directors might have 38 people working for her. Those 38 people would be indicated by a number of boxes below the Assistant Director's box and connected to her box by solid lines. The other Assistant Directors would also have people working for them. We do not show them to simplify the example. If you run a museum and take issue with our organization chart, it is only an example.

The organization chart in Exhibit 6.2 shows a possible organization of a grant-funded project. All we can tell without more explanation is that this project has a Project Director that is in overall control. Working directly for the Project Director are a Technician, a Psychologist, and an Interviewer. The Psychologist has three counselors working for her. All of these positions are connected with solid lines indicating lines of authority and responsibility. Note also the Advisory Board off to the right. It is connected to the Project Director by a dashed line, and is on the same level as the Project Director. The positioning of the two boxes shows that the Project Director does not work for the Advisory Board and that the Advisory Board does not work for the Project Director, in the same way that the Technician, the Psychologist, and the Interviewer do not work for one another. The fact that the line between the boxes is dashed indicates that the relationship between the two positions is one of communication, not authority and responsibility. In other words, the Project Director must maintain communications with the Advisory Board and vice versa, but the Board does not exert authority over the functioning of the project. By the same token, the Advisory board does not have responsibility for the project either, but the Project Director does.

EXHIBIT 6.2

Organization of Grant-Funded Project

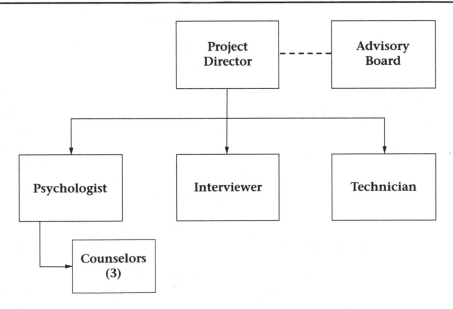

But who manages the Project Director? To whom must the Project Director answer? Who has responsibility for and authority over the Project Director? The answer can vary widely, but one aspect of the answer is always true. Somebody does. No grant-funded project exists wholly on its own. The Project Manager is answerable to someone. The question is, Who is that person? The general answer is that the person responsible for the Project Director is someone in your organization or agency. Your project funded with grant money must plug into your own agency's organization chart somewhere.

By the way, if you really can't see how or where the project plugs into your own organization chart, then something is badly wrong with the project, probably at the most basic level, the mission statement. If you can't find a place to put a project, its mission and purpose must not be aligned with the mission and purpose of your agency. The project should not be undertaken by your agency. The project falls outside of your purview, and your agency really doesn't have the charter to take on such a project.

Let us illustrate a possible organization chart of a nonprofit agency. This agency is responsible, countywide, for alcohol, tobacco and other drug (ATOD) prevention. The agency's normal funding comes from a

EXHIBIT 6.3

Organization Chart: Drug Treatment Program

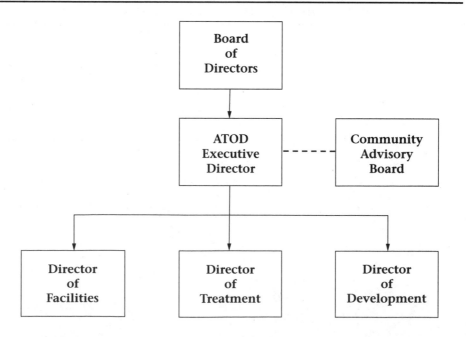

combination of city and county government, the United Way, the community foundation, and a federal formula grant. The organization chart of this agency might look like the one in Exhibit 6.3.

Now, let us assume that the agency has applied for and won a federal project grant in the area of prevention and treatment of teen drug use. The project's approach is technology-oriented and uses telecommunications as a key feature of counseling and training. The organization chart for this project is that shown in Exhibit 6.2.

The questions are: to whom within the nonprofit agency will the Project Director report, to whom is the Project Director directly responsible, from whom does the Project Director draw her authority? The answer is, as high ranking a person as possible. Preferably, the Project Director works directly for the Executive Director of our ATOD agency. If we were to combine the two organization charts, the result might look like the one seen in Exhibit 6.4.

Having your project plugged into your organization as high as possible serves several purposes. First, it shows the grantor that your organization takes the project seriously. The fact that the project is of high enough

EXHIBIT 6.4

Expanded Organization Chart: Drug Treatment Program

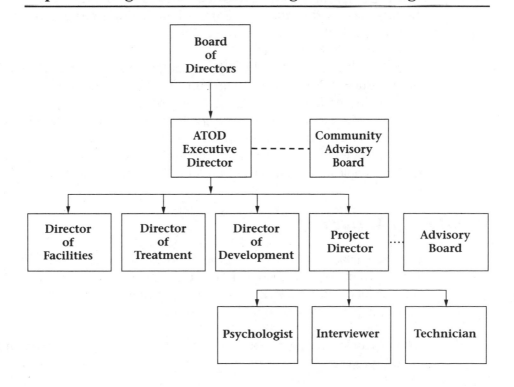

importance for direct oversight by your head person is clear evidence of its priority. Second, this placement puts the Project Director on a par with the first level managers, right under the "boss." This means that when the Project Director attends organizational meetings she is on equal footing with department or division heads, and can therefore expect her share of resources. Finally, this proximity to the "boss" gives the Project Director leverage when working with other departments or offices within the organization. Perhaps the printing office is supposed to provide printing services to the project. If the Director of the project, due to its position in the organization chart, is below the head of the printing office, it may be difficult for the project to get its needs taken seriously against other competing needs. When the Director of the project works directly for the "boss," it only takes one example of the boss clarifying the status of the project for most of those sorts of roadblocks to be cleared away.

Going back to our original definition of management, we said that management is the allocation of resources to accomplish tasks. A few moments' thought could lead us to realize that the Project Director is not the only person in our project who allocates resources. From our organization chart it is quite clear that the Psychologist manages three counselors. What is not, perhaps, as clear is that the Technician and the Interviewer, and indeed the three counselors also must manage. They manage their own time and the resources allotted to them so that they can accomplish the tasks assigned to them. The point here is that everyone is a manager. One person is the head, the Project Director, but everyone has his or her own responsibilities as well.

While it is true that the primary responsibility for project management resides with the Project Director, it is also true that each staff member has his or her own management responsibilities. In addition, the person in the agency who has authority over the Project Director also has management responsibilities. The point is that all management does not fall onto one person. The management chores are divided proportionally among people and positions all up and down the organization chart.

What Gets Managed?

Moving back to the top of the project organization chart—the Project Director—what exactly does this person manage? We can divide what a grant Project Director manages into four categories: project people, project events, project components, and project finances:

- By people, we mean persons that either work with, or participate in, the project.

- By event, we mean an activity that happens in a discrete time frame.
- By component, we mean an activity or set of activities that run for the length of the project, or at least most of the length.
- By finances, we mean money, which includes in-kind as well as cash.

People

The people who might be managed by a Project Director can be categorized into five groups. Briefly discussing the five groups is all we do about this subject here, because Chapter 8 is dedicated to management of personnel. It is probably true that if we were to stick to a strict definition of management, one or more of these categories of people would not be managed but rather coordinated or led or directed. As we have said before though, we are taking a broad-brush approach to the term management. We are including under the heading "management" all leadership characteristics such as communication, coordination, direction, coaching, mentoring, and so on.

Staff. By staff, we mean people who are paid to work on your project. They may be paid from grant funds, your agency's funds, or a project partner's funds. They may be full-time or part-time employees. They may be paid a salary or they can be paid by the hour. This category consists of people who are under direct or indirect control of the Project Director by virtue of the source of all or part of their wages.

Volunteers. By volunteers, we mean people who perform project work of their own free will with no promise of compensation. We mean monetary compensation, since, after all, volunteer work carries its own intrinsic compensation, which for many people is much more valuable than money. Volunteers are under the direct or indirect control of the Project Director because they choose to be. This presents special challenges that are discussed in Chapter 8.

Participants. Participants are members of your target population who are actively participating in project activities. They are the beneficiaries of your project, the people you are trying to help. These are the folks for whom you are doing the project in the first place, for whom you are trying to solve a problem. A person's participation can be voluntary or it can be coerced. People may be forced to participate in some activities of a project while other activities are voluntary. It all depends on the type of organization running the project, the type of target population you have, and the type of project you're running.

Service Providers. A service provider is a person or business that is paid to provide a service to the project. This category is often called contractual services. Services can be such things as cutting the grass, legal representation, building a greenhouse, or cleaning the project facility. The simplest way to discern the difference between staff and service providers is to answer the question: "Who is responsible for withholding taxes." If your agency or a partner's is responsible for withholding taxes, then the person is staff. If the person or company with whom you contract is responsible for their own taxes, then it is a service.

Consultants. Consultants could fit easily under the category of service providers. We separate them because the use of a consultant is usually brought about because we need help with an event or a component of our project with regard to knowledge, expertise, or experience that directly impacts the target population. There are three key features of a consultant relationship. First, the legal relationship between you and the consultant is that of a service provider. Second, the "product" created by a consultant is largely intellectual. Even though a real document may be delivered, the importance of the document is what it contains, not the document itself. This is different than, say, a builder who erects a greenhouse. Third, the "product" is used to benefit the target population. Much more discussion of consultants occurs in Chapter 8.

Events

An event is an activity that occurs at a discrete time and over a fairly short time frame. An event could occur only once during the duration of a project, or it could be repeated on a regular or irregular basis, yearly, quarterly, or just when it becomes necessary. Perhaps a list of activities that can be considered events will help: a trip to a grantor's meeting, a concert, a recital, a community education workshop, a performance, speaking at a convention, holding a meeting of almost any kind, an arts festival, a graduation, a job fair, a group test, a screening, a class, an orientation, a training session, a summer institute, a grand opening, or a fund raiser.

Components

A set of activities, indeed, a set of events, that occur over the length of a project, or at least a good part of that time, can be called a component. Examples of sets of activities that can be considered components are: mentoring, professional development, teaching, training, counseling, curriculum development, treatment, evaluation, documentation, and project management.

Finances

The term "finances" includes all aspects of the management of money. The money in question can be cash or it can be in-kind. The cash can come from the grant, from your organization, from one or more partners, or from revenue generated by the project. The in-kind can come from your agency, volunteers, or partners. Chapter 10 is dedicated to the subject of managing project finances, so we go no further here.

We now have an inclusive list of all the things that are managed during a grant-funded project. The methods used to manage or provide oversight for each separate item in the list might be different, but the end result is the same. The Project Director must allocate those resources at her disposal so as to cause the activities of the project to be accomplished effectively and on time. The outcome of the accomplishment of the project activities, we hope, is that the mission or goal of the project is accomplished.

How Does a Project Director Know What to Do?

This question is one we receive most often. A telephone call from a recent client that we helped with a grant proposal went something like this. "We just got the grant!" Excitement and fear are in the voice coming over the telephone. "What do we do now!?!?" The "now" is drawn out into a plaintive wail, a plea for help. "I'm so excited. I'm so scared. I don't know what to do. What happens now?" Breathless with breakneck speed is the best way to describe this stage of the dialog. And, what is our response? Well, first we celebrate. After all, we are only human, and it is great to win. Once we get down to business, however, our response is always the same: "You do what you said you would do."

Once a grant is awarded, the proposal that generated the grant becomes a contract between the grantor (who has the money) and the grantee (who gets the money). So, what you are expected to do is what you said you would do in the proposal. The following quotation from the Grant Proposal Guide published by the National Science Foundation (NSF) makes this point succinctly. "The administration of grants is governed by the actual conditions of the grant." Three sets of conditions govern the management of a grant: (1) conditions set by the content of the accepted proposal, (2) conditions set by the grantor, and (3) conditions set by federal, state, and local laws and regulations. At this point we are only discussing the conditions set by the content of the proposal.

Your proposal, which was generated from your fully developed project, contains the set of instructions that the Project Director needs. If the

Project Director reads the proposal and does not know what she should do, one of two things is true. The project is insufficiently developed, or the Project Director does not have the necessary knowledge and background to direct the project. The two key items here are a fully developed project described in a proposal and a qualified person. If you have the correct person for Project Director, that person will combine the proposal with her own knowledge, experience, and skill to create a fully realized project.

Let's go back over that, because two very important points are being made here. The combination of your proposal that describes a fully developed project and a qualified Project Director will equal a good project. If either piece is lacking, either the project description or the qualifications of the Project Director, the project is probably in trouble before it begins. A proposal is not meant to be so detailed that any person off the street will be able use it to create a project, but a person qualified to direct the project will be able to do just that. It is the combination that makes it work—sufficient detail in the proposal such that a person with the right background can interpret what is needed.

Assume that you have the correct Project Director. Where in the proposal does she look for direction? Start with the mission or overall purpose of the project. Find that one sentence somewhere in the proposal that cuts to the heart of the issue and sets the direction, the purpose, the vision. Next find the goals and objectives. They are the outline of the project. They give the framework on which everything hangs. Remember that this outline or road map to the project may not be named goals and objectives. It could be named objectives and action plans, or strategies and activities, or any number of other titles. The point remains the same. Somewhere in the proposal is a set of short, organized statements that give the major steps to accomplish the project, and under each of the major steps will be a set of smaller steps. As we know, what these levels are called is up to the grantor, but that they exist is a given. Take a moment and review the previous chapters of this book and *Grantseeker's Toolkit* for guidance if necessary here.

Next, our Project Director needs to hunt down in the proposal the project time line. This will, in graphical form, show what happens when. The time line is as good a short simple tool to get an overall picture of what is going to happen as you can find. The budget comes next. There our Project Director is told how to spend the money. Once the Project Director has the basics (the mission, the goals and objectives, the time line, and the budget), it is time to read carefully the project narrative or project description or project plan; it can be called many things. Here the Project Director picks up detail and nuance. The interaction of components becomes clear. The involvement of partners is explained.

Then the Project Director must pay critical attention to the evaluation plan, the dissemination plan, the documentation plan, and the continuation plan, all of which she will be expected to manage to an effective outcome. To put it simply, "It's all in the proposal."

Outside Regulations

Activities involving people, money, equipment, materials, supplies, and facilities may well be subject to regulation by several layers of government. Those layers could include federal, state, county, village, town, or city regulations. The actual titles vary from state to state and region to region of the country, but the idea remains the same. Many of your activities are subject to regulation by those government entities that have authority over your activities because of your location or because of the type of activities in which you are involved.

Federal Regulations

Federal regulations may apply whether or not your grant comes from the federal government, but rest assured, if you accept federal money, a number of regulations definitely come along with it. To start with, if you pay staff with grant funds (actually, if you pay any staff from any funds), you are expected to fulfill your financial and reporting obligations to the federal government with respect to the payroll withholding tax, social security and Medicare taxes (FICA), and Federal Unemployment Tax (FUTA). You may be required to perform a financial audit at some time or times during the grant period.

If you use federal money to care for children, there are federal regulations about facilities and staff. If you use federal money to care for the elderly, there are federal regulations. If you feed people with federal money, there are regulations about nutrition.

Many more federal regulations may come to bear on your project. The regulations described in the following paragraphs certainly do not cover all that can apply, but they are the ones you are most likely to run into.

Drug-Free Workplace. When you pay a person with federal funds, you are expected to provide that person with a workplace free from drugs. You, as Project Director, are expected to be vigilant that drugs are neither stored, nor used, nor sold on your premises or by your staff. When, as can happen, your project works with drug addicts, you must declare, publicize, and display prominently your drug policy. Having each staff member, volunteer, and participant sign a contract dealing with drug issues may be part of the answer. It certainly provides paperwork to show your attempt to comply with the regulation. A critical aspect of compliance is to have a written policy.

Nondelivery by Applicants for Federal Assistance.   This is a pretty simple regulation. If you don't do what you said you were going to do, you are in trouble. If you said you were going to create curriculum lesson plans, then you need to be able to physically point to the lesson plans and show that they exist.

Debarment and Suspension.   Your organization or agency can be debarred or suspended from receiving federal funds. This debarment or suspension may have nothing to do with your project. It may be some other department or division within your agency, but nevertheless, if your agency is disbarred or suspended, your grant funds will be stopped also. It will be stopped as soon as your granting agency finds out, that is. News doesn't always travel fast through the federal bureaucracy.

Lobbying.   You may not use federal money to lobby the federal government to get federal money, or anything else for that matter. You may lobby. It is completely legal. You may use your money to lobby. You may use my money to lobby. You just can't use federal money to lobby the federal government.

Program Fraud.   The essence of fraud is that we obtained grant money for one purpose and spent it on a completely different purpose. To be fraud, we did it intentionally. Honest mistakes are expected and are handled easily. Fraud isn't an honest mistake or a misunderstanding. It is where an agency gets money to work with the homeless and spends the money on crystal chandeliers. This is where we were supposed to have a computer lab and instead the computers are in the program officer's and worker's homes.

Civil Remedy Act.   The Civil Remedy Act is the enforcement aspect of the nondiscrimination regulations discussed in later paragraphs. The act gives a person who feels that she or he has been discriminated against a remedy or a method of redressing possible injustice.

Environmental Tobacco Smoke.   This regulation is the newest of the entire bunch and means simply that you must banish smokers to the outside, unless you have state restrictions on outside smoking, in which case smokers are just out of luck.

Nondiscrimination.   A listing of the characteristics about which we may not discriminate includes race, color, national origin, gender, handicaps, age, drug abuse, alcohol abuse, and alcoholism. We're not sure how you reconcile a drug-free workplace with nondiscrimination against drug abuse, but there it is. It would make perfect sense if they meant prior drug abuse, and prior alcohol abuse, and prior alcoholism, but that isn't always certain. When, or if, this sort of thing comes up, to be on the safe side, consult with an employment attorney.

Do not let this apparent wilderness of federal regulation scare you away from federal grant money. It is not as difficult to handle these issues as it may at first seem. First, you will receive a packet of information from your granting agency that will explain the regulations with which you must be in compliance. Second, your grant program person is an excellent source of information. If you are unsure about what something means or what to do about it, give your program manager a call. That is why they are there. Third, a wealth of helpful information can be obtained from other organizations or agencies that are already doing what you plan to do. They already have had to deal with the regulation issues. Use their expertise and experience, and save yourself time and trouble.

State Regulations

Your state has its own set of regulations. States are vigilant about tax issues. You must comply with payroll withholding requirements and documentation. You must pay state unemployment tax (SUTA) and keep up with the documentation. You may also be required to pay into a worker's compensation insurance plan. A list of things regulated by states would be enormous, but a few salient issues can be pointed out. When you work with children the issues of facilities, staff, violence, drugs, guns, alcohol, weapons, and abuse are just a few that probably come under some state regulation. There are regulating authorities for most everything. If you provide meals or transportation, if your project is in a building, if you house people who are not your family members, you will have regulations to follow. Check with your related state government agency or agencies. Check with your city or county government office. Again, checking with other service providers in your community gives you a heads up on what to expect. A good maxim is, when in doubt, assume there are regulations.

Local Regulations

By local we mean those government entities smaller than a state, such as a county, parish, village, town, city, incorporated area, or whatever they are called in your locality. In some areas one or more of these entities levy taxes of one sort or another. If they levy payroll taxes, these are to be taken seriously and attended to assiduously, both the payment and the paper work. These government entities are the ones you will work with when building or renovating, usually through building codes and building permits. Check again with your related government agency or agencies, your city or county government, and consult with other providers of similar services in your area. Your small business administration is another good source of information. As with the state, assume there are regulations, not the opposite.

Miscellaneous Management Items of Interest

This section discusses briefly some miscellaneous management topics. We collected them here mostly for simplicity, but also to give you an awareness of some of the detail involved in project management.

Changes in the Project

Even though what you are supposed to do in the project is what you said you would do in the proposal, changed circumstances can make changes in the project necessary. These project changes fall generally into the following five categories.

1. *Transfer of project effort* occurs when you discover that you are doing the wrong or inappropriate thing(s) and want to change what you are doing, or perhaps you decide you are using the wrong participants and want to change who participates.
2. *Change of objectives or scope* most often occurs when a grantee realizes that they have bitten off more than they can chew and want to restructure the project with a tighter focus.
3. *Change in Project Director* can occur due to a variety of reasons: the Project Director resigns, moves away, becomes incapacitated, or proves to be incapable of continuing effectively.
4. *Substantial change in Project Director's effort* means that, for whatever reason, the Project Director will be working a lot less with the project than originally planned or she will be working a lot more. Either way is a substantial change in effort.
5. *Reallocation of funds* means you want to spend the money on something other than what you said in the proposal budget. Usually, the grantor allows you to shift a certain amount of funds among line items, but rarely do they allow you to shift money to or from a personnel budget.

All of these are dealt with in the same way. First, communicate with your grantor, and explain what is happening. Gain your grantor's approval or negotiate an acceptable compromise. Second, submit the changes in writing to the grantor. Remember that your approved proposal is a contract between you and the grantor, therefore serious changes in this contract must be documented. Your written explanation of the change will be appended to the proposal, and the document, as amended, remains the contract between you and the grantor.

Ownership Issues

The question here is, who owns what regarding that which is created with grant funds? The "things" that can be owned are copyrights, intellectual property, and patents. A copyright and a patent are legal terms that refer to the intellectual content of a document or creation. We use concrete examples to simplify this discussion. Suppose during our grant-funded project that we create a training curriculum. Who holds the copyright to the material? In most cases, the grantee does. During our grant-funded project we create a device that greatly simplifies an onerous task. Who owns the patent to the device? In most cases, the grantee does. In those cases where copyright and patents and ownership of intellectual property are going to be held by a grantor, notification of this is made up front in the application guidelines. The time to get this whole issue straight is before applying. If one of the outcomes of your project will be a product that could be copyrighted or patented, you need to discuss ownership with the grantor before you submit the application. After submission, it is too late. You will be held to the grantor's expectations. After all, you signed the application package, and one thing that signature does is to obligate you to the grantor's terms.

One other issue about ownership of product is of some importance. In this book we are discussing grants to organizations, not individuals. As a result, you must be careful about the results of the answer given above that ownership is held by the grantee, because the grantee is going to be an organization, not an individual. Whether a person is able to hold copyrights or patent rights to something created while being in the employ of your organization is a question of policy. The general legal answer is that when a person is paid to develop a thing by an employer, then the work is considered to be "work for hire," and ownership of the product created resides with the employer. This does not mean that everything you create belongs to the organization that employs you, but it does mean that the issue must be clarified up front. Many organizations have a policy that staff maintain ownership. Many businesses allow engineers, scientists, and others to patent processes they create while on company time. The companies find it a useful incentive.

Acknowledgment of Support

When you write news releases, or articles, or publish almost anything about your project, it is always a good idea and at times required that you acknowledge where the money came from to support what you are describing. An example of an acknowledgment statement might look like this. "This material is based on work supported by <grantor's name>." This is short and sweet, but it tells the basics necessary in an acknowledgment statement.

Disclaimer

You might also want to (or be required to) include a disclaimer statement in any material you publish that contains an acknowledgment statement. This statement gets the grantor off the hook if what you say doesn't agree with their stance. A disclaimer statement might look like this. "Opinions, findings, and conclusions or recommendations expressed in this material are those of the author(s) and do not reflect the views of <grantor's name>." With these two statements, grantors get to eat their cake and keep it too. You give credit to the grantor for support of your project, but you absolve the grantor of responsibility for your "opinions, findings, and conclusions or recommendations."

Release of Information About the Grantee

You need to realize that a grantor can release information about your organization and the project that is being run with the grantor's money. This is part of the "game," so don't be surprised by it. The federal government goes even further. Once you are funded, your proposal becomes public information and can be released to anyone who asks. You can protect intellectual property by clearly putting on any page that contains such material that this material is of a confidential nature and is not to be released to the public. Federal agencies will make a good faith attempt to abide by your wishes, but if they fail, they have no responsibility to you, and you have no legal recourse. One additional point here: Proposals that do not get funded remain private. When a proposal you submit does not get funded, it is not available to the public.

Reporting

Grantors may require a variety of reports. They may even state the specific reports required or they may assume you simply "know" about reporting, especially if you've ever before managed a grant project. They may tell you up front that they will make an on-site visit once a year or they may call you one May and tell you to be ready for a visit in June. You should expect to report to the grantor and to your own monitoring agencies and your partners' monitoring agencies and boards. It's a part of the grant process. We discuss reporting heavily in Chapter 7 but, suffice it to say that you need to think of your grant project as an open book. If someone in authority, and the grantor is certainly one of those in authority, asks about a certain component of your project, you should be able to produce evidence of results and/or a report of the same. Sometimes a quarterly newsletter or internally produced general status report will suffice. The safest thing to do with regard to the grantor is ask what reporting they'll expect. If you are still unclear after their response, ask to see a sample report from one of their past awardees.

Participation by Grantor

Your grantor may want to participate in certain project events, such as workshops, kick-off meetings, annual meetings, close out meetings, major public relations or public education events, and special studies. One good habit of successful project managers is to keep the grantor informed of such meetings and issue them an invitation. The grantor attending an event is not the issue. You are keeping them informed and letting them know that you welcome their participation. Your grantor will appreciate that.

Dealing with Foundations

Dealing with foundations is not very different from dealing with any other type of grantor. Here are a few points about dealing with foundations that we have collected from conversations with foundation program people over the years. Remember that we are not discussing how to get a grant; we are discussing what happens after you win one. In fact, you should apply most if not all these principles to any grantor with which you deal.

- Keep the foundation informed. Regular packets of information are in order. Send a cover letter and any items that have been produced since the last packet. Such items could be brochures, curriculum, publicity pieces, recruiting material, or meeting announcements. It doesn't matter what is in the packet as long as you send them on an ongoing basis enough information to keep them up-to-date on the progress of the project.
- Be sure your foundation is on your mailing list. Any time something is mailed out by your project, the foundation should receive a copy.
- Always be honest. The kiss of death in grants is to be less than honest with a foundation. Word will get around.
- Let a foundation know about any problems.
- Never let a foundation be surprised by bad news. Don't let them be blindsided by hearing bad news from a source other than you.
- Acknowledge receipt of the grant (the check) immediately. That means the moment you get it. A fax, an e-mail, a short telephone

message, any method is acceptable, but let the foundation know that you have the money.

- A formal, personalized expression of thanks (gratitude) should follow in due course the immediate notification of receipt of the grant. This expression of thanks and gratitude should come from the highest-ranking person in your organization, and contain an original signature. At the very least it must be a formal business letter. It would be preferable to send along a certificate of appreciation, officially designating the foundation as a "friend of the homeless in My Town." Of course you would use an appropriate phrase.

- Foundations like to see publicity pieces you plan to publish. They like to be informed about events that you are going to hold to publicize the project. In short, keep a foundation fully informed about what is going on. This is important for all aspects of a project, but especially so for publicity events and materials. The image of the foundation is at stake, so do the professional thing, and give them an opportunity to review materials and plans before you go public.

- Don't challenge a foundation about having given too little money. This makes you appear ungrateful for what you got and sets you up for not getting funded in the future. Any foundation can find organizations to which to give money that will be deeply and sincerely appreciative. A foundation does not have to put up with ungrateful grantees. Don't put yourself in this position.

- The biggest No-No in the foundation world is to not live up to the contractual relationship that has been created by the award of the grant. A grant is not a gift. You have promised to do certain things. Those promises are binding on you.

Site Visit by the Grantor

It is not uncommon for a grantor to perform a site visit. This visit is different from participating in events. By site visit we mean a formal, announced visit to the site of a grant project by foundation staff with the purpose in mind of observing the activities, interviewing staff, interviewing participants, reviewing documents, and in general determining if the project is progressing as expected. The outcome of a site visit can have major consequences for continued funding. It is important for you to have your ducks in a row. What is more important is that you not let the ducks get too far out of line right from the beginning of the project. If you have to make a major effort to prepare for a site visit, you are not keeping up with the day-to-day management and administration of the project.

Wise Guy

OK, that's it. This chapter did it for me. I'm speechless. I'm fed up. I'm outa' here. No way am I going to put up with all this—this—this—bovine compost. We don't need the hassle. Just who in the blue blazes do these grantors think they are anyway, demanding all this work? We are regulated up to our ears as it is. Why would I want to take on more?

Wise Lady

As with most everything else on earth, grants are not free. You haven't just won the lottery. They are not gifts to do with as you will. Grants are investments by the grantor, and as any investor keeps tabs on his or her investment, so do grantors. How else will grantors know whether their funding has actually done any good, accomplished anything? Would you continue to give money if you never had anything to show for it? Do you think the grantor's founders or board members—those responsible for their charter—would allow the directors of the grant-making organization to continue if they could never show results? Remember, grant making is their business. This is not just an idle statement. Grant making is truly a business in every way and it is run as such. Investments are the fertilizer, the catalyst, for growth of a crop, to use your rather rude analogy. If you don't want to work, then don't ask for a grant. You're not a good candidate. It's as simple as that.

Conclusion

This chapter introduced a number of management topics, some of which are expanded at length in upcoming chapters. In summary, management is the allocation of resources to accomplish activities. Those resources can be as insubstantial as time and authority or as concrete as pencil and paper. Someone must be in charge of a project, and this someone is often called a Project Director. A Project Director has the overall responsibility and authority to manage the project. Although the Project Director has primary responsibility for project management, everyone involved in a project has her or his own management responsibilities. A Project Manager is managed by someone, preferably by the highest management level person in your organization.

The Project Director manages four categories of things: people, events, components, and money. The road map, the directions, the plan for what a Project Director does is found in the funded proposal. If the plan is incomplete, the Project Director must fully develop the project before proceeding. Project activities may be subject to a number of regulations and laws from federal, state, and local government.

Before delving into specific topics such as management of people, or finances, or events and processes, Chapter 7 discusses documentation, keeping records about what happens. Fundamental to all management is being able to tell accurately what has happened, answering the questions of what, when, where, who, how much or how many, and how much did it cost? Relying on memory is simply not enough. There must be records. There must be documentation.

Documentation: Keeping Records

Most of the people my age are dead.
You could look it up.

Casey Stengel

Introduction

We would only be able to look it up to see if Mr. Stengel was correct if someone, or many someones, had kept records, that is, if documentation existed. Documentation is the fundamental material out of which we form opinions, develop findings, draw conclusions, and make recommendations. Documentation is how we know what has happened. Documentation is what a Project Director uses as the raw material from which to make decisions. Much of what is necessary for a successful project would not be possible without documentation. No evaluation could be done. No information could be disseminated. No financial reporting could be done. No results could be tracked. No decisions about whether to change activities could be made. In short, documentation is the life blood of a project. It is the raw material out of which facts can be mined. From these facts we can decide the future with faith that our decisions are based on solid ground.

But what exactly is documentation? What does a grantor mean when it tells me to document my progress? Is there some definition of a document that I can hang my hat on? These and other similar questions are discussed in the first section of this chapter. Then the next major topic is the answer to this question: Why is it important to keep records? It isn't easy to take on additional work without being convinced that the end is worth the work it takes to get there. We explain why documentation is considered so important by grantors.

Next comes the subject of what to document. On what should we be keeping records? What are the types of things that grantors usually expect to find documentation about? The final topic of the chapter is how to actually do the documentation. We have included many concrete suggestions and guidelines about keeping records.

What Does the Grantor Mean by Documentation?

We kick off the chapter with this quotation from a grantor. In this case the program is a Youth Council Incentive Grant offered by the Governor's Office of the state of South Carolina:

How will program documentation be completed?

In this section, consider what documentation needs to be completed in order to report on the status of your program. It is likely that monitoring or tracking forms will need to be developed to adequately capture your program's progress. Identify who will be responsible for developing, completing, and submitting this documentation. Describe quality assurance procedures that will be used to insure that the appropriate documentation is maintained and submitted in a timely manner.

How will the number of people served be documented?

Consider how you will track the number of contact hours that your program provides. This may be hours spent in training and/or hours the participants actually attend the program. The methods for documenting these hours should also be described here.

*Guidebook for Completing the 1998 Governor's (South Carolina)
Youth Council Incentive Grant Application*

What we have, from this grantor, and indeed from all grantors, is a mandate, a directive, an order, a command. The mandate is that you collect and keep all pertinent information about your project for later use. Keeping documentation is not voluntary. It is mandated by the grantor. It is another of the many work-inducing aspects of getting a grant awarded to your organization. Consideration of documentation requirements may well be an item in your go-no-go decision making.

The short definition of documentation is "any written or recorded material." Another correct view is that documentation is a record, or that documentation is evidence. "A record of what?" is a valid query. "Evidence of what?" is also a valid question. We will get to those answers later. An interesting way to look at the definition of documentation is that three things are necessary and required to produce documentation. The first requirement is that something occurs about which a document can be produced. An occurrence is something that takes place or happens.

What occurs can be as elusive as a thought or as real as a rock, or more correctly the observation of a rock. The second requirement for documentation is that there be a medium on which the occurrence can be recorded. The third requirement for documentation is that there be a means to transfer evidence or record of the occurrence onto the media. We have, then, three items to investigate an occurrence, media on which to record, and the means of recording an occurrence onto the media.

What Is Needed for Documentation

Thinking about occurrences, things that take place or happen, leads us to realize that anything that we can imagine is an occurrence. Anything that happens is an occurrence. In fact, the act of thinking is itself an occurrence. Things occur that no one is around to see; the proverbial tree falling in a forest is an example. The lack of an observer, or listener in our proverbial case, doesn't make the fact of the occurrence any less real. About what, then, can a document be created? A document can be created about anything that happens. Just remember that observing a rock is an occurrence, and thinking about a rock is an occurrence. An example of a "rock" would be a home visit by a social worker or counselor. His or her stream of consciousness notes about what went on in the home visit, the journal where notes are taken about what was said, and the observations of the visitor represent the "thinking about the rock."

The second necessary ingredient for documentation is media on which to place a record or evidence of an occurrence. The most obvious and certainly the most common medium on which records are kept is paper. From paper we can move on to media such as computer disks, audio recording tape, video recording tape, digital recording tape, microfiche, photographic film, photographic paper, cloth, plastic, plaster, leather, wood, metal, glass, concrete, and rock. So far, the most lasting medium has turned out to be rock.

The third necessity for documentation is the means for placing a record or transferring evidence of an occurrence onto the media. This usually involves a person manipulating a process that creates images on media, but a person is not completely necessary. We know of dinosaurs even though people were not around yet. What are our three necessities? First, dinosaurs existed. That is certainly an occurrence. Second, conditions were occasionally such that areas of mud formed, and these areas of mud were capable of accepting imprints and bodies. Third, the dinosaurs walked around leaving footprints in the mud, and the dinosaurs died leaving their bones in the mud. The mud hardened and created fossilized footprints and bones. The result is the documentary evidence that dinosaurs existed. We can see their footprints. We can touch their bones.

Now before you think we've gone on too much of a tangent, we are completely aware that, normally, scientists draw a distinction between a document created by people, and other evidence that is created without the assistance of people. We simply want you to realize that a document can be anything and take any shape or size. Returning to our original definition that documentation is "any written or recorded material," and staying within the realm of project documentation, we can see that the forms that our documentation can take will probably be one or more of those on the following list:

- Paper records
- Computer files (including websites and electronic mail)
- Microfiche film
- Audio recordings
- Video recordings
- Digital recordings
- Pictures, drawings, paintings, photographs

On the enclosed computer disk is a tool for your use called the Documentation Planning Worksheet (0701.doc), seen in Exhibit 7.1. On it, we suggest you indicate to what project goal and objective the occurrence to be documented refers. Then, looking at your project plan, expanded project outline, or simply your goals and objectives, list all the key occurrences you expect to take place. Beside the occurrence, check the box under the type of documentation you plan to collect and keep regarding that occurrence.

To summarize, when we create records about something that has happened or about an observation of something that has happened, we have created documentation. Documentation serves as the memory or the evidence that a thing has happened or that a situation or state existed. Documentation is the way we preserve the present, so we or others in the future can determine what went on.

Why Document?

It is nice to know what documentation is, but it would be great to have a good reason for going to all the effort it will take to produce documentation on our grant project. We get at the reason or motivation for documentation

EXHIBIT 7.1

Documentation Planning Worksheet

Occurrence for Goal _____ Objective _____	Paper	Audio	Video	Computer	Picture	Digital	Microfiche

if we can answer the question, "Why should we document our project?" We leave aside the simple fact that the grantor expects it of you. Most people stopped falling for the "because I said so" explanation around the age of seven or eight. If it did not work for our parents, it probably will not work for the grantor either. In fact, from conversations with grant program managers, it turns out that grantees tend to ignore directions from grantors that grantees either do not understand or that they believe are "busy work."

We document because we (or the grantor or our partners) want to understand what is happening. That fact that seems so very important today, that one fact that we will never forget as long as we live, that overwhelming fact that stands out as the one salient reason that things are going well/poorly—this fact will be long gone from memory a year later when it comes time to write a report. It will have been replaced with more pressing current facts. But perhaps we were correct a year ago when we discovered "that" *critical* fact. The only way we will be able to know a year later is to record the fact, produce a document. Then, when we make later decisions, we can dredge the fact out of a folder or computer file, and we can compare and contrast it with all the other facts collected over time. Now we can make a truly informed decision. We have all the facts to lay before us, not just those that come to mind.

Documentation is the foundation on which all management and decision making is based. Using documentation is the only way to know truly what has gone on, what is currently going on, and by extension, what is likely to happen. Documentation is fundamental to Project Management, Evaluation, Dissemination, Replication, and Continuation.

> It is a capital mistake to theorize before one has data.
>
> Sherlock Holmes
> Sir Arthur Conan Doyle, *Hound of the Baskervilles*

Document to Manage the Project Effectively

From Chapter 6 we have a basic understanding of project management. Using the simplest definition, that project management is the allocation of resources to accomplish activities, we can see without much effort that to allocate resources effectively we need to know accurately and exactly what those resources are. Accomplishing activities does not happen effectively if we do not have clear definitions of what activities to do, in what order, at what times, and what is needed to do them. Perhaps some of us are capable of holding all that information in our heads, but most of us have busy lives brimming with many demands for our attention and our time. The efficient way to manage is to have at the fingertips the information needed to make decisions, to allocate resources. The inefficient, time-wasting way is to sit and think and work to remember what you need to know.

Document to Evaluate the Project Results

With no other activity, except perhaps dissemination, is the existence of documentation so self-evidently important as with evaluation. Every grantor expects to receive a report from you about what happened as you spent their money. This report may be as simple as an end-of-project letter or as complex as a two-hundred-page evaluation report. The level of complexity and the length of what you send to the grantor does not change the simple fact that your grantor wants to know what happened. Grantors do not want polite fuzzy generalities about how much good has been done in the community. Grantors want you to state with confidence that 25 community training sessions were held with total attendance of 8,450 adults, which means that 36 percent of the adults in the community received training on <whatever your project was about>. You can only make statements like this if you have documentation from which you can extract and tally the numbers. The evaluation simply cannot be done without documentation.

Document for Information to Disseminate, to Inform

Dissemination is the process of getting the word out about your project. Grantors make this your responsibility. Just what will you say as you spread the word about the success of your project? Will you trumpet to the skies how good everybody feels about the project? Will you proudly discuss how hard everyone is working on the project? Well, actually, these items have a place in disseminated material, but without hard facts to lend them credence they will fall flat. If you want a reader to believe that the community feels great about your project, you will need to get the evidence, perhaps from interviews or questionnaires. This is documentation. If you want to show that your project motivates people to work hard, you will need evidence you can cite. This is why documentation is fundamental to dissemination.

Document to Provide Guidance for Replication

Most grants are made to fund model or demonstration projects. At the heart of the model/demonstration project concept is that other agencies, other communities will observe your solution and implement it themselves. This is the import of replication, which means reproducing. If another agency or community wants to replicate your solution (your project), how will they know what to do? They will know because they will read the information you put together on how to create and run the project. This is documentation, and it is fundamental to replication.

Document for Evidence to Ensure Your Continuation

Grantors make grants for many reasons. When grantors make grants to fund projects to solve problems, they expect that the solution will continue in place after the term of the grant is over. This act of continuing a project after the grant money stops is called continuation, or sustainability, or institutionalization. We discuss continuation at length in Chapter 17, so for now suffice it to say that one aspect of continuation is to convince others to support the project after the grant money stops flowing. The "other" may include your board of directors, city or county governing boards, the local United Way committee, partners, citizens, and basically anybody who could provide support. When you approach these groups with a request for funding, will they respond to your heartfelt pleas or will they respond to cold hard facts? If you can show that an investment of $10,000 in your project will prevent $200,000 worth of teen vandalism of city property, you have just made a sale. You have gotten continuation funding. And you did it with a presentation of facts. The facts come from your documentation, making documentation fundamental to continuation.

Who Documents?

The flip answer to "Who documents?" is that everybody does. Actually, that answer is not flip at all. It is true. Everyone does document. The Project Director, as in all else, has primary responsibility to ensure that documentation is completed, but much of the actual documentation is done by anybody and everybody involved with a project. The following list shows the different people and organizations and departments that have responsibilities for documenting some part of a project:

- Project Director
- Project staff
- Project volunteers
- Project partners
- Project participants
- Consultants
- Financial office personnel
- Payroll office personnel
- Evaluators
- Advisory boards and committees
- Person with responsibility for oversight of the Project Director

EXHIBIT 7.2

Documentation Planning Worksheet II

Occurrence for Goal _____ Objective _____	Paper	Who/When	Audio	Who/When	Video	Who/When	Computer	Who/When	Picture	Who/When	Digital	Who/When	Microfiche	Who/When

On the enclosed computer disk, we have included a tool for your use called Documentation Planning Worksheet II (0702.doc), seen in Exhibit 7.2. This worksheet is similar to the previous Documentation Planning Worksheet in Exhibit 7.1, only we've added space to include a listing of who is responsible for the documentation and when.

What Is Documented?

It will be helpful to think in terms of the three main "chunks" of time involved in any grant project. The "chunks" are:

1. The application process (before the grant)

2. Project activities (during the grant)

3. Continuation activities (after the grant)

We tend to think only of the middle "chunk" of time, that time when we are receiving the grant. The bracketing times are just as important. If your agency intends to be serious about grant seeking, making grant seeking a process not an event, your agency will make absolutely sure that the periods before a grant and after a grant receive the careful attention they deserve.

Documentation Before the Grant

Attention to and documentation of the activities during the process of applying for a grant will result in two huge benefits. First, when the project development and all other application process activities are properly documented, running the project becomes much easier. The information you need is easily available. Second, if you are turned down for a grant, you can analyze what went wrong much easier if you have documentation on which to fall back. A list of the documents that should be collected from this time frame follows. Remember, many of these documents may be computer files or some other means of recording.

- Grantor's application guidelines (request for proposal)
- All information collected about the grantor during application process
- Project design worksheets
- Project development worksheets
- Minutes from internal planning meetings
- Minutes from partner meetings
- Results of focus groups
- Examples of information gathering tools
- Results of information gathering
- Research data (on the problem and the solution)
- Correspondence with grantor (letter, fax, e-mail)
- Submitted proposal
- Award letter
- Approved budget
- Approved project plan
- Preaward material from grantor
- Grantor's reporting requirements

On the enclosed computer disk and in Exhibit 7.3 is a Pregrant Documentation Checklist (0703.doc) to use to ensure you have kept or know where to find all the information gathered prior to acquiring actual grant funding. The checklist includes the items in the foregoing list along with columns to list where information can be found and/or who has it. A space is provided to indicate if the information is tabbed in a project notebook.

EXHIBIT 7.3

Pregrant Documentation Checklist

Have It	Item Description	In Project Notebook	Where Is It?	Who Has It?
	Grantor's application guidelines (request for proposal)			
	All information collected about the grantor during application process			
	Project design worksheets			
	Project development worksheets			
	Minutes from internal planning meetings			
	Minutes from partner meetings			
	Results of focus groups			
	Examples of information-gathering tools			
	Results of information gathering			
	Research data on the problem			
	Research data on the solution			
	Correspondence with grantor			
	Submitted proposal			
	Award letter			
	Approved budget			
	Approved project plan			
	Preaward material from grantor			
	Grantor's reporting requirements			

We highly recommend keeping a project notebook throughout project development and, in fact, developing notebooks on a number of potential projects as a "hit list" for grant seeking. For a further explanation of this part of the grant process, refer to *Grantseeker's Toolkit*.

Documentation During the Grant

We have already discussed why it is important to document what goes on during a project. The documentation will be the basis for decision making, for evaluation, for dissemination, for replication, and for continuation.

What we now need to do is categorize the types of necessary documentation. Think about project documentation in terms of three categories: financial transactions, events and/or encounters, and processes and/or components.

Financial Transactions.   Documentation of financial transactions seems relatively simple. Remember, though, that the category of financial transactions includes more than the cash transactions that take place as you spend the grant money. There are in-kind contributions to the budget of the project by your organization, the volunteers, and the partners. Your organization or another may expend cash on project activities. There may be revenue generated by project activities. All of these financial transactions must be documented. Chapter 10 concerns financial aspects of the grant project, and in the *Grantseeker's Toolkit,* there are numerous financial forms for planning and capturing financial information. In addition, many grantors have their own required forms and processes. It is critical that you find out, up front what the requirements are and then set up your systems to comply with them.

Occurrences and Events.   "Occurrence" and "event" are words we use as labels to name the project activities that take place only a few times and that extend over a relatively short period of time. Examples of an occurrence would be a trip to Washington, D.C., to attend a grantee meeting, a grand opening gala, an open house, or an arts festival. "Processes" and "components" are words we use as labels to name the project activities that take place over extended periods of time, usually most of the duration of a project. Examples of processes and components would be mentoring, professional development, counseling, training participants, or documentation.

The following list is not complete or inclusive by any means. No list could be, but the length of the list and the variety of items on the list will give you an idea of the types of financial transactions, occurrences, and components that must be documented.

- Grantor's application package (RFP)
- Advertisements for job openings (personnel recruitment)
- Job descriptions
- Applicant resumes
- Job interview results
- Employment contracts
- Temporary worker paperwork
- Equipment order forms

- Materials and supplies order forms
- Contract services order forms
- Consultant contracts
- Purchase orders
- Paid invoices
- Checkbook register
- Canceled checks
- In-kind verification forms
- Audit reports
- Advisory committee meeting minutes
- Project management team meeting minutes
- Partnership or consortium meeting minutes
- Training syllabi
- Training curriculum
- Training material
- Handouts
- Volunteer recruitment material
- Participant recruitment material
- Letters
- Memoranda
- E-mail
- Faxes
- Schedules
- Articles published about project
- Communications from partners
- Brochures
- Announcements
- Descriptions of procedures
- Descriptions of processes
- Pretest results
- Posttest results
- Survey tools (questionnaire)
- Survey results
- Focus group set-up material
- Focus group results
- Incident reports
- Counseling reports/results

Documentation After the Grant

How you handle a grant-funded project after the grantor's money stops flowing will have great impact on future grants. Grantors simply love applicants who can show that they have continued successful projects beyond the term of a grant. The fact that you have done it in the past is strong evidence that you will do it again in the future, only this time it will be with their grant-funded project. You can, of course, simply say that you continued the XYZ project funded by a grant from Mega Foundation. This provides some assurance to a potential grantor. On the other hand, you can quote numbers and facts and statistics, showing by your wealth of detail that the project you are describing is alive and well and providing solid evidence to the potential grantor. Where did you get the numbers, facts, and statistics? You got them from your documentation, of course. The types of documentation that you collect are the same as those listed previously, so we will not repeat the list.

How to Document

Many events, encounters, processes, components, and financial transactions automatically generate documents. Items such as payroll records, canceled checks, test results, publicity material, brochures, training material, and questionnaire responses are examples of documents that are created naturally as a normal outcome or occurrence. All that is necessary is that you collect and save all of this documentation that flows from the activities of your project. This collecting and saving process is one of the keys to maintaining proper documentation. The truth of the matter is that much of the work of documentation is simply the act of collecting and archiving documents, or copies of them, as they are produced and putting them in a safe place from which they can be reclaimed with ease.

The real problems come from the instances in which an activity does not naturally create a document. Here we must create a document that will fulfill our mandate to collect all the pertinent information about our project for later use. Contemplating the creation of documents might well elicit questions such as these: How do I create a document from thin air? Are there any guidelines as to what should appear in a document? How can I know what information to include? Of course there are guidelines, and of course we can figure out what should go into a document.

Going back to our definition, recall that a document is any written or recorded material that provides a record or evidence about something that happened or the state that something is in. Thinking about all the different things that we would know if we observed an occurrence leads us to be able to list the items that must be in an effective document. By effective we mean a document that preserves the essence of what happened for later use. The following numbered items and their descriptions show what pieces of information belong in an effective document. In the following list we use "it" to mean the thing that happened, about which we wish to create a document:

1. **Name:**
   What was it called? Give the name or title or label of the occurrence. Make one up.

   Examples: job-counseling session, quarterly board of directors meeting, medical examination, wrestling match, focus group, or job training

2. **Purpose:**
   What was the reason for it? Give a short explanation of the purpose of the occurrence. This might not be necessary if the Name sufficiently describes what the occurrence was. ,

   Examples:

3. **Date:**
   When did it happen? Include the day of the week and the date (day, month, year).

   Example: Monday, June 30, 1999

4. **Time:**
   What time did it happen? Include start time, stop time, and perhaps elapsed time.

   Example: Start = 7:30 P.M. End = 10:50 P.M. Elapsed time = 3 hours and 20 minutes

5. **Location:**
   Where did it happen? Include the name of the organization in whose facility it happened (if necessary, see examples), the type of facility, the name of the facility, the building and/or room number, street address, city, state, and country if applicable.

   Examples: 1) The Peace Center, 35 North Main Street, Any Town, Any State, USA
   2) University of Know Everything, Erudite Hall, Room 312, 40 Hawthorne Avenue, Any Town, Any State.
   3) The Own Everything Corporation, Corporate Campus, Building 892, Room 3512, We Own It Boulevard, Any Town, Any Place.

6. **Prime Mover:**
   Who made it happen? Include the name of the organization or agency, and one or more names of the people who made it happen, with their titles if appropriate.

Example: Wellness on Wheels Project, Jane Doe, Director (see the note concerning names in the next section)

7. Secondary Movers:

Who helped make it happen? Include the names of the organizations and/or agencies that contributed to the occurrence, as well as the names of the people from those groups who contributed.

Example: County ATOD Prevention Agency, Dr. John Bears Foretipton

8. Leader(s):

Who led it? Include the names and organizational affiliations of the leaders, speakers, presenters, facilitators, performers, counselor, teacher, trainer, interviewer, nurse, lawyer, Project Director, or whoever led the occurrence.

Example:

9. Methodology:

How did it happen? Include a descriptive word or phrase or narrative if necessary to explain the methodology involved.

Example: group discussion, facilitated planning, teacher taught, self study, interactive computer learning, video conferencing, Internet research, or family intervention.

10. Participant(s):

Who participated in it? Include the name or names of the person or people who participated in the occurrence.

Example: John Smith

11. Observer(s):

Who and how many watched it? Include, if appropriate, the name or names of the observers. Include the number of observers in attendance.

12. Activities:

What happened? Include an account of what happened.

Example: "School board members debated the new violence guidelines and scheduled a vote for the next meeting. The budget was voted on and passed. Fourth grade students had hands-on experiences with live sea life. Two miles of roadway was cleaned of trash and debris.

13. Outcome:

What resulted from it? List the outcomes.

Examples: action items, budget requests, recommendations, diagnosis

On the enclosed computer disk, we have included a form to use to capture and document event information. The tool is titled Event Documentation Form (0704.doc), and can be seen in Exhibit 7.4. This complete

0704.DOC

EXHIBIT 7.4

Event Documentation Form

Name of Event _____ Date and Time of Event _____

Purpose	
What is the reason for the event?	
Location	
Where was the event held?	
Prime Mover	
Who sponsored or made it happen?	
Secondary Movers	
Who co-sponsored/helped make it happen?	
Leaders	
Who led—names and organization?	
Methodology	
How was it carried out? Through training, meeting, discussion, Internet research, family intervention, self-study, etc.	

EXHIBIT 7.4 *(Continued)*

Participants Sign in here. Include the following information, please:	
Observers Sign in here. Include the following information, please.	
Activities What happened?	
Outcomes What resulted from the event? Make a list. Budget requests, recommendations, diagnosis, lesson plans, research, plan of action, etc.	

form can be used to document most events or occurrences that do not produce their own documentation just by virtue of their happening.

About Names

At times when you use or collect names on documentation you might need more than just a name. The following list includes the type of information you might need to collect for the people who are named on a document. You will not always need all this information, and issues of privacy and confidentiality come in to play also. The list is just to jog your memory so you don't forget any pertinent information that you might need:

- Title or job function
- Age
- Birth date
- Gender
- Race
- Home address
- Telephone number
- Fax number
- E-mail address
- Place of employment
- Employer address
- Employer telephone number

This list could be limitless. Things you might need to know could include items such as medical conditions, family history, next of kin, information about a spouse and children, language spoken, national origin, religion, what kind of car they drive, what kind of toothpaste they use, and whether the toilet paper in their bathroom comes off the top of the roll or the bottom. The information you need will be governed by the type of project you are running. Just remember to collect it at the simplest and most opportune moment.

Included on the enclosed computer disk is a somewhat more detailed form than the one found in Exhibit 7.4 (0704.doc). The purpose of this new tool seen in Exhibit 7.5 (0705.doc) is to capture information about the people involved in your grant project. It is called the People Information Form and can be used for employees, participants, advisory board members, volunteers, and so forth. There are spaces in the form for you to type in your own category of information to capture.

After reading the numbered items on the list above, it becomes apparent that some of the information that is needed is known beforehand. Just as apparent is that some of the information can only be collected at the occurrence.

Keeping track of all the documentation that is collected is a small, but important issue. The nature of the document will dictate to some degree the method of storage. Paper is most easily stored in filing cabinets, unless the paper is of unusual size, for example a map or chart. Computer files are most easily stored on media such as disks or tape, which themselves are stored in boxes or cabinets.

EXHIBIT 7.5   0705.DOC

People Information Form

Name: _____ Title/Job: _____

Address: _____

City/State/Zip: _____

_____ Male   _____ Female   Birthdate: _____

_____ Caucasian   _____ Asian Descent

_____ African Descent   _____ Hispanic Descent

_____ Native American   _____ Other (describe) _____

Home telephone: _____ Work telephone: _____

Fax number: _____ Pager: _____

E-mail address: _____ Other: _____

Place of employment: _____

Employer's address: _____

City/State/Zip: _____

Relationship to project (employee, participant, job title, volunteer, etc.)

_____

_____

_____

_____

_____

_____

        When it comes to creating a filing system, we suggest that you start simply. Create a few obvious files and begin to put documents into them. As time goes on, you will realize which additional files you need. Perhaps the most elegant method is to analyze what is needed at the start and create all the files right then and there, but we have found that we are almost never correct about what is really needed. We have found that only time and experience teach exactly what files are needed. Let the system take shape of its own accord. The types, the nature, and the quantity of the documentation that you collect will direct you as to how to store and file it. That is, it will direct you if you pay attention and not ignore the task. Boxes of unsorted documents will be the bane of your existence when reporting time comes around. A few minutes a day during the project will save you a week of intensive work at the end.

Wise Guy

OK, so I fibbed. I didn't leave. I didn't quit. And, I'm still here. Oh, and by the way you just listen to me you so-called Wise Lady. I haven't taken any cheap shots at you, so how about you lighten up on me. I'm a busy man with lots of responsibilities. All I'm trying to do is minimize the amount of time that this whole grant project thing takes out of my already busting-wide-open schedule. I'm stuck with the job. My boss made that clear in no uncertain terms. I just need to be able to handle it somehow.

Wise Lady

Usually, the person with the most responsibility in an organization, the most competent individual gets the job of managing the grant project. It's not the way it should be, but it is reality. I suggest that if you use our techniques and methods to fully develop and then organize your project, your headaches will be less and you will find that the grant project won't eat up as much time as you think. It's all in the preplanning and the careful way you create management strategies for and train your grant project staff. Documentation is not a problem if you have your systems in place to capture and store the information. As we've said, the grant project will create many of its own documents. If you discuss the necessity for, and the manner in which the information will be captured with your staff, you'll wind up with the documents you need. After all, if each of the staff knows exactly what to do and what's expected, then your management time is exponentially lessened. What creates a management nightmare is ill-defined expectations for a half-developed project management plan.

Conclusion

One important use of documentation that is only implied in this chapter is worth a clear discussion. That important use of documentation is to track the progress, or the lack thereof, of project participants. If your project works directly with people, you will want to know how those people are progressing toward whatever goal or purpose the project intends for them. The only way to truly know is to constantly monitor and create documents. Then, the information contained in documents created at different times can be compared to see if progress is indeed being made. Of course, it is possible to set up a system in which you do not compare the actual documents, but rather the appropriate data from the documents in a summary form. An example of this method that we all remember is a teacher's grade book. Our teacher didn't collect all our homework in a stack, but rather recorded the grades for easy access. The teacher was creating a document from which he or she could easily compute grades. This process of tracking progress is one of the most valuable uses to which documentation can be put.

Now that we have a general idea of what we need to do to collect documentation, we move along to one of the specific management tasks that a Project Director faces—the management of people. Documentation plays an important role in the management of project personnel, and will continue to play an important role in all the remaining chapters and topics.

## Chapter 8

Managing
Project Personnel

I get by with a little help from my friends.
John Lennon and Paul McCartney

Introduction

In Chapter 6 we say that the heart of management is the "allocation of resources to accomplish things." In this chapter we discuss the allocation of human resources people. A fair number of people do not like to be thought of as a resource. We were facilitating a 2-day planning retreat some years ago. Everyone in the room was a social worker type except for the lone technology expert. Early in the first day, he said with some sarcasm in his voice, "I want you to know that I am not a resource. I am Ted." Everyone got the message. Ted wanted to be considered a person, not an impersonal resource for the social workers to use as they would a computer or a filing cabinet.

Still, people are resources. In fact, people are our most precious resource. People are the only real source of experience, creativity, resourcefulness, and human love and compassion. We can get knowledge from a book, but isn't it much easier and more enlightening to have a person's explanation? We can key our symptoms into a computer and it can give us our diagnosis, but that simply is not the same as a compassionate doctor explaining to us what is wrong and how, working together, we can set it right. Here, although we talk about allocating human resources, we are not thinking in impersonal terms. Rather we view human resources as the most powerful, the most useful, and the only truly indispensable resource in any project.

We have a lot of ground to cover in this chapter. We start with a discussion of the basics or fundamentals of managing people. We set a philosophical foundation, if you will. Next we discuss the management of human resources from each of the different sources of people that can be involved in a grant project. We discuss separately the people from different sources, because the source of the person changes the relationship between the person and the manager. The sources of people that we discuss are paid staff, volunteers, advisory groups, supervisory groups, participants, service providers, partners, and consultants.

Laying the Groundwork

Books on management abound. Visit any bookstore and go to the business section. You will find numerous volumes on personnel management, many of which are excellent. This book focuses exclusively on the management of grant-funded projects. Still, we, of necessity, delve into some of the basics. Getting to the basics involves thinking about the fundamental reasons for conflict between people. After all, we are discussing people here. We may call them managers and staff, but these are people, and when people interact they create people issues, human issues. When you work with people you always have the potential to create the full range of conflict that can arise between two people or between groups of people. This comes with the territory. While people are the only source of human touch, human compassion, and human love, they are also the only source of human anger, human rebellion, and human stubbornness.

At the root of almost all conflict between people of good will whose intention is to work together is a misunderstanding. This misunderstanding usually comes from miscommunication. One person or the other, or both, had different understandings about what was to take place. Another way to say the same thing is that the two people had differing expectations. The result is predictable. When one does not live up to the expectations of another, conflict often arises. The conflict may be delayed for quite a while. What probably will be felt at first is disappointment that a person did not live up to their side of the bargain. In the mind of the other person, however, he or she delivered as expected. As the disappointments accumulate, resentment grows. When the resentment gets to an intolerable level, words are exchanged, often angry words. Words that send a message like this, "You have let me down. You are responsible for all the problems around here, because you do not hold up your end of the stick. I'm sick of it, and I won't put up with it any more."

The other person, working along, believing themselves to be doing OK, is blindsided by these accusations. It is only natural that people, believing themselves wrongly accused, will lash back, will counterattack. The counterattack might sound like this. "I let you down! I'm the one responsible for the mess this place is in! And you say you won't put up with me anymore! I'm the one doing the putting-up-with around here. I never know what's going on because you don't tell me. How can I do my job when you make everything a big secret? Huh? Answer me that if you can?" Of course, nothing like this has ever happened in your workplace, so you will need to trust us when we say that this sort of thing does happen, all too often.

The number one way to prevent conflict and to create a team of people who work together smoothly and efficiently is to set expectations correctly and impart full knowledge from the very beginning. Everyone must know exactly what is expected of them. Everyone must know the "rules of the road." Everyone must have a clear understanding of their place in the scheme of things, their value to the project, and the importance of what they do. Everyone must understand the purpose and significance of the project. Everyone must understand what all the others are doing and their importance to the project. Everyone must understand that the project rises or falls on the efforts of the team, and that the success of the team rises or falls on the efforts of the individual members of the team. Everyone must know that the successful completion of each team member's job is critical to the overall success of the project.

There you have it, a complete course in management in one paragraph. Before moving on, let's start with two givens or assumptions. First, let's take as a given that the people working on your grant-funded project are there because they want to be. Most people who work in the nonprofit world, in education, and in health care are motivated by more than the money. Money is not why a person works in a rape crisis center or teaches kindergarten, or provides hospice care. The people who do these things are motivated by a desire to make a difference, to serve, to be of value to their fellow humans. It is more than likely that the people working on your project are just like this. Second, let's take as a given that the people working on your project team are people of good will and good intentions. You do not have any purposeful troublemakers. If we keep those two givens in mind, the rest of what we say about management will make better sense.

So, we have proposed that the single best way to effectively manage a team is to fully disclose to each and every team member exactly what is expected of them. Dispel any chance of misunderstanding by being completely clear about what each team member is to do, what their relation is to other team members, and the importance of their contribution to the success of the project. This concept may be foreign to some, especially to those old-school manager types who subscribe to the mushroom theory of management. In case you have not heard of the mushroom theory of management, that is when management keeps everybody in the dark and feeds them compost.

Clearing Up Communication

A nagging question is probably arising in your mind about now. "You say we need to tell everybody clearly and concretely what is expected of them; and we need to tell members of the team all about the project and how they fit into the scheme of things and how important their job is, but where do we get that information?" We are glad you asked, because this question takes us back to the source of all information about the project, the proposal.

The source material for informing your project team is the information that you gleaned from your project development process and then summarized into your proposal. In the project narrative you described in detail who would do what, and when, and with what resources. Now is the time that you put that information to its intended use. What you put into the proposal was not an exercise in creative writing. What you put into the proposal is the blueprint for running your project, the assembly directions.

The mission or purpose of your project will explain to your team where the project is headed. The problem statement explains the underlying motivation of the project. The goals and objectives of your project, as an outline of your project, should chart clearly what needs to happen, how it needs to happen, who is to make it happen, when it is supposed to happen, and what result is expected because it happened. The goals and objectives, assuming that they are written as we teach, are your primary source material for informing your project team about what is expected of them.

Included on the enclosed computer disk and in Exhibit 8.1 is a Project Assignment Sheet (0801.doc) to use when planning and carrying out project tasks. The form can be printed back-and-front, one sheet per objective. Project staff members will have their own tasks along with the time frame and deadline for completing the task as well as a listing of resources needed and the budget assigned. There is space to list assistance needed and on the back of the form a worksheet for problems encountered, remedies taken, and recommended changes. This form is appropriate for documentation to the grantor of task progress. More than one Project Assignment Sheet may be needed per objective.

Next, look to the job descriptions. In addition, the time line might clarify scheduling. Finally, the project narrative will flesh out your team's understanding of the project. In short, every team member must read the proposal. If necessary, hold a team meeting in which you, as manager, ensure that all team members are singing off the same page of the hymnal.

EXHIBIT 8.1   0801.DOC

Project Assignment Sheet

Name & Job Function _____ Date _____

Goal _____

Objectives & Tasks	Time Frame	Deadline	Resources Needed	Budget
Obj. # _____				

Assistance Needed	From Whom?

Problems Encountered

_____

_____

_____

_____

Remedies Undertaken

_____

_____

_____

_____

Recommended Changes

_____

_____

_____

_____

As a manager, you will be held to a higher standard than the people who work for you. Following the maxims in the following list will place you firmly on the path to success:

A Baker's Dozen

1. Always remember your purpose, and stay focused on your vision. Your purpose and vision is not to manage a project. The project is a means to an end. The end is to help real people solve real problems. The end is to improve your community, your state, your country, and your world.

2. Anticipate and meet your boss's (can be the advisory board's) needs for information. Never let the boss be blindsided.

3. Never make negative comments about one staff member to another. Your listener will assume you make the same type of comments about her to other staff.

4. Do not play favorites. Treat everyone with the same dignity, respect, and professionalism.

5. You are not your staff's buddy. You are their leader.

6. Do not foster soap operas or play office politics.

7. Back up your staff. If one makes a mistake, it's still your responsibility. Discuss mistakes privately. Publicly, as Project Director, you must take responsibility.

8. Always act, or refrain from action, with the best interests of the project the foremost consideration. Never delay or avoid unpleasant tasks out of consideration for your own discomfort or embarrassment.

9. Never take credit for the accomplishments of your staff. In fact never take credit for any accomplishment. Give credit to staff, to volunteers, to partners, to participants, to the grantor, but not to yourself.

10. Be sure you know how to do a task, or at least the major principles involved in doing the task, before you assign that task. It's hard to lead an effort if you are totally unfamiliar with what's involved.

11. Don't make assignments that you wouldn't do yourself if you had the requisite expertise.

12. Be positive, not sickening, but positive. Nothing is so dangerous to a project as a negative leader.

13. Set a good example. Work as you'd like your staff to work. Handle participants, coworkers, clients, colleagues, as you would like your staff to handle them. In short, subscribe to the Golden Rule and it's hard to go wrong.

Managing the Paid Staff

By paid staff we mean people employed by your organization or agency who work on your project, report directly or indirectly to you, and who are paid wages. These wages are paid either directly from the grant or from your organization or agency budget. When wages of project personnel are paid by your agency, the funds are considered by the grantor to be an in-kind contribution to the budget of the project. A paid staff member can be full-time or part-time. A paid staff member can be paid a salary or hourly wages. You may have claim on all or only part of a paid staff member's time.

You, as Project Director, are one of these paid staff members. You work for someone. The absolute first thing you must do once you are hired is sit down with your supervisor and have a long talk. You need clear direction. You need clarification of your role. You need definition of your responsibilities and your authority. You need to know exactly what your supervisor expects of you. Get a copy of the organization's personnel manual. Get a copy of the policies and procedures. Get a copy of the application guidelines for the grant. Get a copy of the funded grant proposal. Get a copy of all project development information. Get a copy of all correspondence between the grantor and the grantee.

With great care and deep thought read all the material you have collected. Questions will arise. Conflicting mandates will surface. Scheduling conflicts and resource difficulties will come up. Schedule another meeting with your supervisor and get the answers to your questions. Leave nothing to surmise or surprise. But, and this is a very important "but," do not expect your supervisor to solve all of your problems. In fact, you should enter this meeting with suggestions on how to solve each of the problems that you raise. The best tactic is to have alternative solutions to present, giving your supervisor more than an either-or, take-it-or-leave-it approach. Your supervisor might not understand what you are doing, but she will very much appreciate later that you have gone to this trouble. No supervisor likes to be constantly badgered with minor problems. Getting the situation crystal clear from the beginning is the best antidote to management malady.

Hiring Staff

One of the most important tasks a manager ever does takes place before he has any people to manage. That task is selecting team members, hiring people. Admittedly, many times as a Project Manager you will be plunked down with existing staff and have no say in the makeup of your team. This discussion is for those times when you do have control, when you will be hiring the staff. The three basic steps in the hiring process are publicizing the opening, interviewing candidates, and selecting the one(s) to hire. How you publicize an opening depends on the policies and procedures of your organization. If you work for a government agency, you have strict guidelines. How you use the information in the next paragraph will be determined by how your organization expects you to go about the publicity component of the hiring process. In many organizations this task is not the responsibility of the Project Director at all, but rather an office or department specifically set up to manage the hiring of personnel.

Four methods of publicizing a job opening are usually used:

1. Submit the opening to your local Employment Security Commission Office (ESC). An ESC has on file information about people in your community who are seeking jobs. Many organizations make a commitment to their local ESC that they will submit all job openings to them. Response to this method will be by people in your locality.

2. Advertise in the help wanted section of the classifieds in appropriate newspapers. This method will bring responses from people in the circulation area of the newspapers in which you advertise.

3. Advertise in the help wanted section of appropriate professional journals, magazines, newsletters, and newspapers. This will bring responses from a wide geographic area.

4. Advertise in one of the Internet job search sites. This method will also bring responses from a wide geographic area, perhaps from around the world.

Require that a job applicant submit a cover letter with the resume. The cover letter is very important. You can tell a great deal about a person by how they put together their cover letter. Many resume services exist now. The resume may have been put together by a professional, but the cover letter is usually written by the applicant. This is your first glimpse into the real person behind the resume. If applicants call on the telephone, tell them that they must submit a resume and cover letter. When you set up a procedure for screening applicants, do not let aggressive applicants subvert the process. One thing you are doing here is weeding out people who simply cannot or will not follow directions. If a person will not follow directions while applying for a job, how well do you think they will follow directions after they have the job?

One good technique we have used is to develop a list of questions pertinent to the project for the applicants to answer and send with the resume. We always ask the applicant why they want the job. Answers can be very enlightening. Requiring answers to a short set of questions accomplishes several things. First, you get a better idea of the applicant's communication skills. You have a glimpse into their mind-set and thinking. In addition, this weeds out a lot of not-so-serious applicants who just want to send the same cover letter and resume around to every potential employer in the contiguous states. This should remind you of our admonition not to shotgun proposals to potential grantors.

Schedule interviews with applicants whose cover letters, answers to questions, and resumes make them appear to be likely candidates. We strongly suggest that you create a written interview format. This will mean that you ask the same questions of all the applicants, and you will be able to compare with some degree of accuracy the responses of different people. Another important reason for using a written format during interviews is that you will not forget things. Also, the applicant will see how seriously you take the process. The interview sets the original tone for eventual employees.

Do not make hiring decisions until you have completed all the interviews. This is in fairness to the applicants and to your project. Even if you are certain that you found the perfect person on the first interview, the other applicants deserve the opportunity to prove you wrong. After all, you might actually be wrong. You will never know about that top quality person waiting and eager out there, unless you interview them all.

Once you complete the interviews, it is time to make the selection. One method that works well is to look at the information that you now have on each person (cover letter, resume, answers to questions, and interview results) and eliminate the applicants who are obviously wrong for the job. Now, take two applicants' material and rank the applicants against each other. Physically place one applicant's material in a position superior to the other one. Pick another set of material and rank the applicant with regard to the two just ranked. The new one could go below both, above both, or in the middle. Keep doing this for all the remaining applicants. Eliminate all but the top two or three. One of them is your new staff member.

Orienting New Staff

Once you have a staff, albeit just one person, the education and communication process must start. The process of setting expectations begins. To be effective, this process needs to be organized and carried out by you with purpose and resolve. From your organization you will need the Personnel Policy Manual and any Policies and Procedures manual or handbook that might exist. From the project, you will need the following items:

- Mission statement
- Goals and objectives

- Project plan
- Job description

Take as much time in conversation as is needed to be totally positive that the new staff member understands the purpose of the project, the goals and objectives, and what part he or she is to play in the success of the project. Several discussions might be helpful. An ongoing dialog is essential until the new staff member has participated in the project long enough to feel secure about understanding the project.

A set of items usually covered in a Personnel Policy Manual will be of great importance to your new staff member. Don't be surprised or put off when you are asked questions about items on the following list. These things are uppermost in the minds of most people when they take on a new job. An interest in these issues does not show selfishness or disregard for the work that they will do. Most people work better when they understand what is going to happen. These items are an important part of the everyday life of every working person:

- First pay check
- Regular pay day
- Probationary period
- Expense account
- Expense reimbursement
- Holidays
- Vacation days
- Sick days
- Personal leave days
- Health plan
- Insurance
- Dental plan
- Education plan

These policies often differ dependent on whether a person receives a salary or an hourly wage. Policies can also often differ dependent on whether a person is employed full-time or part-time. If you work for a large organization, you might be able to direct employees to an office or division that handles such inquiries, but in most small and medium sized agencies, a Project Director is responsible for passing the word to project staff about these issues.

Once your team members fully understand what is expected of them, assuming that you chose skilled and motivated people, they can get to work. As their manager, it is your responsibility to provide them with all the tools and resources they need to accomplish what you require. You cannot expect a person to staple a report in the upper left corner if they do not have access to a stapler. You cannot expect a person to write effective, elegant, and persuasive text if their workspace is in a noisy walkway. You cannot expect perfect spelling in documents if your staff does not have access to a dictionary or a spell checker on their word processor. You get the picture. If you want peak performance from your staff, then provide them with the tools, resources, facilities, and time that it takes.

In addition to being responsible for supplying stuff, it is your responsibility to motivate your staff. This is where leadership comes into the picture. Under the topic of leadership, here are a half dozen more maxims:

A Leader's Half Dozen

1. Create esprit de corps. Give your project staff a reason to be proud of what they do. Make it fun. Keep it positive. Spend some money, even if it's your own.

2. Party on "company" time rather than personal time. (How many of you secretly hate company picnics on the weekend?)

3. Create a recognition system that rewards a variety of things such as best new idea, most case files processed, fewest data entry errors, and best cookies brought in for snacking. What you choose is not really important. It is the recognition that other people noticed that is important. It's the laughter and cheering when the winners are announced each week or month that is important. Motivation is light stuff. If is uplifting stuff. The old style of motivating through fear and intimidation is counterproductive. You could announce that all holidays and vacations are canceled until morale improves. You could pick your hardest working, most productive staff member and fire him as a lesson to the rest. You could do these things and your staff will fear you, but they will not respect you. They will not work for you willingly and joyfully. They will not go that extra mile that is needed around every project from time to time. Attention to morale and motivation is part of a manager's job. This aspect should be planned and scheduled as carefully as any other aspect.

4. Be flexible, but not a pushover. If a staff member is fifteen minutes late because his child suddenly had to be taken to the doctor, just forgive the time and don't charge it against his leave. If it happens repeatedly, then a disciplinary remedy is necessary early on, before things get out of control.

5. Don't just meet for meeting's sake. If there's a reason, create a realistic agenda, announce the meeting in plenty of time to accommodate

schedules, get to the point, and then adjourn. Plan the meeting carefully so that staff feels their time is not wasted. Also, don't have meetings only when something is wrong. Meetings are for the purpose of informing everyone in the meeting at once, to gain input on a well-specified topic, or to straighten out a group problem that can't or shouldn't be handled individually.

6. Don't allow verbal dumping and don't you do it either. We call it verbal dumping when someone walks by a desk and says, "oh, I need that client report on Monday morning." Another example is, "just so you know, I made that call to Mr. Jones." The dumper has just gotten rid of a fact or task and loaded it on a coworker, thus accomplishing several things. The dumper has relieved his conscience. The dumpee has been interrupted, has had her train of thought broken. Now the dumpee has to find an appropriate piece of paper on which to record your tidbit so she doesn't forget it. Verbal dumping is unfair to the dumpee and creates free-floating anxiety and resentment as the dumpee tries to remember what you said as you strolled by the desk. If you have something important to say, then write it down. Send a memo, make a list, send e-mail, but don't verbally dump it in a coworker's lap.

Performance Reviews and Disciplinary Action

It may be necessary for you to perform performance reviews on your staff. If your organization or agency does not mandate performance reviews, it is still a good idea to set up a system yourself. The idea is simple. On a regular schedule, usually once or twice a year, you take time with staff members to critique their job performance since the last review. This is a time for staff members to set goals for themselves. It is a time for you to offer constructive criticism and suggestions for improvements, and to give your assessment of how well they met their own goals from the last review. In many organizations, raises in pay are tied to the outcome of these performance reviews.

As much as we would like to ignore the fact, every once in a while it is necessary to discipline a staff member. Again, the policies and procedures of your agency should provide you with guidance. The guiding principle of all discipline should be proportionality. Do not let the discipline get out of line with the infraction.

And then comes the bane of every manager's existence, firing someone. Dismissing a staff member is as traumatic on the person doing the firing as it is on the person being fired. You will, no doubt, have trouble with that statement until it becomes necessary for you to deprive someone of their job. Sit across a desk from a living breathing person, a person with family and interests and dreams for the future. Look that person in the face, and tell them that they no longer have a job. It is one of the hardest things any manager ever does.

The path that leads up to the actual dismissal may be long and tortuous. If you work in a large organization or for a government agency, there are extensive policies and procedures to follow. In general all these policies follow this basic pattern. Before you can fire someone they must first have been warned that their performance is not measuring up. If their performance remains unacceptable, the person must be counseled, and the consequences of continued poor performance made perfectly clear. They must know that continuing in the same path will lead to dismissal. This counseling usually puts a person on some type of probation for a set time period. At the end of the probationary period, the manager must either remove the person from probation and fully reinstate the employee, or the manager must dismiss the employee. There are many variations on this theme, but the basics remain the same, warning, probation, decision point. There can be levels of warnings, or there can be a certain number of warnings that must be accumulated. The process can take a very long time, or it can be accomplished in just a few days. It all depends on the policies of your organization. The most important issue here is the documentation. Every step of the process must be completely documented. Once you set foot on the path of dismissal, you probably want to get the employee to sign a document every time you take one of the actions toward dismissal. You simply cannot afford for the dismissed employee to be able to misunderstand or misrepresent the reasons for the dismissal.

Please pardon another commercial for complete planning and specificity in job description and task assignment. Not only does this avoid miscommunication and misunderstanding that can lead to dismissal, but if dismissal is appropriate, the lack of following specified processes and procedures has likely been documented.

Let's not end our discussion of managing paid staff on such a negative note. If you have gone through the hiring process we recommend and you have set up and communicated the appropriate staff expectations, you are not likely to find yourself in a disciplinary situation.

Managing the Volunteers

The major difference between paid staff and volunteers is the most obvious one, the difference you thought of immediately. Volunteers are not paid. They get no wages for their work, so they are not employees. This makes the management of volunteers a whole different ball of wax than the management of employees, right? Sorry, but that is not completely correct. It is true that you do not need to deal with pay and benefit issues, holidays and vacations, sick days and personal leave. But, most of the rest of management stays about the same. You still recruit, interview, and select the right volunteers to work on the project. You still have the same requirement to set expectations clearly and completely. You must motivate. You still must monitor performance. You may need to administer discipline, and you may need to dismiss a volunteer. Also, the management maxims still apply.

The tendency is to let volunteers get by with the kinds of things that would get an employee fired. Things such as tardiness, absenteeism, sloppiness in performance of work assignments, insubordination, failure to adhere to project policy, inappropriate dress or appearance, personal hygiene, and abuse of drugs or alcohol. Many project managers feel that they have no "hold," no authority over volunteers. Not true. Your project offers to volunteers something they can get nowhere else, the chance to do something they love, the chance to make a difference in their community, the chance to touch and change lives, the chance to be needed, the chance to give meaning and direction to their lives. You and your project have a lot to offer, do not ever forget that.

It is true that there is competition out there for volunteers. Most not-for-profits count on volunteer work to some degree. Hospitals usually have volunteer programs. Schools use volunteers for a variety of purposes. Brownie Scout, Girl Scout, Cub Scout, and Boy Scout leaders are all volunteers. Docents at museums and historical sites are often volunteers. There are Foster Grandparents and Big Brothers and Big Sisters. You probably can think of many more situations in which volunteers perform valuable services. All this does not indicate a shortage of volunteers. What it proves is that a huge number of your fellow citizens do volunteer work on a regular basis. There are plenty of volunteers out there. It is up to you to find them and attract them.

Recruiting the Right Volunteers

Finding the volunteers you need is the first task in the management of volunteers. We recruit volunteers with publicity in the right places. For example, your organization might already have a mailing list of people interested in your cause. A letter mailed to the people on this list explaining your need for volunteers may garner you all the recruits you need. One avenue for obtaining volunteers is for you to volunteer yourself. Volunteer to speak at the meetings of the various service organizations in your community about the need for and the purpose of your project. Explain how your project is going to make a difference. And at some point you make an appeal for volunteers, or for help in obtaining volunteers.

As Project Director, never pass up the opportunity to get before a group of people and spread the word about your project. This serves a number of purposes including information dissemination and the possibility of obtaining help in continuing the project. As quickly as possible after becoming Project Director you need to develop a presentation about your project. Make the long form about an hour long, with a shorter version of about thirty minutes, along with a shortest version of about ten minutes. This will allow you to speak before almost any group regardless of the time they allot to you.

Once you begin to have a flow of volunteer applicants, treat them just as you would potential employees, with the exception that you might not want to require a resume. You absolutely must institute an interview process. An interview checklist must be created and used during all volunteer interviews. The content of the interview checklist will change depending on the responsibilities for which the person is volunteering. Mentors must be put through a much more rigorous screening than the folks who will stuff envelopes.

Setting Goals for Volunteers

Once you have selected your volunteers it is of the utmost importance that you have an expectation-setting session. You might have more than one volunteer attend at a time, but the sessions must be held with the same care given to the content as was given for paid staff. Right up front explain fully and openly what you expect. Do not shy away from holding volunteers to standards. A good volunteer does not object to standards and policies that are reasonable and fair for the circumstances. If you cannot explain a policy or standard in such a way that your volunteers, in good faith, can understand its utility, you probably need to investigate whether the policy or standard is truly appropriate.

Place each volunteer securely in the organization somewhere. They need to know without doubt or confusion the one person for whom they work. Working for something as fuzzy as the "project" will lead to problems later. Bringing volunteers on board and not giving them compete and detailed direction can result in the volunteers making it up as they go along, and you might not like what they make up. It will not be the volunteers' fault. They did the best they could. You did not tell them any better. Providing clear, unambiguous directions is up to you and up to the staff member to whom the volunteer reports.

Once volunteers are fully briefed and understand what is expected of them, have each volunteer read and sign a statement to that effect. The discipline of having to create this document will force you and your staff to carefully think through what it is you expect from each volunteer. Be as complete and detailed as possible. You can use this document as the handout material in the expectation-setting sessions. This will provide you with a set agenda for the session and ensure that nothing is left out.

Training and Monitoring Volunteers

Volunteers probably need training. They need to be included in any relevant staff training. They may need special training. For example, what if your project includes a mentoring component and mentors are volunteers. You absolutely, positively, must have a well-developed and highly specific training session for mentors. A well-meaning, but ill-prepared volunteer mentor can do real damage to participants. Whatever the role of your volunteers, they must have the tools to do a good job and that includes knowledge and skill. They provide the desire to help, but you must provide the knowledge and teach the skill.

You and your staff must monitor the performance of volunteers. Set up a simple process based on the job description that the volunteers signed. You might want to interview members of the target population with which the volunteer interacts. You might want to tally sign-in sheets for dates and times of volunteer work. You might want to observe the volunteer at work. And, you will certainly want to have regular performance review sessions.

Volunteer time must be tallied. It's a part of the in-kind contribution for your project (see Chapter 10 for a definition and discussion). Normally the grantor requires time sheets. On the computer disk enclosed with this book (0802.doc) and in Exhibit 8.2 you will find a time sheet that can be used for any volunteer or hourly employee.

If it becomes necessary to reprimand, discipline, or dismiss a volunteer, do not put it off. Once you realize that such action is needed, move quickly. If you notice that something is wrong, so do other members of your project team. Any hesitation on your part to hold every person involved with the project to the same consistent and high standards, regardless of position or person, can be interpreted by team members as a lack of care and commitment by you. You are getting paid to direct the project. The uncomfortable tasks come along with the happy ones.

Managing Advisory Groups

Most projects of any size have at least one advisory group that can be called a board or a committee, or a panel, or some other such term. An advisory board can be made up of representatives from populations and organizations that have an interest in the performance and outcome of your project. An advisory group can also be made up of specialists, available to provide expertise for you and the project. The one aspect of an advisory group that remains constant is that they advise, not direct. The Project Director does not work for the advisory group, and neither does the advisory

EXHIBIT 8.2 0802.DOC

Project Time Sheet

For week beginning on _____

Name _____ Job Function or Title _____

Task	Location	Date	Start Time	End Time	Signature	Supervisor

group work for the Project Director. The job of the advisory group is to give advice to the Project Director and through her to the project itself.

What makes advisory groups important is that the membership is invariably comprised of movers and shakers in the community. These are people who you want to keep on your side. Also, advisory group members often represent populations about which you might have little knowledge. They offer you the opportunity to take the pulse of the community in a way perhaps otherwise denied to you. And finally, if your advisory group is made up of experts in the field of your project, you can go to them with problems and expect to gain valuable insight from their experience and expertise.

When we say that the Project Director must manage the advisory group, we do not mean manage in the normal sense. What we mean is the relation between the project and the advisory group needs to be managed carefully. Members of the advisory board might not have been involved in the original creation of the project and the proposal that subsequently won the grant. This means that the advisory group may well have ideas of its own that do not fit within the strictures of your grant-funded project. It is your job not to let the advisory board pull the project off course.

We recommend that you always hold a well-planned orientation session for members of the advisory board. They need to understand the purpose and constraints of your project. Also, they need a firm understanding of their role as advisors (not managers). If you appropriately set expectations, you will have few problems with your advisors. Consider also including them in selected training sessions and meetings.

It is your job to keep the advisory group informed about the activities and progress of the project. As we said before, never let the advisory committee be blindsided, particularly about anything negative. Hold regular meetings and keep them informed about issues within their interests, expertise, and purview. Day-to-day personnel matters are not within their scope of influence. Decisions may be announced, but the advisory board is not the place to discuss personnel supervision.

You must walk a fine line. While reporting to the advisory group and while consulting the group on appropriate issues, you still must not let them run the project. You must listen to them and accept their advice, while at the same time you must ignore advice that runs counter to the purpose, goals, and objectives of the project. That is your job. You must use the advisory group to gather information. You must use the advisory group to better understand the problems and perceptions in your community. You must use the advisory board to get expert advice and counsel. But, you must not let the advisory board run the project. That is not its job. It is your job. Never let the advisory board, no matter how impressive their resumes, run you.

Managing Supervisory Groups

It often happens that the ultimate authority over a project resides in a supervisory group made up of representatives from each of the project's partners. This situation is one with which many people in the nonprofit community will be familiar. For all practical purposes the supervisory board acts just like the board of directors of a nonprofit, and the position of Project Director corresponds to that of the Executive Director of a nonprofit. Anyone who has held the position of Executive Director of a nonprofit can tell you that managing the Board is a major part of their job.

Again, we do not mean management in the sense of oversight and direction, but rather in the sense of maintaining a useful working relation in which the supervisory group and the Project Director work together toward a common end. The same points that we made with respect to advisory groups apply here also. It is quite possible that one or more members of the supervisory group were not involved with the original project development or proposal creation that won the grant. When this happens, misunderstandings can arise. It is the Project Director's responsibility to educate the supervisory group about the legal relationship between the project and the grantor.

As Project Director, you are a staff member of the project, and you work for the supervisory group, so you must take direction from it. But again, it is incumbent on you not to let the supervisory group pull the project off track. Remind them that they have contractual responsibilities to the grantor.

Keep the group fully informed. You never want them to be surprised with bad news coming from the community. You want the group to hear any bad news from you first. This prepares them for the inevitable questions they will be asked by members of their organizations. You will make fast friends of supervisory group members if you always prepare them ahead of time for situations for which they may be called to answer uncomfortable questions. Fore warned is fore armed. It is your job to both warn and arm. The biggest mistake of a Project Director is to try to hide from or avoid his or her supervisory board.

Letting your supervisory group head know about emergencies is not all the reporting you must do. Supervisory groups can get really cranky when not kept informed about progress and activities. After all, they have ultimate project responsibility. It is an excellent idea to prepare as detailed and lengthy a report as possible for each meeting with your supervisory group. The time necessary to compile the report can be kept to a minimum if you realize ahead of time what information you will need and plan your documentation around gathering everything you will need in an easy-to-access format. Be meticulous and be detailed. Make a copy for each group member. Never, ever hide less-than-glowing information from your supervisors. It will only be worse when the information eventually comes out. Also, if your supervisory board becomes accustomed to you telling them the whole truth all the time every time, they will not look over your shoulder nearly as much as they will if they suspect that you are not being totally forthcoming. Honesty is the best policy—the only policy.

If you keep your supervisory group fully and honestly informed, if you protect them from being blindsided with bad news, and if you educate them into the arcana of grantor/grantee relations, you will have managed well. You will have established the kind of open, trusting working relationship that will work both to your and to their benefit and will ultimately benefit the target population that you both intend to serve.

Managing Participants

You are the subject matter expert when it comes to the participants in your project. We would not presume to tell you how to manage in an area about which you are the expert. After all, participants could be infants or they could be elderly, pregnant, or postmenopausal, school dropouts or PhDs, participants could speak a foreign language or perhaps not speak at all. The range of potential project participants (target population) is as great as the differences and possibilities inherent in the population at large. Any one of us could be a participant in some grant project or other. The range of problems that projects attempt to solve is equally staggering. Still, commonalities among such divergent participant target populations can be found, at least with regard to project management.

One management task that remains constant regardless of who participates in a project is the maintenance of participant confidentiality. The information that you collect on your project participants is confidential. It is private. Unless participants specifically sign a release form, you are responsible that the information you possess about them is available only to project staff members who have a legitimate project-related reason to access the information. For all others this information is off limits. It is not difficult to design a security system that prevents inadvertent disclosure of confidential material. One place to be careful is with information stored in computer files. The tendency is to provide adequate security for paper files (after all, a locked filing cabinet usually suffices), while neglecting security for access to the same information contained in computer files. The simplest method of protecting such information is with password access. The problem with passwords is that many people become quite careless about them, even going so far as to write them down for safekeeping somewhere on the same desk on which the computer sits.

On the enclosed computer disk (0803.doc) and in Exhibit 8.3 is a security checklist to help you and your staff think about and plan to ensure the privacy of your project's participants.

Another common management task related to participants is to ensure that the project is providing the expected benefits or that sufficient adjustments are being made to do so. The participants, after all, are the focus of the project. They are the most important element, and definitely not just guinea pigs for your staff's amusement. They are people and they have a problem or you likely wouldn't be working with them. Everything possible must be done to maintain respect for them and to ensure they are treated with dignity.

It is very important that all persons in contact with participants are specifically oriented or trained in your procedures, communication methodology, and manner in which you expect participants to be treated. Don't make the "everyone knows that" assumption. Assume good intentions. Assume ignorance, but not stupidity. Assume the need for training or orientation.

Your chief responsibility as a Project Director is to closely monitor staff, volunteer, advisory, and supervisory interaction with participants. This bears repeating. Your main responsibility as a Project Director is to see that all communication and interaction with participants is appropriate and private. As Project Director, you should be known to the participants and should visit sites and be present during as many meetings and events as possible, given your other tasks and duties. It is a big mistake to make assumptions regarding participants. Find out for yourself.

More than this we cannot say regarding participant management because of the limitless possibilities posed by the number and variety of characteristics. However, security, privacy, dignity, and the need for training and close supervision are common issues in working with any group of participants. The Golden Rule applies.

Managing Service Providers

The management of service providers can be summed up in one phrase, "get it in writing and don't pay until they live up to their commitments." In reality it is a little more complicated than that, but if you follow the principle, you will not go far wrong. The first key in procuring a service is to know what you want. Before approaching a service provider define to yourself exactly what you want accomplished. Decide how much money

EXHIBIT 8.3 0803.DOC

Project Information Security Checklist

Place Check	Project Information Security Checklist
	Participant profiles, including basic name and address information, are kept in a locked filing cabinet. Key(s) are limited and available only to those who have specific authority to review this information.
	Test or evaluation results are kept in a locked cabinet in a locked room. Key(s) are limited and available only to those who have specific authority to review this information.
	Participants' health, social, and/or economic conditions are kept in a locked cabinet in a locked room. Key(s) are limited and available only to those who have specific authority to review this information.
	Personnel files, including basic name and address information, are kept in a locked filing cabinet. The Project Director (or personnel manager) has the only key.
	Keys are kept in a key box with a lock. The Project Director of his/her assignee is the only person with a key to the key box.
	No keys are kept on personal key chains.
	No keys are left where a person could take them and make duplicates.
	Keys are clearly and indelibly stamped "do not duplicate" so that stores that make keys will be warned not to make copies.
	Computer records of participant profiles are kept only on an authorized computer that is passworded by the Project Director. Passwords are not written down and they are changed regularly and frequently.
	Computer records of test or evaluation results are kept only on an authorized computer that is passworded by the Project Director. Passwords are not written down and they are changed regularly and frequently.
	Computer records of participants' health, social, and/or economic conditions are kept only on an authorized computer that is passworded by the Project Director. Passwords are not written down and they are changed regularly and frequently.
	Computer records of personnel files, including basic name and address information, are kept only on an authorized computer that is passworded by the Project Director. Passwords are not written down and they are changed regularly and frequently.
	Agency electronic mail addresses (those paid for with agency or project funds even though they are used by staff) are passworded by agency or project directors and regularly monitored for security purposes so that no private information is shared. Staff members who change passwords are subject to severe disciplinary action.

EXHIBIT 8.3 *(Continued)*

Place Check	Project Information Security Checklist
	Policy manuals clearly state that a breach of security can result in dismissal and potential prosecution of the person(s) responsible for that breach.
	Microfiche files are kept in locked cabinets. Key(s) are limited and available only to those who have specific authority to review this information.
	Areas where participants are interviewed are private and soundproof so that unauthorized persons are not privy to private conversations.
	Staff has been informed and trained on privacy issues and procedures.
	Advisors have been informed and trained on privacy issues and procedures.
	Supervisory group members have been informed and trained on privacy issues and procedures.
	Volunteers have been informed and trained on privacy issues and procedures.
	All staff, advisors, supervisory group members, and volunteers have signed a statement that they understand privacy issues and procedures and will abide by same.
	No secure records, whether kept on paper, computer, film, or microfiche are removed from the project premises.
	Reports contain no specific references to a particular participant, but are made up from generalized statements and statistics.

you are willing to spend. Decide when you want the job completed. Approach the service provider with a complete, detailed, and written job specification that explains as completely as possible what you want done. You may need to call in an authority to help with the specification document if you do not have a background or experience in what is necessary to complete the job. Someone in your project "family" probably has the necessary expertise. Do not forget volunteers and participants.

Choose which service providers to approach based on reputation, time in business, and recommendations from satisfied customers. A check with the Better Business Bureau can quickly tell you if a particular service provider has many complaints filed against it. Do not be put off by one or two complaints. Every company in business occasionally runs into a customer that is impossible to satisfy, and anyone can file a complaint regardless of whether the gripe is justified. When a service provider has been in business for many years, that simple fact provides a strong indication that they do provide a quality service. No business stays in business for very long if it sells poor products or a poor service. It always catches up with them. Most small businesses fail within the first 2 years. Those that last past 10 years can almost always be counted on to be reliable. And, of course, the positively best way to check on the ability and capacity of a service provider is to talk with previous customers.

Have the service provider submit a bid in the form of a firm estimate including materials and labor and all other costs. Structure your request for a bid so that the service provider has to answer a series of questions. Provide all bidding service providers with the same bid packet so that each is bidding on exactly the same service. Have them refer to your specification document in the estimate and append it to the estimate. The estimate must include a specific time when the job is to be completed. The estimate must be signed by a person with the appropriate authority to make it binding on the service provider. Also require the bidder to submit to you a set of references. References, in this case, are names of people or organizations that have been provided with the same type of service you are interested in. Take the time to talk with several people on the list. A key question to ask is whether the person would hire the service provider again if they needed similar work. When you decide to accept the bid, do so in writing. Save all correspondence and paper work.

Once work starts, you are completely within your rights to make regular site visits to inspect progress. If something seems amiss to you, ask. If you do not get an answer that satisfies you, go to the next higher person in the service provider's chain of command. Keep at it until you are satisfied. You are paying the bill with somebody else's money, your grantor. You have a responsibility to the participants, to your project, your organization, and the grantor to ensure that the money is spent wisely. Do not let service providers intimidate you. You are in charge. You can stop work at any time if the quality of the work is unacceptable, if the quality of the materials is less than what you are paying for, or if the behavior of the workers is objectionable (let's be reasonable and allow a certain leeway here). You have a document on which to fall back. The estimate with your job specification document attached protects you against any problems. That is, it will protect you if you carefully thought the job through before creating the job specifications.

That, as they say, is all there is. Here are the steps to managing a service provider in order and in a short format:

1. Know exactly what you want.
2. Create a job specification document (bid description, work order, or bid packet).

3. Obtain bids that incorporate your job specifications.

4. Get references and check with them.

5. Respond to the bid you accept in writing.

6. Oversee the work regularly.

7. Be in charge; they are working for you.

8. Pay only when the work is completed to your complete satisfaction.

Managing Partners

Management is probably the incorrect word here. Maintaining good relations is more accurate. You will not "manage" your partners unless they fulfill a job function directly under your supervisory umbrella, but you must manage the relationship between you and them to ensure that it remains strong. You might be asking, "Just who are these partners you keep talking about?" Good question. When you apply for a grant of any size to the federal government or to most foundations, the grantor expects you to bring other organizations and agencies into the project to work with you on solving the problem. Many state grant programs also require a grant applicant to include other organizations or agencies to work with the applicant to implement the project. But, plenty of state grant programs, some smaller local foundations, and many corporate grant programs do not require partnerships. Because these smaller, more local grant programs are the ones with which most groups begin their grant seeking, you may not be familiar with the requirement to work with partners. Rest assured, when you go after funding for larger projects, the grantor is going to require that you have partners, and usually more than just one. It's a trend that is spreading as the need to ensure nonduplication of services, as well as the desire to provide for better services through cooperation grows.

But there are other reasons a growing number of grant makers want to see partnerships. They believe that nonprofit agencies, public service agencies, schools, hospitals, government human service agencies, law enforcement agencies, and institutions of higher education have become too insular, too inward looking. As a result, these grantors use their grants to attempt to foster communication and cooperation among agencies in a community by making partnering a mandated part of any project that they fund.

These same grant makers also believe that broad-based solutions work better than single-action solutions. For example, your library wants to start an after school program to give latchkey kids a safe, secure place to do their homework before their parents return home from work. A grantor probably will want your library to partner with one or more agencies that can provide additional services for your participating children, perhaps supervised outdoor physical activities, or tutoring, or supervised social activities, or any of a long list of possibilities. By making it a requirement to receive a grant that applicants must work with partners, grantors force broad-based approaches onto agencies that might not otherwise use them. This is an example of a grantor's agenda at work. They use their money to affect the change that they believe is necessary.

This is why, much earlier in the book, we cautioned you to be absolutely positive that going after a grant is in the best interest of your organization. The aims of the grant program must match the mission and at least one goal of your organization. Otherwise, implementing the grant project will pull your agency off its proper track, and you will find yourself doing things that you really did not intend to do, just to get the grant.

The identity of your partners was established during the project development phase, as you were developing the proposal. So, generally you know who your partners are when you begin a project. There is the real possibility that you have established only some of the partnerships you will eventually need. It is common in grant projects to begin a project with a few partners and intend to recruit additional partners. This partner recruitment aspect of your project is probably an objective all on its own, with its own activities and with funds allocated in the budget to support the partner-recruiting activities.

A very important point must be made here. Always only choose partners who are compatible with your organization and project's mission and who will work well with you and your project team. Partners should be chosen as carefully as you'd choose a spouse. After all, you will live with that partner for the duration of the project. You don't want to have to divorce a partner.

To be a real partner, an agency has committed in writing to a real and concrete involvement in the project. This involvement must be to do something or provide something. Partners are not cheerleaders. Partners participate. The participation could be referrals, such as a court system referring juveniles to your violence prevention program. The participation could be allowing access to information held by the partner, but normally available only for a cost (access to database information). The participation could be facilities, or expertise, or people (staff, advisory, supervisory, and volunteer), or training, or consulting, or supplies, or money, but the one common feature of all true project partners is that they contribute something of concrete value to the project. Kind and positive words (cheerleading) do not a partner make (although they certainly help). Action makes a partner.

As the Project Director, you know the involvement of each of the partners. The involvement of the partners is written into the project development and into the proposal. The involvement is also explained in the letter of commitment from each partner. These letters of commitment, sometimes called letters of support, usually are found in the appendix of a grant proposal. Your job is to ensure that the partners live up to their commitment and to expand that commitment if at all possible.

The rule to remember when dealing with partner agencies is to "make it worth their while." You do this by constant and repeated acknowledgment to a partner agency about the important contributions that they make and the impact that those contributions are having. You "make it worth their while" by constantly and repeatedly letting the community know about the important contributions that partner agencies make to your project, and therefore to the good of the community. You "make it worth their while" by giving the credit for all the related good things that happen to your partners. If you expect to receive, you must give. What do you have to give? Praise, good words, and credit, that is what you have to give. Give it lavishly, often, and in many different ways.

Under the category of making it worth their while, remember partners should contribute significantly to project success. They certainly should reap direct benefits from the knowledge and information gained, as well as from the participants' progress. They should be full members of the team, not just folks "up with which you surely must put." If the partner's people are fulfilling the same job function as a volunteer, then treat them like a volunteer. If their people are fulfilling the same job function as an advisor, then treat them like an advisor. If the partner has supervisory responsibility for an entire component of a project, then treat them as such. It's not hard. Partnerships, when approached correctly, can significantly expand your project capabilities and intellectual capital.

Look at things through their eyes. Why should a partner agency continue to work with you when you never let them know about the positive impact that their contribution is having? What will "make it worth their while" if you take all the credit for the project's success? Why should they partner if they are only included at arm's reach?

Several maxims should be apparent without having to state them, but here they are anyway. We sometimes forget to do them in the rush of day-to-day life, but once you are a Project Director, they become part of your job description.

A Baker's Dozen

1. Choose partners that are compatible and willing to commit to significant contribution.
2. Don't look upon partnerships as a burden. Find ways to involve partners constructively.

3. Keep partners fully informed about all aspects of the project. Expect and require they keep you informed about project components for which they are responsible.

4. Treat partners as full members of the project. They are. Treat them as you would advisors, volunteers, service providers, and supervisory group members, for they frequently fulfill some or all of these responsibilities. Treat them as you would treat any other person fulfilling the job function they and their staffs fulfill.

5. Meet face-to-face on a regular schedule with all partners, and deliver a written report to them at each meeting. Partners should also call meetings concerning their components of a project.

6. Make sure that partners hear any upcoming bad news from you first. Use telephone, fax, and e-mail. Do not wait for the partner meeting. Do not let partners get blindsided by bad news.

7. Never lie to a partner or withhold information from a partner. Require the same in return.

8. Never avoid a partner. Keep them "in the loop." Require the same in return.

9. In your public presentations about the project, be sure to include praise of the partners.

10. In every dissemination piece, include the contributions by your partners.

11. Whenever you mention your partners in any correspondence or promotional literature, send a copy of the correspondence to the partners. Actually, you should have approval of partners before using their names.

12. Express your appreciation to your partners.

13. Include partners in training and other relevant programs.

Perhaps about now you are getting sick and tired of what you might see as a Pollyanna approach to things. That is understandable. We suggest, however, that great, good deeds are seldom done by folks with negative outlooks. We suggest that the way to solve problems is to focus on what can be done, rather than on what cannot be done. We suggest that the way to get along best with any person or group of persons is to always deal with people as you would like to be dealt with yourself. You want people to be honest with you. You want to know bad news before a possible adversary hears it. You want to know what is going on, to be kept informed. You want to know that what you are doing is appreciated. So does everyone else. It is a simple but powerful principle, perhaps the most powerful that any manager can master.

Managing Consultants

Managing consultants is much like managing service providers. After all, a consultant is a service provider. We only separate them because of the difference in what they provide. Service providers usually, but not always, provide a physical or technical service, such as building something, or cleaning something, or providing T1 line communication capacity, or mounting your web page, or installing wiring, or drug testing, or security. Obvious exceptions to the physical or technical definition of service providers would be an accountant or a lawyer.

A consultant, on the other hand, usually provides a service that is largely intellectual in content. The following list shows just a few typical needs for which we might hire a consultant:

- Create curriculum
  - For your staff
  - For your participants
- Train staff
  - In a highly technical skill or knowledge where you need outside expertise
  - In an awareness-building knowledge or skill
  - When you want outside reinforcement for your internal processes and procedures
- Create plans
  - Technology
  - Facilitation of strategic planning—an outside facilitator can be very valuable
- Project evaluation
  - May be required
  - Can help with project credibility and provide an outside view and guidance

The pattern for working with consultants is similar to working with service providers. One major difference can be that your service providers probably are located in your community, while the consultant you need may reside in another part of the country. This makes the search for the right consultant more trouble—not difficult, just more time consuming. The first step in obtaining a consultant should not be a surprise—you need to define exactly what you want from the consultant, completely and in detail. This information will be formatted into a document that we call a spec sheet. Once you know what you are looking for, you can begin looking.

The first and best place to look is to the consultants who have provided you top quality service in the past. If they did a good job then, they probably will continue to do so. The next place to look is the consultants who successfully worked for you in the past. Yes, we just said that. Even if your trusted consultants are not right for a particular job, they are still a valuable resource. They can provide you with leads to consultants who could be right for the job. Consultants who have been in business for a while develop a network of fellow consultants whom they trust. Also, no consultant wants to stick a valuable customer with a dud. You should be able to count on your consultant to not lead you astray, certainly not on purpose.

If you have tried the first two methods and still cannot find the right consultant, ask your grantor. Over time, grantors also develop a network of consultants whom they trust. The folks who gave you the grant will certainly not lead you astray on purpose. If you still draw a blank, ask trusted colleagues in your profession. Another source is your national or state professional association. Such associations often maintain lists of approved consultants, ones that have received high praise from members of your association. The one thing that all these methods have in common is that they use either your direct experience with a consultant or the experience of someone else. This is a key feature of any consultant search. Use a method that prescreens your potential consultant. Methods you do not want to use include any type of advertising, whether in a newspaper, magazine, or on the Internet. Depend on leads from people or organizations you know and trust.

Assume that you have uncovered a few potential consultants. The first thing you want from them is their resume with a cover letter, and a list of past clients. In the request for a cover letter, ask the consultants to discuss their approach to the type of help that you need. A careful reading of the cover letter will tell you a great deal about the consultant. The resume is not so important. The list of clients is crucial, because you are going to call some of them and ask if they would hire this consultant again the next time they need the type of expertise that the consultant provides.

Once you narrow the field, send to the consultants still on your short list a copy of the spec sheet for the job. Also send a cover letter instructing them to respond with a firm bid for the work described in the spec sheet. Have them refer to the spec sheet in the bid and append it to the bid as the ultimate authority about the job. Make it clear that you expect time frames and that you expect the bid to be signed by the consultant. For those consultants who have submitted acceptable bids, arrange a conversation, preferably face-to-face, but over the telephone will do. You already know that the consultant can do the work. You already know the cost is reasonable. So what is the conversation about? It is to ensure that you get along personally with the consultant. It is not necessary to be bosom buddies, but it is essential that you feel comfortable working with the consultant and that the consultant feels comfortable working with you. Only personal conversation can ferret out whether the working relation will work.

Respond in writing to all your applicants, but especially to the one who submitted the winning bid. Keep copies of all paperwork and correspondence, including faxes, e-mails, and computer files. Now comes the tough part. It simply does not matter that the consultant is more educated than you, that she has more experience than you, or that she knows more than you. Even if all true, it is irrelevant when it comes to project management. You are still the boss. You are the one in charge. You are responsible for the project. Yes, of course you should listen to the consultant when the subject is in his area of expertise, but you did not hire the consultant to run your project or to give advice outside his area of expertise, so stay in control.

Do not hesitate to terminate the contract of a consultant who makes you feel uncomfortable or for whom you develop distrust. The progress of the project is your responsibility, and you must make hard decisions from time to time. Always act in the best interest of the project, not to make yourself feel comfortable or to avoid distasteful tasks. Except for legitimate expenses, pay the consultant only when the work is completed to you satisfaction. The steps for hiring a consultant are listed below in order and in a short format:

1. Create a job specification sheet (bid packet, work order or description, scope of work).
2. Look first to consultants with whom you have worked in the past.
3. Look next at consultants referred to you by the consultants with whom you have worked in the past.
4. Look next at consultants referred to you by trusted sources.
5. Require a resume, a cover letter, and a client list.
6. Talk to several past clients.
7. If on short list, send spec sheet.
8. Require a signed firm bid, with spec sheet appended.
9. Talk personally with any consultant you may hire.
10. Accept a consultant's bid in writing.
11. Remain in charge.
12. Pay when services are completed satisfactorily.

> ### Wise Guy
>
> Hey, I like this chapter. It tells me that I can boss everybody around, even my own boss, and especially that nosy advisory committee. They really cramp my style and waste my time. Maybe I can find something to agree with in here after all.

> ### Wise Lady
>
> ARRGGGH! There you go again, just when I think I have you straightened out. You don't exist on an island (even if there are those who wish you did). The advisory committee is a help to you. It's seldom that you have at hand all the expertise and intellectual capital you need to perform every aspect of a project to maximum quality. The advisory committee should be carefully selected to help fill the gaps. You would not be my choice as Project Director. You confuse bossing with leading. You confuse dominating with directing. You need to become a team player to be successful as a Project Director.

Conclusion

By this time it ought to be obvious that managing people is as much an art as a science. After all, people are human with human needs, human fears, and human faults. Before we despair, however, remember that people also have human compassion, ingenuity, love, and faith. We may be flawed, but we are still magnificent. People are the stuff from which the future is built. As the manager of a grant project, you hold a great responsibility. If you work well with all your project people, you can change lives. You can create a better future. But first you must treat all those people with the respect, dignity, and courtesy with which you expect to be treated. We have moved all the way back to an ancient truth. This truth is expressed by every great faith in varying terms and ways. The central truth remains that you get back what you give. If you want respect from your staff, respect them. If you want courtesy from your participants, be courteous to them. If you want your people to pick up trash on the grounds, go out at lunch and pick some up yourself. You must do what you want others to do.

Now that we know a little about working with the people involved with our project, we turn to the management of the things that happen during a project. Chapter 9 details the things or occurrences or events or activities or components that happen during the course of a project. We lay out an organizational scheme into which you can place the various parts of your project. And, we will give you guidelines on how to hold events.

Managing Events
and Components

In every enterprise consider where you would come out.

Publilius Syrus, Maxim 777, First Century B.C.

Introduction

Our definitions of event and process (project component) are arbitrary. We use them for convenience sake. Do not look for them anywhere else. You will not find them, at least not in the way we use them. We are interested only in projects funded by grants, so we use words that fit what happens during those projects. Everything that happens during a grant project can be considered to be either an event or a component. We use the word "process" interchangeably with component, but component has more meaning within the context of a project.

In this chapter we first define what we mean by event and component and explain their relation to each other. We list a number of things that can happen during a project and classify them as events of components. Importantly, we discuss what it means to manage an event, with a discussion of the pieces that can fit together to make up an event. Then finally we discuss what it means to manage a component and the pieces that fit together to make up a component.

What Is a Project Event?

An event is a happening, an occurrence. In the context of a grant-funded project, an event is an occurrence that takes place over a relatively short period of time. The length of time we set is arbitrary. Some events take minutes to occur. Some take days. Events are discrete occurrences in the sense that they are separate and distinct and can stand on their own. Perhaps the following list will help clarify what we mean by the term *project event:*

- Advisory board meeting
- Supervisory board meeting
- Staff meeting
- Focus group meeting
- Professional development training session
- Participant training session
- Participant treatment session
- Participant diagnosis session
- Participant counseling session
- Presentation at a conference
- An interview
- Administration of a test
- Mentoring session
- An intervention
- Home visit
- Observation session
- Educational event as the sharing of a video
- Audio or video taping session

Another quality of events is that they usually are only named in the proposal. Events usually are not detailed in a grant proposal or in the project development process, for that matter. The assumption of the project developer and the grantor is that the key personnel responsible for managing the project know how to make the named event happen effectively. For example, you normally do not find instructions in a grant proposal or in your project development material on how to hold professional development training sessions. You will find in the proposal a set of facts, from which project staff are expected to be able to hold the training sessions. The information included in the proposal will probably include how many sessions are to happen, which participants and how many are to attend the training, and what is to be taught during the training, in general terms. Also usually included are who will provide the instruction, the general method of instruction, and the method to use to know that the training was effective. The grantor assumes that the project key personnel have the knowledge and experience necessary to actually hold effective training sessions as defined in the project description. The grantor assumes that you, the grantee, know how to plan and hold the events necessary to accomplish the project.

What Is a Component?

A component is a main constituent part of a whole. In our case, the "whole" is our project funded with a grant. So, for our purposes a component is one of the main parts or chunks or pieces of our project. A component extends in time over all or a large part of the duration of the grant. The following list should clarify by example what we mean by project component. We make no claims whatever that this list is inclusive. These are just a few examples of the hundreds, perhaps thousands, of possible project components. If you add specific topic content to an item, such as training of participants in job skills, social skills, technical skills, and so forth, then each of these topics can balloon into an impressive list all by itself:

- Evaluation of the project
- Professional development of staff
- Treatment program
- Participant training program
- Participant education program
- Installation/testing of technical infrastructure
- Creation of training curriculum
- Creation of treatment process
- Creation of education curriculum
- Management of the project
- Project documentation
- Project dissemination action plan
- Project continuation action plan
- Mentoring and role modeling program
- Health screening or testing program

Relation Between Event and Component

It has, no doubt, become apparent to you that there is an intertwined and linking relation between events and components. The relation is extraordinarily simple. It is that components are comprised of events. A number of related events carried out over an extended period of time with a specific purpose or goal or objective is a component of your project.

Managing Project Components

The Basic Concept

While events usually are simply named in a grant proposal, components are more fully explained. In a grant proposal, it is stated simply that the event of traveling to Washington, D.C., and attending the grantee meeting will take place. Money is allocated in the budget for this event. You are expected to be able to figure out the details of how to get to Washington, find lodging, find the meeting place, participate in the meeting, and what to take away from the meeting. A component is explained in more detail. The detail largely consists of naming a series of events that will take place. Often the actual events are not named, but inferred by the thrust of the directions. Thus it is up to the Project Director and project staff to understand about events and to interpret when an event is necessary, as well as what the event is.

For example, your project has a mentoring component. In the proposal, it might be said that the mentoring component is divided into four parts: (1) recruit mentors, (2) train mentors, (3) implement the mentoring, and (4) evaluate the results of the mentoring. The four parts may be explained a bit further something like this:

1. Recruit mentors
   a. The Chamber of Commerce has agreed to include our mentoring component in their established "Be a Role Model" community-wide mentoring project.
   b. In addition, the chamber will allow us to make our recruitment pitch to the entire membership during their regular, monthly meetings.
   c. Our business and industry partners have agreed to allow us to recruit among their personnel.
   d. We have obtained a 30-minute slot in prime time on the cable television company's local access channel, and part of our program will be recruitment of mentors.

This is a typical explanation of part of a project component, in this case recruiting mentors. Thinking about the four items that make up the recruit mentors part of the mentoring component will lead us to realize that a number of events have been prescribed. In item a., for example, including our project's mentor recruitment in with the Chamber of Commerce's establish mentoring program will require meetings and communication to establish the relationship. It will require recruitment presentations before the chamber's group of community role models. Unspoken is the fact that the recruitment presentation itself must be created, perhaps with handouts and visual aids. You will note that in item a., no events are actually named. You must infer their existence from what has been described. The particular events that are necessary will become apparent by thinking through what will have to happen to make the item a reality.

Each lettered item follows a similar course. To complete each item, several events will be planned and executed. The expectation is that once all these events have been accomplished, the purpose of the "recruit mentors" part of the mentoring component also will have been accomplished. How will you know if the job is done properly? You will know because in the "recruit mentors" task sheet, or objective boxes you will have attached a quantity, a measurement, to the task or objective. In this case, the measurement will be the number of mentors you need. When you have recruited that number of mentors you have successfully completed the items and that part of the component. In the same way, when you successfully complete each of the individual events in each of the parts of the mentoring component, you will have successfully completed the entire component.

This is how a project is put together and executed. This is how you manage a project. Take the general components of your project—they may be called goals, objectives, strategies, or any number of names—and break them down into constituent parts. Then break the constituent parts down further into discrete events. Accomplish all the events successfully, and it follows logically that each of the constituent parts will have been accomplished successfully. When all of a component's constituent parts have been accomplished successfully, it follows logically that the component itself has now been accomplished. And finally, when each project component has been accomplished successfully, the project itself has succeeded. The mission, the purpose, the vision of the project is being met, is being accomplished.

This is the essence of how projects are put together and how they are managed. As a Project Director or as a project staff member, one of your responsibilities is to take general instructions from a proposal and break them down into appropriate discrete events. If you have done complete project development before writing the proposal, this job will be much simpler. Looking at the Task Analysis Worksheet in Exhibit 5.5 (0505.doc) will provide you with direction. Details on the process can be found in *Grantseeker's Toolkit: A Comprehensive Guide to Finding Funding.*

Project Organization Generalities

All the foregoing discussion under this topic leads us to this generalization. The first, and most important, part of managing a component of a project is to define the component into its constituent parts and then to further define the constituent parts into discrete events. This simple formulation can give people a great deal of trouble. From participants in our grant-seeking workshops we often get comments like these:

> "It's not possible to know all that needs to be done before even starting!"

> "We'll have a mentoring component, and the details of exactly how we'll do it will fall into place as we go along."

> "There are just too many variables, too many unknowns. We can't plan this thing now. We'll take a wait-and-see approach to how it comes together."

At this point we have some rather harsh words. If you and your organization cannot create a detailed plan for implementing a project component, then you have no business trying to accomplish that component. A major assumption of grantors is that the people and organizations that apply for grants know their business—the business about which they're proposing to do the project. Grantees are supposed to know how to go about their business, in detail. When you fail to give sufficient detail in your proposal, when you fail to break components down into constituent parts and explain the parts, you send a clear message to the grantor that you do not understand what is necessary to accomplish the project or its components. The usual result is to fail to get the grant. If, by chance, you do get the grant, the usual result is a muddled, ineffectively implemented project, or worse, a total project failure.

We need a method, a tool, to help us get organized. If we have done our project development properly, that tool is (are) our goals and objectives along with our task analysis. If a good project outline does not exist, which is all that goals and objectives are, then you can use the format we show here. We purposefully have not used words such as goal, objective, activity, and task, so that we can stay away from the word definition game that takes place around such expressions. We assume that a project has a purpose. We further assume that a project has a set of components. Each of these components is divided into constituent parts. Each constituent part of a component is defined by the events that must take place to accomplish the part. First we list the steps in this process. Then we show a way of putting the information on paper.

1. Define the purpose of the project
2. Define the components of the project
3. Define the constituent parts of each component
4. Define the events within each constituent part

Project Organization Specifics

Define the Purpose of the Project. Two things are necessary to define the purpose of a project: (1) We must be able to name the target population and (2) we must be able to say what we intend to happen to or change about the target population, the expected outcome as it relates directly to the target population. You may have a lot more you want to say about the purpose of the project. That is okay. However, these two pieces of information are what are absolutely necessary, and you may not leave either one out. To get started you can use a formula such as: "The purpose of our project is for <name the target population> to <define the expected outcome>." For public consumption, you will want to wordsmith the formula statement into an elegant sentence. The outcome may come before the target population in the final sentence, or it may be mixed into the outcome. It does not matter. All that matters is that both pieces are clearly defined.

Define the Components of the Project. The components are those large chunks into which the actions necessary to accomplish the purpose of the project naturally group themselves. Again, if you truly cannot see the major groupings of actions necessary to accomplish the purpose of your project, what we are calling project components, then you need to question whether you and your organization have the knowledge and expertise to run such a project. A project divided into its components might look like the one found in Exhibit 9.1. A blank version of the model project for your use is included on the enclosed computer disk as 0901.doc.

Define the Constituent Parts of Each Component. The constituent parts of a component are the groupings of events into which a component naturally divides itself. A series of components divided into constituent parts might look like the one found in Exhibit 9.2 except that you would continue past component three, and continue for as many components as necessary. A blank version of Exhibit 9.2 for your use is included on the enclosed computer disk as 0902.doc.

Define the Events of Each Part. Events are those discrete happenings or occurrences that take place over a relatively short period of time. At this stage, events can simply be given names or labels. Events are the basic building blocks of which projects are constructed. As the subject matter expert about your project and its purpose, you and your organization are expected to know how to accomplish the events. A series of constituent parts divided into events might look like Exhibit 9.3. A blank version of Exhibit 9.3 for your use is included on the enclosed computer disk as 0903.doc.

EXHIBIT 9.1   0901.DOC

Model Project and Its Components

Project Purpose Statement

Component 1

Component 2

Component 3

Component 4

Component 5

Component 6

EXHIBIT 9.2

0902.DOC

Project Constituent Parts

Project Purpose Statement

Component 1

　　Part 1

　　Part 2

　　Part 3

　　Part 4

　　Part 5

Component 2

　　Part 1

　　Part 2

　　Part 3

　　Part 4

　　Part 5

Component 3

　　Part 1

　　Part 2

　　Part 3

　　Part 4

　　Part 5

EXHIBIT 9.3

Project Events

Component 1 _____

    Part 1 _____

        Event 1 _____

        Event 2 _____

        Event 3 _____

        Event 4 _____

        Event 5 _____

    Part 2 _____

        Event 1 _____

        Event 2 _____

        Event 3 _____

        Event 4 _____

        Event 5 _____

    Part 3 _____

        Event 1 _____

        Event 2 _____

        Event 3 _____

        Event 4 _____

        Event 5 _____

    Part 4 _____

        Event 1 _____

        Event 2 _____

        Event 3 _____

        Event 4 _____

        Event 5 _____

    Part 5 _____

        Event 1 _____

        Event 2 _____

        Event 3 _____

        Event 4 _____

        Event 5 _____

Much More to Know

Defining the purpose of the project, the components, the parts of the components, and naming the events that take place in the parts of the components generates a lot of information. It also generates a complete overview of the project's organization. It does not, however, generate enough information to enable you to run the project. For example, using this process, we may not know the person who is responsible for events, parts, and components. Using this process, we may not know when events, parts, and components are supposed to happen. We may not know what resources it will take to accomplish the events, parts, and components. We may not know where things will happen. And, we definitely will not know how much it will cost to do all these things. Filling in these details is the purpose of the project development process. Having these details at your fingertips is fundamental to managing a project effectively. Additional discussion and tools to help with this process can be found in Chapter 5, specifically Exhibit 5.5 (0505.doc), the Task Analysis Worksheet.

If we make the two assumptions that your project is fully developed and that the proposal contains all the information that the grantor requested, then the information contained in the items in the following list is your management blueprint. This information will tell you all you need to know about how to run your project. If the information is missing or incomplete, you will need to create it, using our project development process:

1. Problem Statement: the full description of the target population.
2. Mission Statement: the expected overall outcome of the project.
3. Goals and Objectives: the structure of the project. It will describe the components (goals) and the parts of the components (objectives).
4. Task or Activity Analysis: this part may not have been required by your grantor. If it doesn't exist, you need to create it.
5. Project Description: the narrative description of the project; will fill in details that may be missing or unexplained in the Goals and Objectives.
6. Time Line: a compilation into one place in graphical format of the "when" information from the Goals and Objectives.
7. Key Personnel Information: tells who will be performing key tasks in the project.
8. Job Descriptions: describe the purpose of each position in the project and serve as the basis for deciding who is the correct person for what position.

9. Management Plan: describes the basics of how the project is to be managed.

10. Evaluation Plan: describes the process by which you will be able to tell if the project is on track and if the expected outcomes of Goals and Objectives are being met.

11. Continuation Plan: describes the activities you will undertake to ensure that the project continues beyond the term of the grant.

12. Dissemination Plan: describes the activities you will accomplish to publicize the project.

13. Budget: gives the summary, in line-item format, of the amount of expenditures and revenue expected on the project. The expenditures may be cash or in-kind, and they may be from the grantor, your organization, project partners, volunteers, or other sources. The revenue comes from income generated by project activities.

14. Budget Narrative: explains in detail what comprises each line item and the purpose of budgeted items.

If any of this information is missing or incomplete you need to gather it or create it. Meeting with the people who originally designed and developed the project may be one source of additional information. What was obvious to them as they were developing the project may not be obvious at all to you as the Project Director. Simply asking the appropriate people may provide you with a wealth of additional detail.

The Nuts and Bolts

Returning to our definition of management from Chapter 6, we recall that management is the "allocation of resources to accomplish things." Answering the logical question, "What are the resources that we allocate?" gives us a short list of general categories: time, money, and things. Expanding these three general categories into workable detail yields this list:

- Time
  - Project Director
  - Staff
  - Volunteers
  - Partners
  - Participants
  - Consultants
  - Service Providers

- Money
  - Purchases
  - Leases
  - Rents
  - Salaries and benefits
  - Stipends
  - Service fees
  - Travel
- Things
  - Equipment
  - Materials
  - Supplies
  - Facilities

Looking again at our definition of management (allocation of resources to accomplish things), the next logical question is: "What are the things we need to accomplish?" Now we know. We must accomplish the project's components. But we also know that to accomplish the project's components we must accomplish their constituent parts. And finally, we know that to accomplish the constituent parts of the project's components we must accomplish the events that taken together comprise the constituent parts. We can now give a fuller and more meaningful definition of project management as it relates to managing project components.

Grant project management is the allocation of the resources of time, money, and things to accomplish the events that make up components. At this point, all we have done is give a general definition of an event and name the events in our project organization scheme. Discussion about the management of project events takes place in the next part of this chapter. It may seem that we should be finished with project components, but we are not. A number of additional considerations are pivotal. The following numbered list of key considerations brings us close to the end of our discussion of the management of project components. Performing the items on this list is the core of managing project components. Keep in mind that management of people and finances also takes place. These major parts of project management are covered in Chapters 8 and 10.

Key Event Management Considerations

Key events, regardless of type or content, retain similarities. Knowing these similarities makes management of a number of different events easier to organize. The list below shows several common management considerations for key events.

1. Each event must take place at the proper time.
2. Events must take place in the proper sequence.
3. Documentation of events must be collected and stored in an easy-to-retrieve manner and with proper security.
4. Information or material that results from an event must be collected and stored in an easy-to-retrieve manner and with appropriate security.
5. When an event, or events, depends on the outcome of a previous event(s), ensure that the information or material exists and that it finds its way from one event to another.
6. Regularly debrief event participants to learn quickly about difficulties.
7. When difficulties are encountered, analyze the problem and change the event procedure as needed for the next time.
8. Publicize the event as appropriate.
9. Apprise appropriate stakeholders regularly and fully about the accomplishment of events, problems encountered, and the changes instituted to correct the problems.

To accomplish these management tasks efficiently and effectively, we need the guidelines and procedures in the following list. As you can see, a fully developed project and the well-crafted proposal that results from that fully developed project contains all the information you will need to manage project components. They provide the raw material from which to compile all you need to know about how to manage project components.

1. Detailed project schedule, showing dates of events, sequence of events, and which events are dependent on others (time line)
2. Method of documenting each event (documentation plan)
3. Clear definition of the result, information, or material that is to come out of each event (goals and objectives and task analysis)
4. Method of storing and retrieving documents, information, and materials generated by events (documentation plan)
5. Method of checking on performance of events (evaluation plan)
6. Method of using information about performance of events as feedback to correct problems (evaluation plan)
7. Methods of publicizing events as appropriate (dissemination plan)
8. Methods of reporting progress to stakeholders (management plan)

Managing Project Events

So far we have defined project events as basic building blocks. When the correct building blocks are properly positioned and appropriately fitted together into a coherent whole, the edifice we build is what we are calling a project. The number, range, and diversity of possible project events are staggering. Think of all the different sorts of organizations and agencies that can obtain grants. Pick a number. Think of all the different types of projects that just a single individual nonprofit can implement. Pick a number. Then, think of all the different events that can happen in just one project. Pick a number. Multiply the three numbers together and you get a small sense of the number of events it is possible to hold. Interestingly enough, however, the huge number of possible events does not prevent there from being an amazing consistency about what it takes to hold an event.

Look over the content of the items in the following list, and ask yourself this question. "If I am knowledgeable about and experienced with the type of event to be held, and if I am knowledgeable about and experienced with the subject matter content of the event, and if I am given the information on this list, will I be able to hold the event?" If you can say "yes," then we have succeeded in illustrating the common elements in all events. Understanding the event itself and the content of the event is your job. You are the subject matter expert. Here are the common elements involved in holding any event:

1. Title of event
2. Date of event
3. Time of event
4. Duration of event
5. Location of event
6. Type of event
7. Purpose of event
8. Methodology used in event
9. Expected outcome of event
10. Responsibility for event
11. Leader(s) of event
12. Participant(s) in event
13. Observer(s) of event
14. Resources needed for event
15. Outcomes

EXHIBIT 9.4   0904.DOC

Event Management Worksheet

Event Title _____

Type of Event _____

Purpose of Event _____

Methodology _____

Expected Outcome(s) _____

Responsibility for Event	
Organization	**Contact Person**
Name	Name
Address	Title
	Address
Phone	Phone
Fax	Fax
	E-mail

Event Partner	
Organization	**Contact Person**
Name	Name
Address	Title
	Address
Phone	Phone
Fax	Fax
	E-mail

EXHIBIT 9.4 *(Continued)*

Event Partner	
Organization	**Contact Person**
Name	Name
Address	Title
	Address
Phone	Phone
Fax	Fax
	E-mail

Date(s)	Time(s)		Location
	From	**To**	

Leader(s)* of Event _____

_____

_____

 *Speaker, presenter, trainer, teacher, doctor, nurse, attorney, counselor, therapist, performer, master of ceremonies, performance group, artist, etc.

Describe and/or name participant(s) _____

_____

_____

Describe and/or name observer(s)   _____

_____

_____

EXHIBIT 9.4 *(Continued)*

List Resources Needed for Event				
Facilities	**People**	**Equipment**	**Materials & Supplies**	**Contractual Services**

Pre-event Tasks
1.
2.
3.

Event Tasks
1.
2.
3.

Postevent Tasks
1.
2.
3.

Describe Actual Outcome(s)

Wise Guy

Hmmmmm. Frankly, I am blown away by the idea that all the different things we do during a project have common elements. I guess the same is true about just about everything we do. The concept is a wonderment, and makes my brain hurt. It just seems to me that every little thing you want to do has its own peculiar set of rules, and somebody keeps them all a secret, at least from me.

Wise Lady

Yes, there is a lot going on in every project. In fact, that's why we have developed a number of hopefully helpful tools to capture information. We don't actually expect every Project Director to use every tool, but we do suspect that most Project Directors will find some of the tools helpful in organizing and managing the project. Many experienced Project Directors will have already made up tools of their own. The important thing to remember is that you must have a plan and a system. And, no, you can't just wing it. And, yes, everything—every profession, every hobby even—has its own set of rules. You can't play baseball or football or a game of golf unless you know and apply the rules. Getting grants is not easy. Money is not just handed out on a silver platter. Part of this is simply because it's a highly competitive field, thus the necessity for structuring the process so that only the very best projects with the best chances to affect change are tested and tried. Projects take time to implement and it takes even more time for results to settle and mature. Grantors can't just make project awards willy nilly—they don't have enough money or time to waste. But they try hard to tell you the rules. They publish information, they answer questions, and they refine and define their processes. Can you imagine how frustrating it is to them for folks to submit proposals without first having bothered to check to see if there are proposal guidelines, a request for proposal, or some sort of proposal requirements? What about those "Dear Occupant" proposals that circulate around from time to time? You know, the ones that have been written in general and then sent to a bunch of funders. What about the potential grantee that fails to read directions? It's not because the grantor is not trying to communicate. Many times it's because applicants fail to listen, or even worse, they fail to ask.

We have included the worksheet seen in Exhibit 9.4 on pages 195–197 to help with collecting all the information necessary to hold and manage an event, whether the event is a counseling session, a concert, or an arts festival. The Event Management Worksheet is file 0904.doc on the disk.

To repeat, two assumptions are necessary to make this list work. The first assumption is that the person holding the event is knowledgeable and experienced with the logistics and mechanics of the type of event. The second assumption is that the person holding the event or occurrence is knowledgeable and experienced with the subject matter content and the methodology of the event.

Time and again we have said that you are the subject matter expert. You are, of course, but nevertheless, you probably are getting tired of the refrain. After all, you know from experience that situations often arise about which you, the staff of your organization, and even with considering your volunteers and your partners, do not have the necessary knowledge and expertise to handle. When the event is necessary to the completion of the project, you will need to obtain outside knowledge and experience. This is the genesis of the decision to hire a consultant or perhaps a service provider. You can find the discussion of the process for hiring and managing consultants and service providers in Chapter Eight.

Conclusion

We have delved as deeply into the project as a whole as we will go. We now have a clear organizational scheme for a project. We know the parts of a project and proposal from which we can create the organizational scheme. We now know the information that we need to hold events, the building blocks from which everything else in a project is created. We understand that if we do not possess the knowledge and experience to handle a type of event or the subject matter content of an event, we can hire consultants or service providers to fill the gap or we can develop a relationship with an expert partner. Hiring someone means we must spend money, which brings us to the topic of the next chapter, project finances.

In Chapter 10 we discuss a number of topics, all of which concern project money—money that can be in either of the two forms money takes in a grant project, cash or in-kind. Defining money, getting money, spending money, tracking money, making money, accounting for money: It is going to be money, money, money. The shame of it is that none of the money will be ours. It is other people's money, and we are responsible for it.

## Chapter 10

Managing
Project Finances

A good reputation is more valuable than money.
Publilius Syrus, Maxim 108, First Century B.C.

But as for me

I'll bet my money on the bobtail nag—
Somebody bet on the bay.
Stephen Collins Foster, *Camptown Races*

Introduction

The short version of everything you are going to read in this chapter was written more than two thousand years ago. One way to say it is quoted in the foregoing epigraph from the Maxims of Publilius Syrus. Another form is: "Spend the money exactly as you said you would." The two parts of the proposal in which you stated specifically how you would spend the money are the budget and the budget narrative. As a result, what you spend money on during the project is based totally on these two parts of the proposal. The way you handle the finances, however, is based on the grantor's directions, your organization's procedures, acceptable accounting practices, federal, state, and local regulations, and prudent exercise of your fiduciary responsibility.

The first topic is a general discussion of the parts of a budget and the definitions of a few financial terms. The next topic is another general discussion about the various types of direct expenses found in budgets. Then come a few generalities about handling grant funds. After our general discussions we focus on several specific topics, including payroll, sales tax, purchasing services, purchasing expensive items, purchasing materials and supplies, and building things. We end the chapter with a discussion about revenue generation.

The Project Budget

Project Budget or Grant Request?

The first new fact to deal with is that the project budget is not the same as the grant request. A project budget includes all the costs of implementing the project. The grant request is the amount of money that you are asking the grantor to give you. The second new fact to digest is that a project budget is always larger than the grant request. There are no exceptions, none, ever. In order for the project budget to be the same as the grant request, the organization implementing the project and all the other people and organizations involved in the project would contribute absolutely nothing.

Here is the same thought in different words. For the project budget and the grant request to be the same, the following must be true. Zero contributions, other than the grant, are made to the running of the project. By zero we mean none. By contributions we mean help or aid of any type, size, form, shape, or fashion—in person, on paper, via computer, it does not matter. In addition, the "zero contributions" must be made by every person, every group of people, every organization, every agency, and every partner involved in the project. In short, nobody can give anything to the project. We say again, the likelihood of this being the state of things is extremely remote.

It is very possible that a grantor will not ask you for the project budget, but only for an accounting of how you will spend the money given to you in the form of a grant. This accounting usually is called the budget, or even the project budget. However, the fact is that you are accounting for how you will spend the granted money (budget), not giving the total budget of the project. This all too common confusion between the project budget and the portion of the budget that the grant covers can be the source of much confusion.

A total project budget is the total of five sums: (1) the grant request, (2) your organization's contribution, (3) your partners' contributions, (4) your volunteers' contributions, and (5) revenue generated by the project. The grant request, when awarded, is cash. Your organization's contribution can be cash or in-kind or both. Partner's contributions can be cash or in-kind or both. Volunteer contributions are in-kind. Revenue generated by the project is cash. When putting a total project budget together, there is no distinction between cash and in-kind. Both are funds spent on the project. Clear evidence of this is that when a grantor requires "matching funds," the funds can be cash, or in-kind, or a combination of both. If a grantor requires a match consisting of cash, the phrase will be "cash match."

Cash

We know what cash is, so we do not need to define it. Cash is physical money, bills and coins. Cash is also an entry in a bank's computer, which allows us to write checks to obtain what we want. Physical money does not have to change hands. We generate a piece of paper called a check. Our computer then talks to their computer, and the transaction is done. We lost cash, according the entry in our bank's computer. The other party gained cash, again, according to an entry in a bank's computer. Both of the parties also have an accounting system in which entries are made—entries that match those made by the respective banks. At its simplest, an accounting system can be a check register.

In-Kind

First Draft of Definition. In-kind can be a real mystery. The definition of in-kind is "the value of contributions of stuff made to the project." OK, OK, "stuff" is not precise enough to use in a definition. For the sake of keeping it short and simple in this first go-round at the definition of in-kind, we did not list all the "stuff" that can be contributed. Anyway, Shakespeare used the word stuff. In *Henry IV* he writes, "A deal of skimble-skamble stuff." In *Julius Caesar* he writes, "Ambition should be made of sterner stuff." In *The Tempest* he writes, "We are such stuff as dreams are made on." (By the way, "skimble-skamble" means rambling, incoherent, nonsensical.) The last word on "stuff"—if a word is good enough for Shakespeare, it is good enough for us. Taking apart the first draft of our definition of in-kind gives us four concepts to understand: value, contribution, stuff, and project.

Stuff. We will get right to the stuff. As you might rightly assume, stuff, in this case, means anything and everything that you can possibly think of. The stuff or things that can be contributed to a project include people's time (in the form of service performed for the project), real property, equipment, materials, supplies, facilities, services, travel, and all or part of otherwise approvable indirect costs. Can you think of any possible type of contribution that will not fall into one of the listed categories? If you can, we would like to hear from you. Please visit our website and leave us a message (<polarisgrantscentral.net>). Actually, we would like to hear from you regardless. Come visit us. One more interesting point can be made about the stuff that can be contributed. One particular type of stuff can never be an in-kind contribution, never under any circumstances. That one thing is cash. Cash is cash, regardless of the source.

Real property is actually a legal term that has a precise meaning. Real property is land, including the buildings or improvements on it and the land's natural assets such as soil, trees, minerals, and water. People's contributed time comes in many guises. A few examples of people's contributed time are employee release time; foregone stipends, honoraria, and allowances; unremunerated services (foregone wages); and volunteer work. The rest of the items that can be contributed are self-explanatory except for the waiver of all or part of otherwise approvable indirect cost. Also, in the next section of this chapter is a discussion of each of the categories of contributions.

Contribution. The condition that makes the provision of stuff into a contribution is that the provider of the stuff is not remunerated. The recipient of a contribution does not pay the provider for the contribution. A contribution is given freely. Contributions, and therefore in-kind, can come from all the people and organizations that participate in a project. These people and groups include: the applicant organization, partner organizations, volunteers, service providers, project participants, and any other person or group involved with the project.

Value. The value of a contribution is the amount of money that it would cost to purchase, lease, or rent the "stuff" being contributed. When real property is contributed, we are interested in the fair market value of the land, building, or other real property. Fair market value is an important term to understand with regard to in-kind contributions. The definition from Grants Policy Directive 1.02 from the federal Department of Health and Human Services is:

> *Fair Market Value*—The price that a prudent person would pay for property, services, or other assets at a particular time under the free market conditions in the conduct of competitive business.

When equipment and facilities are contributed, the value of the in-kind contribution is computed based on how much it would cost to obtain similar equipment and facilities for a similar length of use. The original price of the equipment and facilities is not relevant. The usual source of such cost information is the marketplace. Go to a source of renting or leasing equivalent equipment and facilities, and obtain the costs for the appropriate time of use. This is the value of contributed equipment and facilities. When materials and supplies are contributed, the value is the cost to the contributor of the materials and supplies. When travel is contributed, the value is what it would have cost to purchase the travel in the marketplace. One source of contributed travel is donation of frequent flyer miles. When services are contributed, the value is the market value of the services performed.

When it comes to people's time, the source of the people and the method of the contribution determine the method of calculating value. Note the differences among the following examples. If people are released with pay from their normal jobs to contribute their time to a project, the cost of the wages and fringes paid to the released employees by their employer for the time spent on the project is the value of the contribution. This applies to any organization or agency, profit or nonprofit, private or government, including the applicant's organization.

If people are released with pay from their normal jobs to contribute their time to a project, and the method of releasing the people is that their employer replaces them with temporary help, the cost of the temporary help is the value of the contribution. An example of this arrangement is the use of substitute teachers paid by the school to release teachers to participate in a project.

If volunteers perform work for a project, the fair market value of the work performed is the value of the contribution. An easy-to-see example would result if a medical doctor volunteered to clear brush to create a nature trail. The value of the doctor's time is the amount that the work would be worth on the open market, in this case, the amount that a brush-clearing specialist would charge for the same work. The value of clearing brush may be $8.00 to $10.00 an hour; therefore the value of the doctor's time is $8.00 an hour. Assume the same medical doctor spends an hour a week providing medical procedures to project participants at no cost to the project. Now what is an hour of the doctor's time worth? The hour is worth probably a couple hundred dollars. The value of contributed time is determined by the value of the job performed, not the person performing the job.

Final Definition of In-Kind. Putting together all we have learned into one, long-winded definition of in-kind yields the following: An in-kind contribution to the budget of a project is the fair market value of contributed real property, time, equipment, materials, supplies, facilities, services, travel, and the waiver of all or part of otherwise approvable indirect costs. Here's the official version:

> *In-Kind Contribution*—The value of non-cash contributions directly benefiting a grant-supported project or program. . . . In-kind contributions may be in the form of real property, equipment, supplies and other expendable property, and goods and services directly benefiting and specifically identifiable to the project or program.
>
> *Grants Policy Directive 1.02, Federal Department*
> *of Health and Human Services*

The difference between our definition and the official one is that we list more types of contributions, where in the official version they use the phrase "other expendable property, and goods and services" which covers a multitude of sins. In the place of their phrases "directly benefiting a grant-supported project" and "specifically identifiable to the project or program" we say "contribution to the budget of the project." Note the insertion in the official definition of the phrase "non-cash contributions," a point we make much earlier and which is necessary to the official version because of the two-sentence structure. We use a one-sentence definition and a cash contribution would not fit into the list of contributions anywhere.

Indirect Costs

For most of us, the concept of indirect cost, often called overhead, is one of the abiding mysteries of the budgeting process. We begin with an official definition and then try to clarify what the definition actually means with the use of plain language, we hope. The term "overhead" is often used interchangeably with indirect costs. An accountant or a business manager, especially in manufacturing, will tell you that indirect costs and overhead are not the same thing. They are correct. The grant world uses the terms interchangeably, but most of the rest of the world does not. So, when you are discussing the budget with business and industry partners, be careful for the misunderstandings that can arise about the use of the terms *overhead* and *indirect costs*.

> *Indirect Costs*—Those costs that are incurred for common or joint objectives and therefore cannot be identified readily and specifically with a particular sponsored project, program, or activity but are nevertheless necessary to the operations of the organization. For example, the costs of operating and maintaining facilities, depreciation, and administrative salaries are generally treated as indirect costs.
>
> *Grants Policy Directive 1.02, Federal Department of Health and Human Services*

We need to clarify a misunderstanding that can revolve around one of the phrases used in the foregoing definition. That phrase is "administrative salaries." Or, phrased another way, administration of the grant. What does it mean to administer a grant? A generally accepted truism is that you manage people and administer money and things. For the purposes of this book we are adding administrative responsibilities in with management requirements. On a very large grant project with plenty of staff, the Project Director may have an assistant who handles all the administrative details, leaving the Project Director free to manage people. In most projects, however, one person, the Project Director, does management tasks and administrative duties. One source of misunderstanding over the use of the words "administer" or "administration" is the huge field of education. In education, managers (school principals, deans, and district supervisors, for example) are called "the administration." In fact, much of what they do is management, but in education, both K–12 and higher, administration combines management with administrative tasks. Here is a definition of administration:

> *Administrative Requirements*—The general business management practices that are common to the administration of all grants, such as financial accountability, reporting, equipment management, and retention of records.
>
> *Grants Policy Directive 1.02, Federal Department*
> *of Health and Human Services*

It is apparent from reading the definition of administrative requirements that even Health and Human Services, which claims to separate the two, uses the terms interchangeably. After all, the definition tells us that we will administer "equipment management." The whole thing gets more tangled the deeper you dig. Usually when grantors use the term "administration," they mean the management of money and things. All the use of the terms *administration* or *administrative costs* or *administrative salaries* does is draw a distinction between two areas of management, the area of people management and the area of managing everything else. Most project managers do both.

Getting back to indirect costs, our definition tells us that indirect costs are "costs that are incurred for common or joint objectives," and that the costs are "necessary to the operations of the organization." A clear and common example of an indirect cost is the payroll department, assuming you have one. If your small nonprofit does not have a payroll department, think back to a time when you were employed by an organization that did have one. Is keeping up with everyone's pay and taxes "necessary to the operations of the organization?" You bet it is. Are the costs incurred by an organization to maintain a payroll department spread across several projects, departments, divisions, or offices? Yes, they are. Are the specific costs incurred by your organization to provide payroll services to a particular entity or activity within your organization difficult to identify? Of course they are. Then the cost of the payroll department can be considered an indirect cost. To be an indirect cost, a few discrete conditions are necessary.

When Is It an Indirect Cost? The cost of an activity can be considered to be an indirect cost if the following statements all are true:

1. The purpose of the activity is spread over several projects, divisions, or activities within an organization.
2. It is difficult or impossible to identify or compute the cost of the activity for each individual project, division, or activity.

3. The activity and therefore the associated cost are necessary to the operation of the organization.

Indirect costs are computed by using a percentage called the indirect cost rate. The indirect cost rate is computed by your financial people, hopefully using generally accepted accounting practices. One last point here: grantors establish a limit on the amount of indirect cost that you can request in your project budget.

Finally we get to the business of the "waiver of all or part of the otherwise approvable indirect costs." This means that if you waive (do not claim, do not ask for or request) indirect costs when a grantor allows indirect costs, the amount of indirect cost that you waive becomes an in-kind contribution of your organization to the budget of the project. Here is the same idea but using different words: If the grantor allows you to claim indirect costs, but you do not claim them, then the amount of indirect cost that you did not claim becomes an in-kind contribution by your organization to the budget of the project.

Let us get one last thing completely straight in this section. Indirect cost is one thing. In-kind is totally different. Indirect cost refers to a type of expense incurred by an organization in its day-to-day operations. In-kind refers to donations or contributions. There is one circumstance where indirect costs can be turned into in-kind, but that does not make them the same.

Direct Costs

Definition. We defined indirect costs before direct costs which is backward from the usual order. It happened because indirect cost was mentioned in our definition of in-kind, so we dealt with it there. Now, we can tell you that there are two and only two types or categories of costs in a budget, direct and indirect. We know what indirect costs are. Now we deal with direct costs, a much simpler situation. Here is the definition of direct costs:

> *Direct Costs*—Those costs that can be specifically identified with a particular project, program, or activity.
>
> *Grants Policy Directive 1.02, Federal Department*
> *of Health and Human Services*

That is simple enough. All direct costs fit into one or more of these nine categories: (1) personnel and fringe, (2) travel, (3) stipends, (4) honorarium, (5) services and consultants, (6) real property, (7) equipment, (8) materials and supplies, and (9) facilities. In absolute terms we could use fewer categories, but more categories make explanations easier. In many budget forms you will see a line item named miscellaneous or other. Our counsel is always to put zero in this line item. What exactly is the money you put into miscellaneous really for? The surmise of the grantor is that you are not sure you computed the budget correctly, so you added a little slush fund in there under miscellaneous or other. If pressed, many people will admit that this line item is their "contingency fund." This tells the grantor that you are unsure of your budget, or that you do not have faith that you can find and compute all the costs involved in your project. What follows in this section is a short discussion of the nine categories of direct costs.

Personnel and Fringe.   This cost is for paid personnel. Paid personnel can be full or part time. They can be paid a salary or hourly. The key to putting a person's wages into this category is that your organization or perhaps a partner organization is responsible for withholding taxes. If you withhold taxes, the person is an employee. Wages paid to employees go in this category.

Fringe refers to the amount of cash it costs your organization for an employee over and above the employee's wages. Fringe is made up of several items, all paid by the employer. These items include the following: matching social security tax, matching Medicare tax (these two together are known as FICA), State Unemployment Insurance (SUTA), Federal Unemployment Insurance (FUTA), Workers' Compensation Insurance, and any benefits provided by your organization such as health care, life insurance, dental care, and retirement fund. Your organization may pay all or only some of the fringe items listed.

Fringe is calculated as a percentage of wages. Your payroll people know your fringe rate. The fringe rate can run from as low as around 10 percent to as high as 50 percent. It is important for you to know about fringe. If you request $20,000 in your project budget for the Project Director and neglect to request the additional 32 percent fringe that your organization will be forced to pay in cash, then the Project Director will not receive $20,000 but a smaller amount after the fringe is taken out.

Many, if not most, grantors require that you use grant-paid staff to supplement not supplant existing staff. Here is how one official statement goes:

> *Supplant*—To replace funding of a recipient's existing program with funds from a Federal grant . . . grant statutes and regulations frequently prohibit this practice.
>
> *Grants Policy Directive 1.02, Federal Department*
> *of Health and Human Services*

An example scenario can go like this. You are a school district. You get a grant. You hire a teacher using funds from the grant. You put the teacher into a classroom, thereby freeing up the teacher who was in the classroom to do whatever you want. You have just converted project grant funds for a specific purpose into general funds for your organization with which you can do whatever you want. This is supplanting, and "grant statutes and regulations frequently prohibit this practice." The same scenario can be repeated for any other type of direct cost item such as equipment or materials and supplies.

The same aversion to supplanting exists among nonfederal grantors. Corporate grantors, foundation grantors, state grantors all "frequently prohibit this practice." Do not be misled because we used only a federal example as our definition. The concept of converting a grantor's project funds into general operating funds for your organization does not appeal to grantors of any type.

Travel. Travel costs include all the costs involved in getting from one place to another, including eating and lodging during the trip. The kinds of costs that can be incurred during travel are numerous, but still can be listed with confidence. Travel itself is usually thought of as being either on the ground or in the air. Project budgets generally do not include trips on boats. The obvious exception is if your project involves marine, lacustrine, or river studies, research, or activities. Finding the cost of traveling by air is simple. It is the cost of the ticket(s). Travel by ground, however, can involve quite a few options. Ground travel can be accomplished by your car, by a rental car, by taxi, by limousine, by hired car, by train, by subway, by bus, by rapid transit train, or by shuttle (hotel variety not space variety). Cost of meals and lodging is simple. It is the cost to eat and the cost to lodge. Intimately entwined with both air and ground travel as well as lodging and meals is the expense of tips. Remember to include tips in a travel budget. Other travel expenses that often get overlooked are parking and tolls.

Stipends. The subject of stipends stands by itself because of the amount of misunderstanding about what a stipend is. You might be surprised by what the dictionary has to say. *Webster's New World Dictionary* says that a stipend is "a regular or fixed payment for services; any periodic payment, as a pension or allowance." The dictionary goes on to say that the synonym is "wage." You probably do not think of a stipend in this way as it relates to a grant-funded project. In general, the use of stipends in a project is viewed two ways. The divide, as with so many other things, is between higher education (and by extension, most health care related projects) and the rest of the nonprofit world including public and private K–12 education. Higher education and many health-care organizations use stipends in a way that would fit the following definition:

> *Stipend*—A payment made to an individual under a fellowship or training grant in accordance with preestablished levels to provide for the individual's living expenses during the period of training.
>
> *Grants Policy Directive 1.02, Federal Department
> of Health and Human Services*

The rest of the nonprofit world tends to use a stipend as a sort of partial payment or thank you for attending a training session, almost a bribe. A common use of stipends is when an organization sets up a training session outside normally paid hours, such as at night, or on the weekend, or in the case of teachers, in the summer. The stipend is paid to participants as an incentive or as a "sorry-we-did-this-on-your-time-but-take-this-and-we-hope-the-money-makes-it-all-right" sort of peace offering.

The two uses of stipends do have two things in common. They both are associated with training and they both use "preestablished levels" of payment. Preestablished level simply means an amount set ahead of time, not a reimbursement for actual living expenses.

Honorariums (Honoraria).

An honorarium is an interesting little payment that can occur from time to time during a grant-funded project. Honorariums are usually made for a speech or presentation or performance. The root word is honor, and the basic concept is that this payment is made to honor a person for some service rather than actually paying them for the service. The actual definition is "a payment as to a professional person for services on which no fee is set or legally obtainable."

The situation normally is something like this: You are holding the grand opening gala event for your project, and you invite the single most famous and expert person in the world on the subject of your project. To your surprise she says yes. She also says that she will be glad to say a few words to the assembled hordes. The day comes. She shows up. She speaks. And, you present her with an honorarium for her presence and her words. The payment is not recompense or payment, because there is no contract. You do not owe her anything. The payment is to honor her for her contributions to the field, her status, the status she lends to the occasion, and for her kindness in speaking to the assembled hordes. Some folks use the words honorarium and stipend interchangeably. They aren't really interchangeable as you see.

Services and Consultants.   First, clearly understand that consultants are service providers. We name them separately only to be absolutely sure that we know exactly where they belong. In general, services are "useful labors performed by an individual or organization on behalf of others." Perhaps the simplest way to explain what services are is to list a few. We make no claims that the following list is complete; you will be able to think of many more. Services can include "useful labors" in the following fields:

- Renovation
- Construction
- Cleaning
- Legal
- Bookkeeping
- Accounting
- Landscaping and grounds maintenance
- Training
- Publicity
- Advertising
- Video production
- Audio recording and production
- Technology
- Communications
- Delivery
- Stenographic services
- Printing and reproduction
- Framing and display

It is true that your paid staff perform services for your organization. In fact, we all perform services all the time, for our employer, for our family, for our friends, and for others. Services for which you pay a service provider or consultant are legally different from services performed by paid staff. The difference is that service providers and consultants are not your employees. You do not withhold taxes or pay fringe on the amount that you pay to a service provider or consultant. The legal relation between you and paid staff is that of an employer and employee. The legal relation between you and a service provider is contractual. This results in the term "contractual services" often being used on budget forms and in grant application packages. When you see the phrase "contractual services," it refers to services. Be very careful about how you use contractual services. There are Internal Revenue Service (IRS) rules about just who is a contractor and who is an employee. Be sure you understand the differences and abide by the rules. You certainly do not want to get it wrong. Even if you are tax exempt, the contractor is not and you are both carefully scrutinized. You can get a description to use for reference from your Certified Public Accountant or from the IRS directly. In fact, you can now get most of the information you need from the IRS website online.

Real Property.   Real property is land, including the buildings or improvements on it and the land's natural assets such as soil, trees, minerals, and water. This definition brings up the fascinating point that we can create real property, and we can increase the value of real property. If we add improvements to a tract of land such as roads, sewage system, water system, and access to electricity, we have vastly improved the value of the land. The improvement is in financial terms. In aesthetic terms the tract of land may not have been improved at all. From the viewpoint of a naturalist or environmentalist, the land may have been ruined. If we build a building, we create additional real property on the existing land, and perhaps again increase the value. Making improvements and constructing buildings is done with the application of services, such as some listed in the previous topic.

Equipment.   Defining exactly what is meant by the term "equipment" can be trickier than you might think. Items considered equipment in one organization can be considered to be expendable in another. Is an electric drill a piece of equipment? Is a bathroom scale a piece of equipment? Is a chair a piece of equipment? Most of you would probably say that each of these items is certainly equipment, but are they equipment from the viewpoint of grantors? The dictionary is no help at all. It says that equipment can be "supplies, furnishings, apparatus, etc.," which just confuses the issue. Falling back on a grantor's definition, which is always wise considering that we are discussing grants, we find that one official definition of equipment goes like this:

> *Equipment*—The tangible nonexpendable personal property charged directly to an award having a useful life of more than one year and an acquisition cost of $5,000 or more per unit. However, consistent with recipient policy, lower limits may be established.
>
> *Grants Policy Directive 1.02, Federal Department*
> *of Health and Human Services*

This definition allows us to define the four characteristics of equipment from the viewpoint of grantors and organizations. The four characteristics are: (1) the item must be nonexpendable, (2) the item must be personal property, (3) the item must have a useful life of some defined term, and (4) the cost of the item must meet or exceed an established amount.

1. The item must be nonexpendable. Nonexpendable means that the item does not become "used up" during its use, or that the item has too much value to discard after use. Clear examples of expendable items that are "used up" are batteries, pencils, drill bits, paper, food, and computer ink cartridges. Examples of expendable items that could be reused but may be discarded after use are paper clips, plastic utensils, rags, and binders.

2. The item must be personal property. This characteristic refers to the legal distinction between two types of property, real and personal. For all practical purposes personal property is anything that is not real property, which has already been defined. A practical example is that the building that houses your organization is real property. Everything in the building is personal property. The things may not belong to a person, but the legal term for them is personal property. From a legal viewpoint, any legal entity such as a nonprofit or a corporation exists as a legitimate "person," in and of itself, with regard to property rights. Some of the personal property in the building can be equipment. The relation between equipment and personal property is the same as the relation between oaks and trees. All oaks are trees, but all trees are not oaks. All equipment is personal property, but all personal property is not equipment.

3. The item must have a useful life of some defined term. The "term" is usually defined in years, from as low as one year to as many five. Each organization can set its own term. An important financial consideration for the length of the term is depreciation and the rate at which the IRS allows you to depreciate the cost of equipment.

4. The cost of the item must meet or exceed an established amount. This amount is in dollars. The lowest established amount we have seen is $50, which is unreasonably low, and the highest we have seen is $5,000 in the foregoing definition, which is unreasonably high.

We can see now that many things we thought were equipment no longer are. Our drill, our bathroom scale, and our chair from the first paragraph in this section would not be equipment according to Health and Human Services. They do not cost enough.

Materials and Supplies. This category of direct expenses is another that seems simple on first glance. We know intuitively and practically what supplies are. Supplies are expendable items such as ink, paper, chalk, laboratory chemicals, pencils, food, soft drinks, and toilet paper. But, what is a computer diskette? A diskette is cheap so it cannot be equipment, but it can last a long time so it is not exactly expendable either. What is wire that we install in the wall for our computer network? It certainly is not equipment, but wire is not exactly expended either. It sits in the wall for years doing its job. Consulting with our official source of definitions we find this:

> *Supplies*—All personal property excluding equipment. . . .
>
> *Grants Policy Manual 1.02, Federal Department*
> *of Health and Human Services*

The ellipsis in the foregoing quotation is standing in for a list of other items that are personal property but are not equipment. This list is not important because none of us would consider intangible property such as a patent or a copyright or a debt instrument to be supplies, so we omitted that part of the definition to keep it clean and simple. Using this definition our diskette and our wire are supplies, but many organizations draw a distinction between supplies and materials. Often, items such as computer diskettes and wire are classified as materials. Other items often called materials are books, computer software, the stuff with which we build things such as wood, glass, plastic, and metal (building materials), and video, audio, and digital tape. Most budget forms published by grantors combine supplies and materials into one line item.

Facilities. Facilities are real property, either yours or someone else's. Facilities are usually equipped with personal property that is needed and appropriate for the activities that occur in the facilities. Facilities can be purchased, leased, rented, or used at no cost (in-kind). Examples of facilities are offices, a museum, a laboratory, a library, a playground, an exercise room, a hospital, a park, a computer center, a video studio, a fishing pond, a health clinic, and the list could go on practically endlessly.

Handling the Grantor's Money

When the grant arrives, via check or electronic transfer, you should assign it its own account number, create a new account number in your chart of accounts, and debit/credit the entire amount of funds you received into that account. Whether you debit or credit the account depends on whether you are an accountant who understands double entry bookkeeping or a person who is using accounting software. What we common folk call a debit, an accountant calls a credit and vice versa. Any cash you receive from any source that will be expended on the grant project is also assigned to that account.

Your project budget shows you how the cash total is to be expended. Normally, grantors require a budget that has several line items, often divided by the types of direct cost expenditures explained in the previous section, or some similar arrangement. This line-item budget serves as your project budget. It tells you how much you can spend on each type of direct expense. The budget narrative provides the detail of exactly how the money in each line item is to be expended.

Make all expenditures by check, never with cash. The one exception to the no cash rule is the use of a petty cash fund for small purchases. "Small purchases" means exactly that, usually under a set amount. Twenty dollars is a normal cutoff point. Set up the fund by writing a check to cash and annotate the check as for petty cash. Every time—with absolutely no exceptions—cash is expended, a receipt must be obtained. This procedure allows an accounting of receipts in hand against the checks written to petty cash. The sum of all receipts and all cash on hand must always equal the amount of checks written to petty cash.

Keep authority to spend money as concentrated as possible. Staff members need to be able to obtain the stuff with which they do their jobs, but the purchase of things should be centralized, with all spending authority residing in one person or a small group of people. One way to show financial responsibility is to require two signatures on checks. This provides a double check on expenditures.

Require complete documentation on all expenditures of any size and any kind. Many transactions naturally create such documentation, but for those transactions that do not, you can use the tools we have included on the disk. File 1001.doc is a form that you can use to document financial transactions. Complete documentation of each transaction is complete protection for you. It is not busy work; it is important work. If you have complete documentation of all financial transactions, it does not matter what questions or problems or accusations come up later. You can prove exactly where every penny went. You are safe and secure. Because of this simple fact, grantors wonder about organizations that cannot produce documentation of financial transactions. There are only two reasons for missing documentation. One is that the money was spent in ways the grantee does not want known. Two is that the grantee is sloppy and inept at handling the finances. Both are unacceptable to grantors. Exhibit 10.1 shows a completed example of this record of expenditure.

EXHIBIT 10.1   1001.DOC

Record of Expenditure

Name of Person Wishing to Purchase Item/Title *N.R. Self, Guidance Counselor*	

Site Address *Beacon Street Location, 22 Beacon, Pleasantville, NC 29987*

Telephone and e-mail *889-777-9090   nrself@beacon.org*

Quantity (ea/cs/hr) *2 ea*	Description of Item(s) *Grantseeker's Toolkit: A Comprehensive Guide to Finding Funding, ISBN 0-471-19303-8, reference books for grantseeking.*

Category (check all that apply)

_____ Equipment	_____ Supply	__X__ Material
_____ Facility Rental	_____ Services	_____ Consulting

Purchase or rental amount (including tax) *$39.95 each, no tax* *$ 5.25 shipping* *$45.20 total*	Purchase Order Number *625349*
	Purchase Order Preapproved By: *A. Countant*
	Date of Purchase or Rental

Date of Order *8/4/2002*	Date of Receipt *8/10/2002*

Company from which item was purchased/location *Polaris Corporation, 800-368-3775, SC, polarisco@aol.com*

Are bids required? _____ Yes __X__ No	If you answered "yes," list below from whom bids were taken:

EXHIBIT 10.1 *(Continued)*

Reason for purchasing or renting the item? *To learn how to acquire grant funding for counseling project and one to put in the library.*
Reason for the chosen bidder? *Not applicable*
Who received the item(s)?   *Nancy Self*
Were the items in good condition? If not, please explain below. *Yes*
If the items were not in good condition, what was done to remedy the matter?

Signature of Purchaser or Renter ___*Nancy R. Self*___

Date _____*8/04/2002*_____

Approved By ___*Sue Pervisor*___

Date _____*8/04/2002*_____

Up to now in this topic we have looked at finances from the viewpoint of the grantor, but other authorities, both governmental or organizational, take an intense interest in how we handle money. Government authorities include the federal government, state government, county or parish government, city, town, or village government, and any other levels that may apply in your location. Organizational authority is the authority to which you answer within your own organization. If you are a school, it may be the district office. If you are a branch of a large nonprofit, it may be the main office. If you are a division in a hospital, it may be the hospital administration. If you are a typical grant project, it will be the applicant organization in the next office.

You are responsible that your financial transactions meet all applicable federal, state, and local laws and regulations. You are responsible that your financial transactions meet all the grantor's rules and regulations. You are responsible that your financial transactions meet all your organization's policies and procedures. It sounds like a lot, but under normal circumstances, all you must do is spend the money exactly as you said you would and keep records on how you spend it.

Regular Financial Reports

As manager of a project, you must require regular financial reports that detail the current balance in the grant account, the balances in the budget line items, and all expenditures since the last report. A complete series of these reports record in outline form the financial life of your project. How often you produce this report depends on the project, but monthly is the minimum. You may need to produce this document yourself. Exhibit 10.2, also included on the disk as file 1002.doc, shows one way to produce such a report. Your report may differ depending on the line items in your budget.

Payroll

As the manager of a project you have three possibilities for handling payroll. First is that your organization has a payroll office or person and that is where payroll will be handled. Second is that the project will set up a payroll office and handle payroll with its own staff. Third is that a service provider will be contracted to handle payroll. Regardless of the method, managing payroll is relatively simple. The process of payroll accounting is refined and exact. The practitioners of this process operate with exactness and precision. They must. They are handling a thing that is very important to a lot of people—their money. The payroll people are directly answerable to every employee who gets a check. That keeps the payroll people very focused.

Your job is to ensure that all the associated paperwork is completed and properly filed and that necessary financial transactions are taking

EXHIBIT 10.2 1002.DOC

Monthly Financial Report

Month	Date Submitted
Project Title	
Grantor	
Project Director	

Beginning Balance $	Ending Balance $	Amount Expected $

Summary of Expenditures by Line Item							
Equipment	Supplies	Materials	Rent	Services	Consulting	Personnel	Overhead
$	$	$	$	$	$	$	$

Total for Month $ _____

Balance Remaining by Line Item							
Equipment	Supplies	Materials	Rent	Services	Consulting	Personnel	Overhead
$	$	$	$	$	$	$	$

Total Remaining $ _____

Submitter's Signature _____

Date _____

Approved By _____

Date _____

place. One transaction to be aware of is the internal transfer of funds from the main grant account into the payroll account(s). Other transactions that must take place are deposit of taxes withheld from employees and deposit of employer contributions to such programs as FICA, SUTA, and FUTA. If your employees are covered by such things as health care, insurance, and a retirement plan, you must ensure that payments are made from your grant account in a timely fashion.

Paperwork that is important includes filing W-2 forms with the Social Security Administration, issuing W-2 forms to employees, obtaining completed W-4 forms from employees yearly, quarterly SUTA reports, and maintenance of payroll tax deposit receipts. The federal government and your state government have absolutely no sense of humor when it comes to all this various payroll-related paperwork. See that it is done correctly and filed on time. Save yourself and your organization the huge amounts of time and grief it will take to straighten out a mess once it happens.

We have included on the disk a tool for managing payroll operations (file 1003.doc). It is a checklist of payroll-related issues, transactions, and paperwork and is shown as Exhibit 10.3. As a project manager, you need to ensure that these items are happening correctly and on time.

Sales Taxes

In some states and localities, nonprofit organizations are exempted from the payment of state, county, and city sales taxes. If this is true for your locality and if you are part of an established nonprofit, you already have the requisite paperwork. Of importance are the official document and the number assigned to your organization. This number is often referred to as your "tax exempt number." It is unrelated to your exemption from federal income tax under a 501(C)(3) or 509(A) status, and it is unrelated to your federal employer identification number (EIN), which is to a company or nonprofit what a social security number is to a person. It is the number that identifies you to the IRS.

Purchasing Services

Purchasing services is a simple exercise in getting it all in writing. We discussed this topic in detail in Chapter 8, but for review we repeat the steps:

1. Know exactly what you want.
2. Create a job specification document (bid description, work order, or bid packet).
3. Obtain bids that incorporate your job specifications.
4. Get references and check with them.
5. Respond to the bid you accept in writing.
6. Oversee the work regularly.
7. Be in charge, they are working for you.
8. Pay only when the work is completed to your complete satisfaction.

To provide help with managing the finances of purchasing services we have included Exhibit 10.4 (1004.doc), which is a generic bid request

Exhibit 10.3 1003.DOC

Personnel Reporting Checklist

Place Check	Period	Description
		Transfer of funds from grant account to cover personnel costs
		Deposit of state taxes withheld from employees, file receipts
		Deposit of federal taxes withheld from employees, file receipts
		Deposit of FICA funds, file receipts
		Deposit of SUTA funds
		Deposit of FUTA funds
		Workers' Compensation Insurance payment
		Health insurance payment
		Retirement plan payment
		State withholding reporting
		Federal withholding reporting
		FICA reporting
		SUTA reporting
		FUTA reporting
		W-9 Forms
		W-2 Forms
		W-4 Forms
		1099s
		State Tax Return
		Federal Tax Return

form. If it does not fit for the type of job you need, you can create your own using the disk document (1004.doc) as a guide.

Purchasing, Leasing, or Renting

To purchase a thing is have title to the thing transferred to you in return for a payment. Once the thing is yours you may use it. Leasing and renting allows you to use a thing for an established period of time but does not transfer title. From a legal standpoint, there is no real difference in leasing and renting. People work with different meanings for lease and

EXHIBIT 10.4

1004.DOC

Bid Request

Bid Opening Date/Time _____

Bid Closing Date/Time _____

Bid Request To

Name of Company or Organization _____

Address _____

City/State/Zip _____

Telephone _____ Fax _____

E-mail Address _____

Contact Person(s) _____

All bids will be submitted in writing by the closing date and time to the following:

Bid Contact Person_____

Organization _____

Address _____

City/State/Zip _____

Telephone _____ Fax _____

E-mail Address _____

Number Desired	Date Required	Name & Specification

Further Description

EXHIBIT 10.4 *(Continued)*

Projected Start Date _____   Projected Completion Date _____

Service Specification

_____

_____

_____

_____

Financial Considerations for Items

Is there a discount for prepayment or payment in less than 30 days? _____ Yes   _____ No

If so, what percentage? _____ %

Is there a delivery charge? _____ Yes   _____ No   If so, how much? $ _____

How is delivery accomplished? _____

_____

_____

Is it possible to arrange payments?   _____ Yes   _____ No

If so, what are the conditions? _____

_____

_____

Is there an interest charge? _____ Yes   _____ No   If so, how much? $ _____

Financial Considerations for Services or Consulting

Is there a discount for prepayment or payment in less than 30 days? _____ Yes   _____ No

If so, what percentage? _____ %

Invoicing will be: _____ By the job?   _____ By the hour?

Invoicing will be: _____ Biweekly   _____ Monthly

                     _____ Quarterly   _____ On completion of the job

References

Name of Contact Person _____

Title _____

Organization _____

Address _____

City/State/Zip _____

Telephone _____   E-mail _____

EXHIBIT 10.4 *(Continued)*

Name of Contact Person _____

Title _____

Organization _____

Address _____

City/State/Zip _____

Telephone _____   E-mail _____

Name of Contact Person _____

Title _____

Organization _____

Address _____

City/State/Zip _____

Telephone _____   E-mail _____

Authorized Signature from Bid Letting Organization _____

Date _____   Title _____

Authorized Signature from Bidding Organization _____

Date _____   Title _____

rent, but in the marketplace there is no real difference. The difference we are interested in is between purchase and lease/rent. From now on we use the single word rent in the place of lease and/or rent.

The first consideration when preparing to purchase or rent an item is whether your organization or agency has policies and procedures in place that deal with such transactions. If such policies and procedures exist, you must comply. The second consideration when preparing to purchase or rent an item is whether the transaction is budgeted for in your grantor-approved project budget. If it is, then fine. If it is not, then look for another source of funds for the purchase or rental. The third consideration when preparing to purchase or rent an item is the exercise of prudent fiduciary responsibility.

You have, no doubt, seen that word *fiduciary* before, and you might have wondered just exactly what it means. Fiduciary means to hold something in trust for someone else, to be a trustee or a guardian. As Project Director you hold the grantor's money in trust. That means that you must exercise the same care with the grantor's money as you would with your own. You have a fiduciary responsibility. What this means in practical terms is that you must be a careful shopper and get your money's worth.

You should do all the things that a careful shopper does, such as comparison shop and pay enough to get quality, but not so much that you are wasteful. The best way to shop for things, whether a car and bus or pencils and paper, is to follow a list such as the two that follow.

If It Is a Purchase

1. Define exactly what you need.
2. Find several sources (vendors) for what you need. Compare cost and quality. If the item represents a significant investment, let a bid package and get bids.
3. Check warranties and guarantees.
4. Check to see how easy and how expensive it is to get service on the item.
5. Check to see how long it takes for the average servicing of the item.
6. Ask to talk to someone who owns an item like the one you are considering purchasing.
7. Compare the features of the item you are considering with other items a little more and a little less expensive.
8. Find out about the return policy.
9. Check to see if your item is a new addition to the product line or an established item. Sometimes new additions are discontinued quickly and you are left without parts and service.
10. Ask about service agreements. Compare prices of servicing yourself versus purchasing an agreement.
11. Check on staff training to use the device. Is it free? If not, how much?
12. Make the purchase decision based on a balance of cost and quality.

If It Is a Lease

1. Define exactly what you need.
2. If it is office space or the equivalent or warehouse space or the equivalent, your city or county government will be able to provide you

with statistics of the *average cost* per square foot for such rental space. They can even provide that information by area of the city or county.

3. Find several sources for what you need.

4. Check such things as whether utilities are included. If not, then check to see what the average monthly cost is/was of the utilities for the space you're considering. Your local utility companies can provide that information and the lessor should provide it. You can also ask the last renter.

5. Go see the facility during or at least after a strong rainstorm. Look for signs of leakage.

6. Have a professional inspect the heating and air-conditioning systems, plumbing, and other such systems and structures. It is well worth the effort even if you have to pay a little.

7. Find out what renter's rights are in your city or county. There should be written documentation of local laws.

8. Find out about renter's rights and responsibilities in your state. There should be written documentation.

9. Ask about who pays insurance on the building and on its contents. Normally, you would be responsible for insuring contents.

10. Check with local police about crime and break-ins in the area in which you are considering a lease.

11. Obtain prices or bids from several sources. Be sure each source is bidding on exactly the same thing.

12. Read the list of things to check if it is a purchase and be sure you check off the same items for a lease.

13. Make the lease decision based on a balance of cost and quality.

Building Something

Building something is nothing more than purchase of a large service contract, or more correctly, several service contracts. The process listed under the previous topic Purchasing Services applies here. The complete description of the service you need becomes a description of what is to be built, a much more complex document. Examples would be architectural plans in the case of a structure and blueprints for a device.

The key to any construction project is to hire and rely on experts. Get an experienced contractor who is familiar with your type of construction and give that one person overall responsibility for the successful completion of the job. Have your main contractor deal with all other contractors. Let your contractor purchase all construction materials and supplies. This gives you one point of contact, one person to hold responsible for all aspects of the job. Make successful and on-time completion of the job a financial incentive by including in the contract penalties for late completion and substandard work.

Revenue Generation

The purpose of this topic is not to give you information about holding revenue generating events, but rather to remind you that you must document fully all financial transactions that take place around such an event or component. Also, revenue generated by project events may be in the form of cash so it must be carefully handled and deposited as quickly as possible into a bank account and assigned to your grant line item in your accounting system. Revenue is not necessarily "free" money. What did you say in the proposal that you were going to do with any revenue? That is what you must do with it.

Income Tax Returns

Nonprofits do not pay federal income tax, but they must still file a tax return. Whether you file a state return depends on your state. The basics of the tax return for a nonprofit are simple. You report all income of any kind from any source. You report all expenditures. You do report on a few additional topics but that is basically it. Tell the IRS what came in and what went out. As with most individuals and companies, it will probably pay dividends to have a professional complete your tax returns.

Financial Management Maxims

Summarizing the advice given in this chapter could lead us to produce a list of money maxims. Doing these things could keep you out of trouble.

1. Comply with your organization's financial policies and procedures.
2. Spend the money the way you said you would in the proposal.
3. Document every financial transaction, no matter how small.
4. Use professionals for any job that you are unsure about.
5. Comply with reporting requirements of your grantor, your organization, and federal, state, and local governments.
6. Be thorough.
7. Be on time.
8. Be prudent.
9. Be honest.
10. When in doubt, ask your grantor's contact person or its fiscal officer.
11. When in doubt, *always* ask first.

Wise Guy

I'm still here, but I'm worn down to a nub. There's not much left of me. This chapter could scare me away from the whole grant thing. I don't want the feds coming down on me. The very thought of the IRS sends cold chills down my spine. And the folks at Social Security aren't to be trifled with either. There is too much to remember. What with the feds and the state, county, and city goons waiting to descend on me when I mess up, my staff on me about their payroll checks, and all this stuff about fi-du-fo-fum trust—I just don't know.

Wise Lady

If you're in business or heading up a business of any sort, you are used to dealing with these things to some degree. Yes, it is complicated and it is daunting, however, if you are doing what you said you'd do in the proposal you don't need to worry. If you have questions, financial issues are the easiest ones about which to get advice. You need good advisors. You need to use the advisors provided by the grantor. Any business person or manager responsible for fiscal issues should have an attorney and an accountant as part of the team. These may be only part-time advisors, but they are critical to the smooth running of your operation, and they are critical to you keeping your sanity! It's not necessary that you totally understand all these issues, but that you know when to ask and you're not afraid to do it.

Conclusion

This is an exhausting chapter. Just remember the prime directive. Do what you said you would do. In addition, do not cut corners. Document every transaction. Make prudent spending decisions. Stay up to date. This is one of the more important aspects of your job as manager of a project. Take it seriously. Think of the time you spend as protection. The better you document and keep up, the better protected you are.

With the next chapter we begin a five-chapter trip into the land of project evaluation. If terms like formative and summative and qualitative and quantitative have ever baffled you, just wait. By the time you finish the next five chapters you will be completely confused. Actually, we hope not. We start with a chapter on the fundamentals of evaluation, and then move into more specific topics in succeeding chapters.

## PART III

Project Evaluation

## Chapter 11

Evaluation: The Basics

There is measure in all things.

Satires, Horace, 35 B.C.

Introduction

This chapter begins our discussion of project evaluation, an aspect of the grant process that has grown over the last decade into importance equal to the project itself. This chapter introduces the topic of evaluation and sets the stage for the chapters that follow. Chapter 12 discusses the evaluation process; Chapter 13 tells how to create an evaluation plan; Chapter 14 tells how to perform an evaluation; and finally Chapter 15 deals with how to create an evaluation report.

This introductory chapter discusses a number of topics that lay the groundwork for what is to follow. We answer a series of questions: What is evaluation, what is the purpose of evaluation, and who does the evaluation? We discuss evaluation terminology, defining several worrisome terms. We discuss when an evaluation takes place and we discuss briefly the evaluation as a budget item. We close with three topics: the evaluation plan, doing the evaluation, and the evaluation report.

What Is Evaluation?

Evaluation means different things to different people. Any discussion of evaluation necessarily includes reference to mostly academic sources, because these are the people who spend the most time thinking, studying, formulating, and writing about evaluation. After all, we task educators with the job of evaluating our children's academic progress on a constant and ongoing basis. With that said, the *Education Research Information Clearinghouse (ERIC) Thesaurus* gives as good a basic fundamental definition of evaluation as we will find. ERIC tells us that evaluation is the process of

> appraising or judging organizations or things in relation to stated objectives, standards, or criteria.
>
> *ERIC Thesaurus*

We are aware that "judging" has become a concept with which many people are uncomfortable. However, the type of judging or judgment referred to in the ERIC definition accords with the definition you will find if you look in a dictionary, which is "to form an idea, opinion, or estimate about any matter." This is exactly what evaluation is with the addition of one important element. That element is that the opinion or estimate of the matter must be in relation to "stated objectives, standards, or criteria."

So we have in place the three key elements to an evaluation:

1. We appraise or judge. Other terms that can be used to flesh out the first concept are measure and compare.
2. We have the thing or matter at hand to be evaluated, which can be anything at all. In our case it is our grant project.
3. We appraise, judge, measure, and compare our matter at hand against "stated objectives, standards, or criteria."

You might be wondering about the term assessment, and where it fits in with evaluation. Many educators view evaluation and assessment as different things. Let's take a look. Here is the definition of assessment from the *CREST Assessment Glossary:*

> The process of gathering, describing, or quantifying information about performance.
>
> *CREST Assessment Glossary*

Does this definition of assessment have the three parts that we found in the definition of evaluation? Yes, it does. To quantify means to apply numbers, which enables us to appraise, judge, compare, and measure. The remaining two elements are embedded in the concept of performance. First, some one or some thing must perform, in our case it is our grant project. Second, to perform means to meet requirements, in our case stated or understood objectives, standards, or criteria. For our purposes then, assessment and evaluation mean the same thing.

Summarizing, specifically for our purposes, we see that at its most basic, an evaluation has three elements: (1) the project, (2) a set of prestated standards, and (3) the comparison or measurement of the project against the standards and the formation of an opinion or a judgment.

What Is the Purpose of Evaluation?

Broad Purposes

Evaluation serves two broad purposes. The first is to provide information for project improvement. The second is to provide information that enables stakeholders to understand what has been accomplished. Note the similarities between the two broad purposes. In both cases, evaluation is performed for action-related purposes. In both cases the information provided helps decide a course of action.

Improve Project. Several types of information can be provided by an evaluation for project improvement. An assessment of project activities can determine if the activities are proceeding as planned. It can determine if the project is proceeding on schedule according to its timeline. It can determine if the resources provided for the project are being utilized effectively. It can determine if the services provided by the project to participants are being utilized effectively. And, most importantly, it can provide information from which changes can be made to improve the project as it progresses.

Inform Stakeholders. In general a stakeholder is any person or organization that has an interest in the grant project. The interest may be in the operation of the project or in the outcomes of the project or in both. Stakeholders usually include the applicant organization itself, all partner organizations, the grantor, and any person or organization that contributes significant resources to the project. One important category of obvious stakeholders has been left out, the participants. Project participants have a clear interest in the project, but whether they are included in the information sharing about the project depends on the type of project and the type of participants. Stakeholders are responsible for making the ultimate decision about the project and whether to continue. They must have all the information they can be given so their decision will be informed.

Culture of Evaluation

The purpose of evaluation is to gain knowledge, not assess blame. Mistakes will always be made. Expect mistakes and document them honestly. If an evaluation is to do its job, the information that it conveys must be accurate. Yes, outcomes are important, but honesty is more important. Do not let issues of accountability become such a political game that the evaluation loses its effectiveness because of unwillingness to speak plainly. Assume that everyone did the best that they could and that mistakes are a normal part of any project. Establish a culture of gaining knowledge, not assessing blame.

Who Does an Evaluation?

The Decision

An evaluation can be an inside job or an outside job. For an inside job, people from within the organization running the project do the project evaluation. For an outside job, a person or organization from outside the organization running the project is hired to do the project evaluation. The decision on which route to take depends first, of course, on the grantor's wishes. Often the grantor will tell you to use an outside evaluator. That settles that. Just as often, however, the grantor leaves the decision up to you. In this case, the size of the grant is a good indication of what you should do. On smaller grants, say those below $200,000, the simple economics of spending the necessary money on an outside evaluator makes it impractical. On larger grants, if you want to show clearly that you are interested in the objectivity of the evaluation, hire an evaluator from outside. An outside evaluation lends credibility to the findings.

Inside Team

When the decision is to go with an inside evaluation, it's important to establish a team, not assign one person to the task. The team should be made up of representatives from all appropriate stakeholders, being sure to include participants. A team with representatives from all interested parties, including participants, is one way to show the grantor that your intention is for the evaluation to be as objective as possible. By the way, if the participants are children, be sure to include parent representatives on the evaluation team. If the participants, for whatever reason, are unable to participate in an evaluation, include caretaker representatives on the evaluation team. It would be preferable if at least one member of the team had knowledge and experience in project evaluation, but this may prove impossible and will not prevent people of good will from performing a good evaluation.

Outside Evaluator

If the decision is to hire an outside evaluator, you are hiring a consultant or service provider. See Chapter 8 for a detailed discussion of the process of hiring a consultant or service provider. Your final decision on the choice of an outside evaluator will come down to three considerations: cost, credentials, and experience. The cost must be in line with what you can afford to spend. The outside evaluator naturally must have the educational credentials to give credibility to the work. The outside evaluator must have had experience in evaluating projects similar to yours. If the project is large and complex, you may need to assemble a team of outside evaluators, each team member uniquely suited to assess a particular aspect of the project. The grantor may require a specific evaluation team.

Evaluation Terminology

The language of evaluation comes mostly from higher education—especially research. To practitioners of the art of evaluation the language is precise and clear, but to most of us the language obscures what is, at base, a relatively simple process accomplished by fairly straightforward means. In this section we attempt to explain a series of terms. We picked these particular few terms because of their common use by grantors in their discussion of project evaluations. The purpose is to clarify what is meant by the terms in a practical way that will prove useful to the nonacademic research project manager. As our standard for definitions we will use the National Science Foundation (NSF). This organization is intimately involved on all facets of evaluations. NSF is a major grantor, making hundreds of millions of dollars yearly in grants. NSF is also a major academic player in defining standards. It is one of the elder statesmen in the grants business.

We start with the terms that define the types of evaluation. The two most commonly used are formative evaluation and summative evaluation. First we give a formal definition. Note that an "intervention," in this case, indicates the same thing as our "project."

Formative Evaluation

Evaluation designed and used to improve an intervention

> *User Friendly Handbook for Project Evaluation, Division of Research, Evaluation, and Communication, National Science Foundation*

Formative evaluation is the assessment of ongoing project activities. It begins at project start and continues for the life of the project. Formative evaluation provides information to improve the project. It determines if the project is being conducted as planned, and it assesses progress in meeting the project's goals and objectives. Evaluation specialists will continue and define two types of formative evaluation, implementation and progress. For our purposes we combine the two and call the whole thing formative evaluation. All grantors do, except those focused on higher education research and scientific research. You will often see the term "process evaluation." It is a stand-in, a synonym for formative evaluation.

The next of our two types of evaluation is summative evaluation. Here is the formal definition according the NSF:

Summative Evaluation

Evaluation designed to present conclusions about the merit or worth of an intervention and recommendations about whether it should be retained, altered, or eliminated.

User Friendly Handbook for Project Evaluation, Division of Research,
Evaluation, and Communication, National Science Foundation

Summative evaluation is the assessment of a project's success. It takes place after the changes needed as the result of the formative evaluation have been instituted, after the project is stable, and after the impact of the project has had time to be realized. Summative evaluation determines if the participants benefited from the project, if the project met its goals and objectives, and if the results of the project are worth its cost. You will see three terms used interchangeably with summative evaluation. They are *outcome* evaluation, *impact* evaluation, and *product* evaluation. Evaluation specialists often draw distinctions between summative, outcome, impact, and product evaluations, but the differences interest only specialists in evaluation. For our purposes, they all amount to the same thing.

What is the relation between formative evaluation and summative evaluation, and what do they mean in concrete terms? When the building inspector checks out the wiring, plumbing, and construction of a house at the request of the builder, that is formative. When home buyers check out the same house, that is summative. When the cook tastes the barbecue, that is formative. When the guests taste the barbecue, that is summative. When inspector number eight puts that little piece of paper in the pocket of a coat, that is formative. When a customer tries on the coat, that is summative.

Another set of terms that is rarely used, but which you might encounter are *traditional* and *systems* evaluations. A traditional evaluation is when you simply evaluate to tell the grantor what your results were. Traditional corresponds to summative.

Systems evaluation is when you evaluate to meet the needs of the participants as well as the grantor. Systems evaluation incorporates both formative and summative evaluations.

The next two terms to define are quantitative and qualitative. They refer to the methods or techniques used in an evaluation. Here is what NSF has to say about quantitative evaluation:

Quantitative Evaluation

An approach involving the use of numerical measurement and data analysis based on statistical methods

> *User Friendly Handbook for Project Evaluation, Division of Research, Evaluation, and Communication, National Science Foundation*

Quantitative evaluation centers on numbers. Common techniques for gathering quantitative data are questionnaires, tests, and existing databases. Here is what NSF has to say about qualitative evaluation:

Qualitative Evaluation

The part of the evaluation that is primarily descriptive and interpretative, and may or may not lend itself to quantitative treatment

> *User Friendly Handbook for Project Evaluation, Division of Research, Evaluation, and Communication, National Science Foundation*

Qualitative evaluation centers on words. Common techniques for gathering qualitative data are observations, interviews, and focus groups.

The relationship between formative, summative, quantitative, and qualitative is best illustrated using a matrix such as the following:

	Formative Evaluation	**Summative Evaluation**
Quantitative Techniques	Yes	Yes
Qualitative Techniques	Yes	Yes

From the table you can see clearly the relation between the two sets of terms. You can see clearly that both formative and summative evaluations can use both quantitative and qualitative techniques. The problem comes from the usage of many people of the terms quantitative evaluation and qualitative evaluation rather than calling them what they are, which is techniques or methods. But, now you know.

Another useful table might be one displaying all the different terms that you might run into when different people talk about evaluation. Again, evaluation specialists and academics take strong issue with so cavalierly dismissing the differences between all these different terms, but for the purposes of the normal nonresearch grant project evaluation, what we are telling you is true.

Formative Evaluation	**Summative Evaluation**
Implementation	Outcome
Progress	Impact
Process	Product
Soft	Hard

When Does the Evaluation Take Place?

Data collection for an evaluation starts when the project begins, as soon as any project activities begin. The evaluation continues on an ongoing basis assessing activities as they happen and assessing progress towards goals and objectives as the progress is occurring. However, the creation of the evaluation plan occurs during project development. Normally grantors require an evaluation plan as part of the proposal, therefore evaluation actually starts before even officially asking for grant money. Evaluation must be an integral part of the project. Evaluation is not something that is tacked onto the end of a project to make the grantor happy. Evaluation is built into the project from the very beginning. For example, note that the method of creating goals and objectives that we teach (see Chapter 5 and also the *Grantseeker's Toolkit*) incorporates measurement and results as an integral part. This makes evaluation easier and fundamental to the project.

Evaluation as a Budget Item

An evaluation costs money. Your grantor expects to see funds allocated in the project budget for evaluation activities. These activities can consume from 5 to 15 percent of the project budget, depending on the project and the grantor. Grantors know this and expect it. In fact, failure to budget sufficient funds for the evaluation can be interpreted by the grantor to mean that you do not understand what is necessary for the process. It can reduce your chance of winning the grant. A few typical costs involved in evaluating a grant project are travel, consultant services, reproduction, and delivery.

The Evaluation Plan

An effective evaluation plan produces reliable, objective, and quantifiable data that can be used to determine project results. Reliable data is worthy of trust; it can be depended on. Objective data is unbiased and not prejudiced. Quantifiable data can be expressed in numbers. The creation of an evaluation plan should be a participatory process. All interested parties (stakeholders) should be included in the planning, the implementation, and the interpretation of results.

An evaluation plan states clearly each of six sets of information listed below, all of which are necessary to perform an evaluation:

1. Measurable results are described.
2. Data collection methods are described.
3. Record keeping activities are described.
4. The people or positions responsible for the evaluation activities are named.
5. The times for evaluation activities are given.
6. The reporting procedures are described. Chapter 13 discusses in detail the creation of an evaluation plan.

Doing the Evaluation

Issues of key importance while doing an evaluation are included in the following numbered list. A full discussion of performing an evaluation is found in Chapter 14.

1. Keep disruption to a minimum. Data must be obtained but be aware of the disruption to normal operations caused by the collection.
2. Apply the highest standards of propriety. You are dealing with people's lives.
3. Conduct the evaluation with the highest standards of legal and ethical behavior.
4. Respect and protect the rights and welfare of human subjects.
5. Respect and protect human dignity and worth in all interactions.
6. Ensure absolutely that no one will feel threatened or be harmed.
7. Obtain necessary formal agreements in writing.
8. Be realistic, prudent, diplomatic, and frugal.

The Evaluation Report

An evaluation report is the documentary record of the methods and the findings of an evaluation. Chapter 15 details the process of creating an evaluation report. A few of the questions we answer in that chapter include: What information does a final report contain? Who receives the final report? When will the final report be completed? There are, of course, reports other than the final report. During formative evaluation a steady stream of reports is created on the performance of activities and progress towards the goals and objectives.

Wise Guy

I get this scam. They throw all kinds of complicated terms at you in the hopes of keeping you off balance. It's as though some priestly caste has the ancient holy task to keep this evaluation thing secret from the rest of us. Well, it's working. For me anyway.

Wise Lady

It's like any other profession . . . it has its own jargon. Do you play golf? You do? Well, what do you call it when you manage to hit the ball into the little cup in one less than the number of strikes they predicted? You say you call it a birdie? Doesn't sound silly or strange to you at all does it? Did you stop to think it might sound awfully odd to someone who'd never had any contact with the sport? Well, evaluation is no different. Processes were developed and someone had to call them something. Read on and you will understand the meaning of the jargon and it won't sound so difficult. It really isn't difficult . . . hard work, yes, but difficult, no. It's just a matter of replacing the jargon with words and phrases that are a little more understandable to the lay person.

Conclusion

This chapter has given a broad overview of project evaluation. Evaluation is the process of appraising the performance or worth of a thing or an organization with respect to preset or established standards. The two reasons for doing an evaluation are to monitor the progress of a project and to find if the project is successful. The evaluation can be done either by an inside team or by an outside evaluator hired for the job. Evaluation is not just something done at the end of a project, but is an integral part of all project activities from the very beginning. We have tried to clear up the confusion around the most commonly used evaluation terms. We have set the stage for the detailed chapters that lie ahead.

## Chapter 12

Evaluation: The Process

"Contrariwise," continued Tweedledee,
"if It was so, it might be;
and if it were so, it would be;
but as it isn't, it ain't.
That's logic."

Lewis Carroll, *Alice's Adventures in Wonderland*

Though this be madness, yet there is method in 't.

William Shakespeare, *Hamlet*

Introduction

We have discussed a lot of generalities concerning evaluation. Now we get more specific. By "The Process" we mean the steps you take to create and accomplish an evaluation. One way to look at the evaluation process is to divide it into three phases:

1. Create the evaluation plan.
2. Perform the evaluation.
3. Create and distribute the evaluation report.

This division is useful for understanding the overall process, but misleading in that all three phases together are the evaluation, not just phase two by itself. A more useful way to approach the process of evaluation is to divide it into five steps:

Step 1: Develop the evaluation questions and the criteria.

Step 2: Match the questions with an appropriate approach.

Step 3: Collect data.

Step 4: Analyze data.

Step 5: Provide information to interested parties.

Steps 1 and 2 are central to creating an evaluation plan. Steps 3 and 4 are the performance of the evaluation with respect to the project being evaluated. Step 5 is the creation of the evaluation plan. In this chapter we discuss each of the five steps. In each of the next three chapters we discuss one of the three phases into which we divided the overall evaluation process. *The following quotation contains all the components that we discuss in our evaluation process, although they are not in any kind of order that makes them easy to work with:*

> First, each evaluation plan must include an evaluation design, an implementation plan for the evaluation, and a discussion of how resources will be allocated for evaluation (e.g., budget, staffing, and management). The evaluation design should address the evaluation questions; the methodological approach for answering the evaluation questions; how data will be collected; how the data will be analyzed; and how the evaluation findings will be reported and disseminated. The evaluation should be linked to the overall formulation of project goals and objectives; it should relate directly to the problem, solution, and anticipated outcomes identified in the "Project Purpose" section. Finally, the research questions and data collection plan should take into account each of the "Review Criteria" treated above.

> *Application Kit, Telecommunications and Information*
> *Infrastructure Assistance Program (TIIAP)*
> *National Telecommunications Information Administration*
> *US Department of Commerce*

Develop Evaluation Questions and Criteria

The goals and the objectives of our project are the source material from which we develop evaluation questions and criteria. That is, the goals and objectives will be our source material if they are concrete and specific, measurable, and include expected results. In other words, if the goals and objectives are created the way we teach, you can use them as the basis for your evaluation. You can use them to create the evaluation questions. If, however, your goals and objectives are fuzzy, not capable of measurement, and do not include your expected results, then you need to rework them until they meet these requirements or developing evaluation questions and criteria will be an exercise in frustration. We have discussed this topic previously in Chapter 5. In the *Grantseeker's Toolkit,* we provide examples and extensive discussion.

Developing criteria means that we set the standard for each question. We determine what is "good." We develop a means of telling clearly whether the progress of the project measures up to the intent of each question. This is the measurability that already should be built into your goals and objectives. Our criteria will, of course, change from question to question, but the overall thrust of all our standards is to determine the progress and effectiveness of our project.

The number of questions that possibly can be asked may be very large. We want to limit the questions to those that will provide useful information for the people who expect to act on it. The number of questions we decide to ask determines how long, involved, expensive, and intrusive our data gathering will be. We must ask all the questions that need answering, but we also must limit ourselves to questions that provide useful information to decision makers. Expending valuable and limited project resources on answering questions that fall into the nice-to-know category does not show prudent and frugal use of project resources.

Deciding if a question is useful or just nice to know is simple. First identify the stakeholders, those parties, those individuals and organizations involved in or affected by the project. Second, address the stakeholders' needs. Apply the process like this. For every question you propose, check your list of stakeholders. Ask this question: "Which of the stakeholders needs to know the answer to this question?" If the answer is "none," then discard the question. It falls into the nice-to-know category, and we, being stewards of the grantor's resources, cannot waste time on such a question. Your project is not a study in evaluation. It is not about evaluation; it is about the benefits to the participants. We are not discussing pure research, in which case evaluation may be entirely the point.

As we develop our questions we need to be sure that we include questions that cover the issues of costs, adaptability, and results. These three issues go to the heart of the reasons that grantors make grants. First, no solution, or part of a solution, can be successful in the long run if it is too expensive to implement. So, ask questions about the cost of implementation of the different parts of the project as well as overall costs. One simple but telling measure of cost, one that most project managers shy away from, is simply to determine the cost per participant. Divide the total cost of the project by the number of participants served. When the quotient is a huge amount of money, there may be a problem.

Questions about adaptability go to the grantor's interest in replicating successful solutions elsewhere. Remember that one of the main reasons grantors make grants is to fund model or demonstration projects. Questions about results go straight to the core of the whole reason we are doing the project in the first place. Is the project working? Is it doing the things that we expected it to do? Is it solving our problem(s)? It is easy to see that the answers to these questions could prove embarrassing. People do not want to find that all their hard work has not accomplished what they expected. At this time, the application of honesty and integrity can begin to cost something. In the long run though, remember that one of the purposes of grant projects is to break new ground, to learn, and to discover. If we are not honest with our appraisal of our project, we have not fulfilled our part in the overall grant process. Many times we learn more from what doesn't work than what does. What we need to be sure to find out is why.

It may be helpful to realize that the questions we ask about costs, adaptability, and results, are asked about four different topic areas: behavior, product, performance, and process. Behavior and performance refer to project participants, the target population. Product and process refer to the project itself. These four areas are often found in evaluation literature labeled as objectives: behavioral objectives, product objectives, performance objectives, and process objectives. Looking back at our scheme for developing goals and objectives we find the suggestion that any project can be divided into the following five stages:

1. Set-up
2. Research and development
3. Implementation with target population
4. Manage and communicate
5. Evaluation

Aligning our five stages of a project with the four "objectives" often found in evaluation literature, we come up with this table:

Stages of a Project (Goals of a Project)	Possible Objectives for Each Stage (Goal)
Set-up	Process
Research & Development	Process Product
Implementation with Target Population (there may be more than one of these)	Process Product Behavioral Performance
Manage & Communicate	Process Product
Evaluate	Process Product

Questions about process objectives concern the progress and procedures of a project. Questions about product objectives concern the tangible results of a project, such as curriculum, reports, or training materials. Questions about performance objectives concern the performance of the participants measured against criteria. Questions about behavioral objectives concern the performance of participants from the viewpoint of behavior in three possible areas: cognitive, affective, and psychomotor. If that last little bit, cognitive, affective, and psychomotor, throws you for a loop, find an educator or a person with a masters degree in social work or a psychologist. They understand this stuff and can explain it and apply it. In cases like this, a service contract can be very valuable. You don't have to know everything, you just find someone who does know.

Match Questions with Approach— The Evaluation Strategy

This step is often called evaluation strategy. What goes on here is the matching of each question that you have asked with the most appropriate evaluation approach or method. Evaluators talk in terms of three types of evaluation "designs." The three types of evaluation designs are core, time-series, and comparison group. *Core design* means that the evaluation will examine a single cohesive group. *Time-series design* means that the evaluation will compare current performance and behavior to past performance and behavior. *Comparison group design* means that the evaluation will measure the performance and behavior of an experimental group to that of a control group. It is pretty easy to see that for social program grant projects, the time-series design is the design we use the most. However, we must select the most appropriate evaluation design for each evaluation question.

Remember that we already have created the evaluation questions and the criteria for each question. We have selected our general methodology (evaluation design from previous paragraph). Now we must determine what source(s) can provide the information that we seek. In many cases we must also decide how large our sample will be. It is not always possible to obtain data from all possible sources, so a sample is used. The sample size is largely determined by the importance of the question. The more important the question, the larger the sample size. And finally we must select the data collection technique for obtaining the information from the source(s) that we picked. These four steps are fundamental, so we repeat them in a numbered list format:

1. Select general methodology (evaluation design).
2. Determine source(s) of information.

3. Determine sample size.

4. Select data collection technique.

An overview of data collection techniques yields five general possibilities: surveys, focus groups, test scores, observation, and review of records. Surveys can be of two types, self-administered or interview. Surveys gather data from people on behaviors and opinions. A focus group refers to the technique of bringing a number of people together and asking questions about behavior and opinion. Test scores refers to the results from tests administered to measure knowledge and/or skill. Observation means exactly what it sounds like it means, watching, observing. Review of records means to search through existing documentation to find the necessary data.

Collect Data

The basic principles of data collection are first to keep it as unobtrusive as possible. Next, avoid using people's time and talents when there are alternatives. For example, the technique of observation is labor intensive, time consuming, and expensive. Use of a testing technique may elicit the same data and save a great deal of time and money. And last, never infringe on people's privacy.

Analyze Data

Two questions need to be answered about how the data is to be analyzed: (1) Is the method technically sound? and (2) Is the method suited to the data? Here we are moving into a part of evaluation that can become highly technical. The help of someone trained and experienced in evaluation can be extremely useful with data analysis. The mathematics and the statistics that can be used are usually beyond the ken of people who run grant projects on an everyday basis, which is one reason that grantors often require that a trained and experienced outside evaluator be used. Your project may not require such a person. You may simply be interested in raw data. Our students progressed three grade levels in reading while being taught this curriculum. Our elderly citizens showed an average of 35 percent improvement according to the Heart Healthy Senior Years test after participating in our physical exercise program for 18 months. These statistics stand on their own as far as most projects are concerned. They are comparisons based on pretests or conditions and posttests or conditions.

Provide Information to Interested Audiences

This is the report generation aspect of an evaluation. It is extremely important to realize that evaluation reports should be generated more often than once a year. Most grantor requirements are for a yearly evaluation. However, if you truly want to make your project as effective as possible, you want regular formative or process-oriented (assessment of project activities) evaluation reports that you can use as a feedback mechanism for improving the project as you go along. The formative aspects of an evaluation lose most of their effectiveness as a tool for project improvement if they are reported only once a year. Every two months or every quarter is a good time frame for formative evaluation reports. After all, one of the main purposes of evaluation is to find problems and correct them. This is done better sooner than later.

The next key aspect here is to provide appropriate information to all stakeholders (interested audiences). All stakeholders may not need all the information that you collect, but it is much simpler to produce one report and distribute to all stakeholders. Also, if you give different sets of information to different stakeholders, you might foster the perception that you are trying to hide something. Full disclosure is always best, if sometimes uncomfortable.

The Process

We now have created an evaluation process, although parts of it have not been discussed fully. The major steps that we have not fully discussed yet are covered in depth in upcoming chapters. For reference, a checklist is provided on disk (1201.doc) and in Exhibit 12.1, to walk through the process.

The checklist can be used to ensure that you stay on track while creating, performing, and reporting the evaluation of your grant project. There is one additional item not on the checklist, because this item should have been done before applying for the grant. It is to develop the budget for the evaluation. How to create a budget for a project evaluation is discussed in Chapter 13.

Exhibit 12.1

1201.DOC

Evaluation Process Checklist

I. Develop evaluation questions

    A. Mission, Goals, & Objectives used as source material
Use File 1302.doc for this activity

        _____ Review and refine mission.

        _____ Review and refine goals to ensure specificity and measurability.

        _____ Review and refine objectives to ensure specificity and measurability.

    B. Limit Questions
Use File 1303.doc for this activity

        _____ List stakeholders.

        _____ List interests of each stakeholder.

        _____ List expectations of each stakeholder.

    C. 1. List formative and summative questions each stakeholder needs to know about **costs**
Use File 1304.doc for this activity

        _____ Related to participant performance

        _____ Related to participant behavior

        _____ Related to project product(s)

        _____ Related to project processes

    C. 2. List formative and summative questions each stakeholder needs to know about **adaptability**
Use File 1304.doc for this activity

        _____ Related to participant performance

        _____ Related to participant behavior

        _____ Related to project product(s)

        _____ Related to project processes

    C. 3. List formative and summative questions each stakeholder needs to know about **results**
Use File 1304.doc for this activity

        _____ Related to participant performance

        _____ Related to participant behavior

        _____ Related to project product(s)

        _____ Related to project processes

II. Develop criteria for each question

    A. Specify what constitutes a positive result (What is "good")
Use File 1305.doc for this activity

    B. Assign a measure (how many or how much)
Use File 1305.doc for this activity

EXHIBIT 12.1 *(Continued)*

III. Match evaluation questions with approach
    A. For each question, select general methodology
        Use File 1306.doc for this activity
        _____ Core
        _____ Time-series
        _____ Comparison group
    B. Determine sources of needed information
        Use File 1307.doc for this activity
        _____ Project participant (target population)
        _____ Project personnel
        _____ Outside people
        _____ Project documentation
        _____ Outside documentation
    C. Select data collection technique
        Use File 1307.doc for this activity
        _____ Survey
        _____ Focus group
        _____ Test scores
        _____ Observation
        _____ Records
    D. Define sampling plan (if appropriate)
        Use File 1308.doc for this activity
        _____ Determine the size of the sample
        _____ Determine the sampling method
            _____ Simple random sampling
            _____ Stratified random sampling
            _____ Other

IV. Complete final data collection plan
    A. Assign schedule for each data collection activity
        Use Files 1308.doc and 1309.doc for this activity
    B. Assign number of cases for each data collection activity
        Use File 1309.doc for this activity
    C. Assign person(s) responsible for each data collection activity
        Use File 1309.doc for this activity

EXHIBIT 12.1 *(Continued)*

V. Create or obtain data collection instruments for each data collection activity
   A. Determine if instrument already exists
      Use File 1310.doc for this activity
   B. If instrument does not exist, create
      Use File 1310.doc for this activity
   C. If instrument exists, determine source
      Use File 1310.doc for this activity
   D. Determine cost
      Use File 1310.doc for this activity
   E. Determine date needed
      Use File 1310.doc for this activity
   F. Assign person(s) responsible for creating or obtaining data collection instrument
      Use File 1310.doc for this activity

VI. Collect data
   A. Select data gatherers
   B. Train data gatherers
   C. Pretest instruments
   D. Supervise data gatherers
   E. Archive and store data

VII. Analyze data
   A. Quantitative analysis
   B. Qualitative analysis

VIII. Provide information to stakeholders (answer the questions)
   A. Written report
      See Chapter 15 for guidance with this activity
   B. Meetings (if appropriate)

Wise Guy

I'll admit, things are coming into focus a little bit on this evaluation thing. I've never seen evaluation laid out step-by-step before. It doesn't seem like quite such a mystery now. I have to say, though, that the mention of mathematics and statistics does send shivers down my spine. It's almost as bad as the IRS. But I guess we can hire an H. & R. Block of evaluation the same way we do for the IRS.

Wise Lady

Yes, for the parts that you don't have the expertise to do, either gather in a partner who can contribute that expertise or hire a service provider or consultant who can handle the statistical aspects of the project. Actually, most action (rather than research) projects don't really require a great deal of heavy statistical analysis. It's more a matter of checking to see if you've done what you said you'd do, adding up participant hours and so forth. I'm afraid most grant Project Directors think they have to know it all and they become apprehensive before they ever start. A good manager is really a creative finder, developer, and user of resources.

Conclusion

The first three Roman numerals of our Evaluation Process Checklist—develop evaluation questions, establish criteria for each question, and match questions with evaluation approach—are the heart of creating an evaluation plan. This part of the evaluation should be done while applying for the grant. The evaluation plan is part of the proposal. This much of the evaluation should be done before you ever get one penny of the grantor's money.

Roman numerals four and five, data collection and data analysis, are activities that are performed during the project. In these phases, the action is in evaluation, people are tested, interviewed, and observed, records are researched, and our experts haul out their heavy guns of math and statistics, if that is necessary.

Roman numeral six is the reporting function of evaluation. It should be clear now that reporting is not exclusively putting together the year-end evaluation report, but rather is an ongoing procedure that must begin early and continue regularly. Reporting on the formative aspects of the project allows us to make midcourse corrections to keep the project on track and better ensure success.

## Chapter 13

Evaluation:
How to Create
an Evaluation Plan

A mighty maze! But not without a plan
Alexander Pope, *An Essay on Man*

Introduction

This chapter is handled quite differently from the remainder of the book. Instead of explaining, we show. Creating an evaluation plan does not need much explanation. With a few exceptions we have already discussed the pertinent background in the previous two chapters. In some cases, the appropriate discussion takes place in the next two chapters. Explaining how to create an evaluation plan with narrative would make a relatively simple process appear to be terribly complicated. Instead, we use a series of completed forms to illustrate the process.

Project Mission, Goals, and Objectives
Are Starting Point

In Chapter 5, we stepped through the basics of the process of establishing the mission, the goals and objectives, and the tasks of a project. The logic of this, or any other, organizational scheme is that the mission identifies the target population and defines the ultimate outcome we expect for that target population. The goals are statements of the major steps that it will take to accomplish the mission. Objectives are statements of the steps it will take to accomplish the goals. Tasks are the small steps or activities that it will take to accomplish objectives. We start with a broad mission and work our way down to small concrete steps or activities. If our thought process has been on target in selecting goals, objectives, and tasks, then after we accomplish all the simple tasks we will have accomplished the objectives. When we have successfully accomplished the objectives, we will have completed the goals. And, when we accomplish the goals, we will have made headway on accomplishing the mission of the project.

We also spent a great deal of time discussing the issue of labels or names for the organizational blocks into which a project is divided. The outcome of that discussion for you should have been the realization that although the parts of a project can be given a number of labels or names, the organizational scheme of all projects is the same. Any and every undertaking organizes itself naturally. We may not see the organization at once, but it is there and can always be seen with hindsight. Any undertaking begins with a reason for the undertaking. Next come the major steps it will take. Next comes dividing each major step into smaller steps, and then perhaps even dividing the smaller steps into baby steps. The names we give to these levels of organization *are* up to us, or more correctly it is up to whom we work for, or what field we work in, or what the grantor to whom we are applying expects. Exhibit 13.1 illustrates this organizational scheme while leaving out labels.

In Chapter 9 we detailed another organizational scheme based on the following set or labels or names: purpose–component–constituent part–event. For all practical purposes, the purpose corresponds to mission. Component corresponds to goal. Constituent part corresponds to objective. Event corresponds to task. Or, what is more correct is that they could correspond. It could be that in your mind the labels should look like this: purpose–component–event–task. The necessity here is to leave behind your preconceived notions of what exactly is meant by the terms activity, or task, or event, or goal, or objective. Suspend any worries about the correct use of these labels, and realize that the only authority is the grantor.

Exhibit 13.1

Example Organization Chart

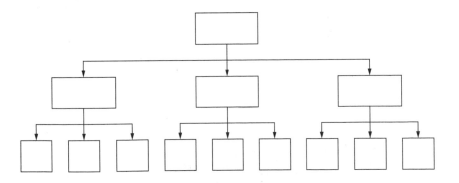

EXHIBIT 13.2 1302.DOC

Goals and Mission Worksheet

Mission of Project	
Target Population	**Ultimate Outcome**
Senior citizens at risk for heart disease	Significant decrease of at-risk factors for heart disease in participating group, thus increase in overall health, longevity, and quality of life

Goal One

	Do What?	Using What Approach?	By When?	With What Measure?	With What Result?
	Recruit and hire	Targeted ads and approved process	June, 2004	3 professionals, 5 paraprofessionals, 1.5 support needed	All hired, all qualified

Objectives for Goal One

	Do What?	Using What Approach?	By Who?	With What Measure?	With What Result?
1	Define job and write job specs	Use ABC model and recommendations of Board of Advisors	Dr. Iman X. Pert	9.5 jobs	Jobs defined and specs written and approved
2	Publicize jobs	State network, AMA, Internet, medical net	Dr. Iman X. Pert	9.5 jobs publicized	Qualified applicants acquired for each job
3	Interview applicants	Approved process	Dr. Iman X. Pert, members of Board of Advisors	Applicants for 9.5 jobs interviewed	9.5 job positions filled with qualified personnel

Goal Two

	Do What?	Using What Approach?	By When?	With What Measure?	With What Result?
	Renovate senior center and equip	Use ABC model for center set-up, approved contractor, standard bid process for equipment	September, 2004	Use ABC model as standard with exception that our center is 1/3 larger and will accommodate 30 more participants	All equipment recommended in ABC model is installed and working, center renovations complete and to spec

EXHIBIT 13.2 *(Continued)*

Objectives for Goal Two

	Do What?	Using What Approach?	By Who?	With What Measure?	With What Results?
1	Excavate and pave track	Contractor, city code approved model	Rhoda Workforce, Inc., City Planning Department	Half-mile track paved	Inspected track ready for use
2	Center kitchen renovated and equipment installed	Contractor, city code approved model for institutional kitchen	N. O. Fry Kitchen Contractors, sanitation and city planning	One institutional kitchen to serve a maximum of 150 people	Kitchen passes inspection and is operational, ready for use
3	Weight room renovated and equipment installed	Contractor, city code inspectors	I. Ron Pump, Inc., city planning department	Weight room set-up including padding for maximum of 25 people	Weight room passes inspection, all equipment is operational, safety mats installed and ready for use
4	Classroom renovated and equipped	Volunteer painters, donated school desks and chairs, donated A/V equipment	Pleasantville Volunteers Unlimited, Johnson School, Audie Owe Shoppe, Ltd.	Classroom seating 80 at tables and chairs, lectern, basic presentation audio-visuals	Classroom inspected and ready for use
5	Examination room renovated and equipped	Health care community partners' donations and labor	General Hospital, Heart Healthy Clinic, volunteer painters, city inspection dept., hospital association	Examination room to accommodate two examiners and two examinees	All equipment operational and sufficient space for heart risk examinations to take place simultaneously
6	Swimming pool renovated and equipped	Contractor, city code inspectors	H. O. O. Werks, Pool Builders, Inc., city planning department	Fiberglas surfaced pool, pool exercise equipment, safety equipment for a maximum of 45 people	Pool passes inspections including chemical, operational, and safety and is certified

Goal Three

	Do What?	Using What Approach?	By When?	With What Measure?	With What Result?
	Publicize and enroll	Local media including local TV and radio spots, ministerial association, community action groups, and all medical personnel	September, 2004	75% capacity enrollment by opening day	85 participants actually come to classes during the first week of operation

EXHIBIT 13.2 *(Continued)*

Objectives for Goal Three					
	Do What?	**Using What Approach?**	**By When?**	**With What Measure?**	**With What Result?**
1	Create enrollment process	Best practices format	Center staff led by Dr. Iman X. Pert	Enrollment process established	Forms and procedure in place to accept enrollees
2	Create and submit newspaper ads	Use volunteers with local ad agencies	Anna Sistent, H. Weir Outhere Agency, U. C. Us Agency	Three ads created	Three ads appear in triad newspapers for four weeks
3	Record TV and radio spots	Professional and paraprofessional staff with volunteer ad agency staff and volunteer TV and radio staff	Anna Sistent, H. Weir Outhere Agency, U. C. Us Agency, WUAL, WYNT	3 radio and 2 TV spots recorded	All spots used daily for two weeks on local stations
4	Press release written and distributed	Use Center staff with review by volunteer ad agency personnel	Anna Sistent, Dr. Iman H. Pert, H. Weir Outhere Agency	Three press releases written, list of all community leaders in database	All community leaders announce the new program
5	Meetings with community	Invitations sent, meeting planned, agenda set, meeting held	Dr. Iman X. Pert, Center Staff, Board of Advisors	Four community meetings held for 158 community leaders	158 community leaders fully informed about new program and announce enrollment
6	Meetings with medical community	Invitations sent, meeting planned, agenda set, meeting held	Dr. Iman X. Pert, Center Staff, Board of Advisors	Four community meetings held for 9 major community health care groups	Medical community fully informed about new program and enroll patients
7	Implement enrollment procedures	Center support staff answer phones and mail and confirm enrollment	Center support staff	125 people are enrolled initially with an additional 10 per week thereafter for project year one	Enrollment is adequate to support the goal of attendance during the initial week and weeks to follow

Goal Four					
	Do What?	**Using What Approach?**	**By When?**	**With What Measure?**	**With What Result?**
	Implement project	Screening, lecture, modeling, mentoring, practice, repeat, evaluate	September, 2005	60% of participants show consistent attendance for a complete 10-month program	90% of these participants decrease manageable at-risk factors by 75% overall

EXHIBIT 13.2 *(Continued)*

		Using What Approach?	By Who?	With What Measure?	With What Result?
	Do What?				
1	Perform initial medical screenings on potential participants and develop Individual Development Plans	Heart Healthy Indices and best medical practices	Medical staff including physicians and nurse practitioners	Each participant has been screened and those that don't fit appropriate guidelines or have too high a danger factor according to indices are eliminated. There is an individual development plan (IDP) on each accepted participant.	Best medical practices and insured and maximum safety standards for all participants. All participants are at high risk of heart disease according to the HHIndices. All participants receive an IDP along with appropriate counseling.
2	Hold information classes	Lecture, demonstrate, practice, demonstrate, practice	Professionals and paraprofessionals	28 classes held per week	All participants attend and complete all classes
3	Hold swimming exercise programs	Prequalification, demonstration, practice, repeat, close-monitoring	Professionals and paraprofessionals	18 classes per week, 12 day and 6 night classes	All participants attend some form of water exercise
4	Hold weight sessions	Prequalification, demonstration, practice, close-monitoring	Professionals and paraprofessionals	20 day sessions per week and 12 night sessions	All participants regularly participate in weight sessions
5	Track sessions	Prequalification, demonstration, practice, close-monitoring	Professionals and paraprofessionals	Track available from 6 a.m. to 6 p.m. during the day and from 7:30 p.m. to 9 p.m. in the evenings	All participants participate in track sessions daily
6	Meals & classes	Nutrition staff and volunteer restaurant chefs and personnel	Professionals and paraprofessionals	Breakfast and lunch served daily for a maximum of 150 at each sitting, classes precede or follow each meal	All participants eat at least one meal at the Center daily and participate in accompanying class
7	Examinations	Heart Healthy Examination procedures followed	Physicians and nurse practitioners	Initial screening and weekly follow-up for project duration	All participants are screened no less than weekly during project year one

Objectives for Goal Four

EXHIBIT 13.2 *(Continued)*

Goal Five				
Do What?	**Using What Approach?**	**By When?**	**With What Measure?**	**With What Result?**
Manage	Supervision by qualified doctor, nurse practitioner, and counselor, as well as an expert advisory board	Ongoing	All project components are completed, all tasks, objectives, and goals completed, revisions made as indicated and approved	Implementation is as proposed and successful completion is indicated in evaluations

Objectives for Goal Five					
	Do What?	**Using What Approach?**	**By Who?**	**With What Measure?**	**With What Result?**
1	Supervise staff	Weekly group meeting, monthly individual sessions, annual comprehensive evaluation	Dr. Iman X. Pert, Board members as necessary	48 weekly sessions, 12 individual sessions for 10 staff members, 10 annual evaluations	All staff are appropriately evaluated and necessary improvements accomplished, merit recognized
2	Supervise volunteers	Monthly group meetings, discussions with supervising staff during group sessions, individual sessions when necessary	Professional staff in each area	12 group sessions, weekly staff meeting discussions, individual sessions as needed	Volunteer program runs smoothly and necessary improvements accomplished, merit recognized
3	Maintain buildings, grounds, equipment	Monthly inspections, adherence to daily maintenance procedures, weekly grounds maintenance	Joe Grasso, grounds maintenance, all professional and paraprofessional staff, all volunteers	12 monthly inspection reports each from building and grounds supervisors, and from each area leader on equipment	Buildings, grounds, and equipment are consistently in order and maintained to appropriate specification
4	Program operation	Weekly and monthly progress reports	All professionals and area leaders	48 weekly reports and 12 monthly reports from each of five areas of operation	Program operates consistently according to best practices and project plan
5	Participants	Monthly regular coffees, walk-throughs by supervisors, questionnaires, reports from attending physicians and workers, suggestion network	Dr. Iman X. Pert, Board of Advisors, area managers, evaluation teams	12 coffees, weekly walk-throughs, 4 questionnaires, ongoing suggestion network and outside reports	Participants have positive attitudes and problems are handled appropriately and quickly

EXHIBIT 13.2 *(Continued)*

	Do What?	Using What Approach?	By When?	With What Measure?	With What Result?
6	Dissemination	Operations manual compiled for each area and made available, regular progress reports published via network, Internet, professional journals	Dr. Iman X. Pert and professional staff, support staff member for Internet publishing	Monthly progress reports published, operations manual available for a publishing fee at year end	Interested organizations and persons have access to sufficient information
7	Documentation and security	All medical procedures are documented to best practices standards, all patient records according to AMA standards, operations and procedures in databanks and locked filing rooms according to approved security standards	All professional staff, security officer, AMA analyst	Every aspect and area of project operation is appropriately documented. There is a complete medical record for every enrolled person including initial and subsequent screenings. For every full term participant, there are 49 medical screenings (initial and 48 weekly).	Complete medical records are available on every participant showing activity and progress. IDPs are updated weekly. Every aspect of the project can be tracked and followed so that it can be modeled and duplicated as well as to afford maximum opportunity for revision and success.
8	Continuation	Commitments by partners are insured. Membership fees on a sliding scale is implemented. Consulting by the professional and paraprofessional team is contracted and fees are used to offset personnel costs. Appropriate subsidized funds are applied for and accounted.	Dr. Iman X. Pert, Mooney Bags, CFO, support staff	At least $256,789 in operating funds are available for project years three and four	The project, if successful, is continued and self-sufficient

Goal Six					
	Do What?	Using What Approach?	By When?	With What Measure?	With What Result?
	Evaluate overall program	Advisory board and expert outside team	Quarterly and at year end	Comprehensive reports published	All evaluations are completed on time

EXHIBIT 13.2 *(Continued)*

	Do What?	Using What Approach?	By Who?	With What Measure?	With What Result?
Objectives for Goal Six					
1	Advisory board quarterly review	Professionals submit summary reports from each area of operation, Center Director submits a management report	Advisory board members and Dr. Iman X. Pert	All aspects of the project have operated according to plan and revisions approved and made where necessary	Project operations and management are approved by the advisory board and a report is composed
2	Outside evaluator quarterly review and observation	Professionals submit summary reports from each area of operation. Center Director submits a management report, team members observe program	Outside evaluation team members and Dr. Iman X. Pert	All aspects of the project have operated according to plan and revisions approved and made where necessary	Project operations and management receive a favorable report by outside evaluation team and a report is published
3	Advisory board reviews all quarterly records and reports	Week-long retreat format	Advisory board members and Dr. Iman X. Pert along with appropriate professionals	All aspects of the project have operated according to plan and revisions approved and made where necessary	Project operations and management are approved by the Advisory board
4	Outside evaluator annual review of all quarterly records and reports and observation of program	Professionals submit summary reports from each area of operation, Center Director submits a management report, team members observe program	Outside evaluation team members and Dr. Iman X. Pert	All aspects of the project have operated according to plan and revisions approved and made where necessary	Project operations and management receive a favorable report by outside evaluation team and a report is published
5	Grant maker evaluation	All reports are submitted to the grant maker and the grant maker visits program and observes operation, interviews personnel and participants	Grant maker team and all professional staff	All aspects of the project have operated according to plan and revisions approved and made where necessary	Project operations and management receive a favorable report by outside evaluation team and a report is published

The creation of your evaluation plan is based on your goals and objectives, assuming that when you constructed them, you included expected results and measurement. If you do not have measurable and result-driven goals and objectives, or whatever you call the two largest steps in project organization, you need to create them to go any further with the evaluation plan. In many works about project evaluation, writers assume that your goals and objectives are in such sorry shape that the first task they assign is to "clarify the goals and objectives of the project." We have no need for that. Our goals and objectives are clarified already. They were clear before we even submitted the proposal, right? If, however, your goals and objectives by any other name do not include all the parts we discussed in Chapter 5, go back and fix them now. On the following pages we have given a complete set of mission, goals, and objectives for an example project. The first page shows the project mission with the goals. Following pages show each goal with its objectives broken out underneath. You may need to go through the exercise yourself of constructing a mission, goals, and objectives for your project. To help you with this exercise, we have included the forms we used to create our example project goals and objectives seen in Exhibit 13.2 on the disk (1302.doc).

Identify Stakeholders and Their Interests

One more set of information is necessary before we formulate the evaluation questions. We need to know who our stakeholders are and what their interests and expectations are. We use this information to focus our evaluation efforts and to limit the number of evaluation questions. The number of evaluation questions that could be asked is so large that it is absolutely necessary to limit evaluation questions to those that need to be answered. Focusing on the stakeholders provides us with guidelines for deciding what questions to include and which to exclude. For our example project, that information is found in Exhibit 13.3 and on the disk (1303.doc).

Restating the mission of our example project will help us understand why the stakeholders listed in Exhibit 13.3 (1303.doc) have legitimate and reasonable interests in the outcome of our project—in other words, why they are stakeholders in the first place.

Ask Evaluation Questions with Respect to Goals and Objectives and Stakeholders

Now we have enough information to ask the evaluation questions. The two tables in Exhibit 13.4 (1304.doc) continue with our example project and show how this works out. To be sure that we include both formative and summative evaluation measures we use separate tables, one for each. To recap, *formative evaluation* is the assessment of ongoing project activities. *Summative evaluation* is the assessment of a project's success. We have picked illustrative goals and objectives with which to work, but, of course,

EXHIBIT 13.3  1303.DOC

Identifying Stakeholders and Their Interests

Mission of Project	
Target Population	**Ultimate Outcome**
Senior citizens at risk for heart disease	Significant decrease of at-risk factors for heart disease in participating group, thus increase in overall health, longevity, and quality of life

Stakeholder	Contact Person	Interests and Expectations
AARP	Ms. Jane Doe	Improve length and quality of life of members
Insurance Companies	[various]	Reduce costs
HMOs	[various]	Reduce cost of health care
County Hospital	Ms. Chair O. Board	Reduce case load, indigent care costs, and emergency room (ER) use
State Medicare	Ms. Addie M. Estrator	Reduce costs
Our Agency	Ms. Chair A. Board	Show effectiveness of agency, justify continued funding
Grantor (HHS)	Ms. Mon E. Tor	Find model that works to replicate

you need to complete the process for all goals and all objectives. We find it helpful to number the questions. This allows easy backtracking and reference among the various forms to come. To help you with asking the evaluation questions we have included forms on the disk (1304.doc).

It is important to note that in Exhibit 13.4 we have not asked all the questions that can be asked about the goals and objectives chosen to illustrate the process. Many additional questions, no doubt, will occur to you as you look at the example, especially if this project is in your area of expertise. Remember, we are not trying to construct a real program, but rather we are trying to illustrate how the process of creating an evaluation plan works. Therefore, the lack of mental and emotional components in the project is just to simplify things and keep the size manageable.

Develop Criteria

Each evaluation question must have a benchmark, a criteria that determines if the goal, objective, task, or activity under consideration has

EXHIBIT 13.4   1304.DOC

Evaluative Question Worksheet

Formative Evaluation			
Goals & Objectives **Process Related**	**Stakeholder**	**Evaluation Questions**	
Goal 3		**#**	**Question**
Publicize & enroll	All	1	Did this model of publicity and recruiting work?
Objective 3: TV and radio	Insurance Companies	2	Which is more effective in reaching the target population, TV or radio?
Objective 5: Meetings with citizens	All	3	Are meetings an effective recruiting tool?
Objective 6: Meetings with medical community	HMOs	4	Does keeping the medical community informed help recruiting?

Summative Evaluation			
Goals & Objectives **Outcome Related**	**Stakeholders**	**Evaluation Questions**	
Goal 4		**#**	**Question**
90% of participants with 75% decrease in risk factors	All	5	Does this model reduce at-risk factors significantly?
Objective 3: Water exercise	All	6	Did participants continue with this mode of exercise as compared to the others?
	All	7	Did participants show improved mobility?
Objective 6: Nutrition education	Grantor	8	Did eating habits change?

succeeded. We must be able to know what is "good," what is acceptable, what is OK. The basis of the criteria we chose is the measurement built into the goals and objectives. This step develops the standards with which you will compare the outcome of the data collection process. We continue with our example project using the forms found in Exhibit 13.5. To help you with this task we have included forms on the disk (1305.doc).

EXHIBIT 13.5

1305.DOC

Worksheet to Develop Criteria

	Formative Evaluation Measures	
#	**Evaluation Question**	**Criteria**
1	Did this model of publicity and recruiting work?	85 participants in first week
2	Which is more effective in reaching the target population, TV or radio?	Number of project participants who got message from which source
3	Are meetings an effective recruiting tool?	Number of project participants compared to attendance at meetings
4	Does keeping the medical community informed help recruiting?	Number of project participants who are referrals from medical community

	Summative Evaluation Measures	
#	**Evaluation Question**	**Criteria**
5	Does this model reduce at-risk factors significantly?	90% of participants decrease manageable at-risk factors by 75% overall
6	Did participants continue with this mode of exercise as compared to the others?	All participants attend and participate
7	Did participants show improved mobility?	20% improvement in mobility
8	Did eating habits change?	50% of participants significantly change eating habits

Match Evaluation Questions with General Evaluation Strategy

From Chapter 12 we found that there are three basic evaluation strategies: core design, time-series, and comparison group. The purpose of this step is to decide which general evaluation strategy is appropriate for each of our evaluation questions. Exhibit 13.6 and the file on the disk (1306.doc) will help you with this step.

EXHIBIT 13.6

Evaluation Strategy Worksheet

	Formative Evaluation Measures		
#	**Evaluation Question**	**Criteria**	**Strategy**
1	Did this model of publicity and recruiting work?	85 participants in first week	Time-series
2	Which is more effective in reaching the target population, TV or radio?	Number of project participants who got message from which source	Time-series
3	Are meetings an effective recruiting tool?	Number of project participants compared to attendance at meetings	Time-series
4	Does keeping the medical community informed help recruiting?	Number of project participants who arc rcferrals from medical community	Time-series

	Summative Evaluation Measures		
#	**Evaluation Question**	**Criteria**	**Strategies**
5	Does this model reduce at-risk factors significantly?	90% of participants decrease manageable at-risk factors by 75% overall	Comparison group
6	Did participants continue with this mode of exercise as compared to the others?	All participants attend and participate	Time-series
7	Did participants show improved mobility?	20% improvement in mobility	Comparison group
8	Did eating habits change?	50% of participants significantly change eating habits	Time-series

Determine Source of Data and Collection Technique

For each evaluation question, determine the source of the information (data) that can answer the question. The type of information (data) that you are gathering and the source of the data will determine the appropriate data collection method. *Remember that data collection methods can be categorized into five types: surveys, focus groups, test scores, observation, and review of records.* Put that information on a form such as Exhibit 13.7. To help you with this task we have included forms on the disk (1307.doc).

Determine Sampling Plan and Timing

Combining the data collection method with the source of the information creates an evaluation activity. For example, if the source of information is the "Project Director" and the data collection method is "interview,"

EXHIBIT 13.7

1307.DOC

Determining Source of Data Collection

Formative Evaluation			
#	Question	Source of Information	Data Collection Method
1	Did this model of publicity and recruiting work?	Enrollment records	Review of records
2	Which is more effective in reaching the target population, TV or radio?	Participants	Survey
3	Are meetings an effective recruiting tool?	Participants	Survey
4	Does keeping the medical community informed help recruiting?	Participants	Survey

Summative Evaluation			
#	Question	Source of Information	Data Collection Method
5	Does this model reduce at-risk factors significantly?	Examination results	Review of records
6	Did participants continue with this mode of exercise as compared to the others?	Project records	Review of records
7	Did participants show improved mobility?	Participants	Mobility Test
8	Did eating habits change?	Participants	Survey

EXHIBIT 13.8 1308.DOC

Form to Determine Sampling Plan and Timing

Formative Evaluation			
#	Evaluation Activity	Sampling Plan	Timing of Activity
1	Review enrollment records for number of participants	None	Monthly
2	Survey participants for TV versus radio	None	When enter project
3	Survey participants for opinions on meetings	None	When enter project
4	Survey participants for referrals from medical community	None	When enter project

Summative Evaluation			
#	Evaluation Activity	Sampling Plan	Timing of Activity
5	Review examination records for reduction in risk factors	None	Quarterly
6	Review project records for participation in water exercise	None	Quarterly
7	Administer mobility test to participants	None	Biannually
8	Survey participants on eating habits	None	Quarterly

then the data collection activity is "interview Project Director." Next we need to settle on a sampling plan if one is appropriate to the evaluation method. We also decide when the evaluation activity will take place. We continue with the example project in Exhibit 13.8 (1308.doc).

Establish Schedule and Assign Staff

Once we establish the schedule and assign staff to be responsible for collecting the data, we have all the information we need to create our final data collection plan. Many grantors require that you use both quantitative and qualitative measures. A column in the final data collection plan allows you to show which data collection activities correspond. One more column asks you to state the number of cases, the number of times you will do this data collection activity. We continue with the example project in Exhibit 13.9 (1309.doc).

EXHIBIT 13.9 1309.DOC

Final Data Collection Plan

#	Data Collection Activity	Type of Method*	Sampling Plan	Scheduled Collection	Number of Cases	Collection By
1	Record review	Q_2	None	Monthly	1	PD
2	Survey	Q_2	None	On entrance	# participants	DC
3	Survey	Q_1	None	On entrance	# participants	DC
4	Survey	Q_2	None	On entrance	# participants	DC
5	Record review	Q_2	None	Quarterly	1	PD
6	Record review	Q_2	None	Quarterly	1	PD
7	Test	Q_2	None	Biannually	1	PD
8	Survey	Q_1	None	Quarterly	1	PD

* Q_1 = Quantitative; Q_2 = Qualitative

Create or Obtain Data Collection Tools

A discussion of the different types of data collection tools is found in Chapter 14. Here, we will only say that you must have the proper data collection devices, tools, or instruments. You may decide to create the tools, or you may use existing tools from within your own organization or from a partner, or you can purchase tools available in the marketplace. We have continued with our example project and illustrated in Exhibit 13.10 how it would look if you made decisions about data collections tools. One small point about purchase of tools may be helpful. What you purchase might be the license to use a tool, not the tool itself. This is common with tests obtained from vendors. Blank forms are included on the disk as file 1310.doc.

Data Analysis

At some point you need to determine the data analysis technique that will be used for each collection of data. It may make more sense to you to have done this step much earlier. We put it here to keep the order of tasks in this chapter in line with the order in which an evaluation is actually performed. Data collection occurs before data analysis. Exhibit 13.11 (1311.doc) is an example of how this step will look.

EXHIBIT 13.10 1310.DOC

Data Collection Tools Log

#	Data Collection Activity	Collection Tool	Q?	E?	P?	Source & Cost if P? is Yes	C?	When Needed	Staff
1	Record review	Monthly Report	1	N	N	n/a	Y	End of PM-1	PD
2	Survey	Questionnaire	300	N	N	n/a	Y	Project Start	Eval
3	Survey	Questionnaire	300	N	N	n/a	Y	Project Start	Eval
4	Survey	Questionnaire	300	N	N	n/a	Y	Project Start	Eval
5	Record review	Quarterly Report	1	N	N	n/a	Y	End of PM-3	PD
6	Record review	Quarterly Report	1	N	N	n/a	Y	End of PM-3	PD
7	Test	"Mobility machine"	1	Y	Y	EYZ, Inc. $8,000	N	PM-6	PD
8	Survey	Questionnaire	1	N	N	n/a	Y	End of PM-3	Eval

Q? = Quantity Needed?; E? = Exist?; P? = Purchase?; C? = Create?; PM = Project Month

Evaluation Matrix

We have developed a great deal of information. Now we must overcome the problem inherent in communicating fully a complex set of information. Our solution is certainly not the only solution, but we think you will find it has the benefits of being complete and easy to understand. In Exhibit 13.12 we have illustrated the forms you will find on the disk as file 1312.doc.

Evaluation Budget

Developing a budget for an evaluation is the same process used to develop a budget for any part of a project.

EXHIBIT 13.11 1311.DOC

Determination of Data Analysis Technique

#	Evaluation Question	Data Collection Method	Analysis Plan
1	Did this model of publicity and recruiting work?	Record review	Numerical tallies
2	Which is more effective in reaching the target population, TV or radio?	Survey	Frequency distribution of responses
3	Are meetings an effective recruiting tool?	Survey	Frequency distribution of responses
4	Does keeping the medical community informed help recruiting?	Survey	Frequency distribution of responses
5	Does this model reduce at-risk factors significantly?	Record review	Matching results with comparison group
6	Did participants continue with this mode of exercise as compared to others?	Record review	Numerical tallies
7	Did participants show improved mobility?	Test	Matching results with comparison group
8	Did eating habits change?	Survey	Percentages selecting various responses

Budget Development Process

1. List an activity. This unit could be as large as a goal or as small as a task. The smaller the activity chosen, the more accurate the costs developed will be.

2. List all the resources needed to accomplish the activity. Resources fall into the following categories: (1) personnel and fringe, (2) travel, (3) stipends and honorarium, (4) services and consultants, (5) real property, (6) equipment, (7) materials and supplies, and (8) facilities; can come from the project, your organization, volunteers, or partners; can be purchased or rented; and can be either cash or in-kind.

3. Determine the quantity of "units" of the resource needed. For personnel this will be time measured in units of hours, days, weeks, months, or years.

4. Determine the unit cost for each resource.

EXHIBIT 13.12

 1312.DOC

Evaluation Matrix

Summary Matrix of Data Collection & Analysis Plan											
Goal	#										
Objective	#										
Data Collection Activity	**Data Collection Method**	**T**	**Standard**	**Sampling Plan**	**# C**	**# P**	**Schedule**	**Person**	**Analysis Type**	**Person**	

Objective	#										
Data Collection Activity	**Data Collection Method**	**T**	**Standard**	**Sampling Plan**	**# C**	**# P**	**Schedule**	**Person**	**Analysis Type**	**Person**	

T = Type of Evaluation Measure with Qn = Quantitative and Ql = Qualitative
C = Cases;   P = Participants

EXHIBIT 13.13

 1313.DOC

Development of Evaluation Budget

Data Collection Activity									Data Analysis

Personnel & Fringe (project staff, partner staff, volunteers)

Position	Qty	Source	Cash In-kind	# Cases	Define Unit	# Units	Unit Cost	Total Cost
							Resource Total	

Travel

Trip Description	Qty	Source	Cash In-kind	Air Cost	Ground Cost	Meals Cost	Lodge Cost	Total Cost
							Resource Total	

Stipends & Honorarium

Description	Qty	Source	Cash In-kind	# Cases	Define Unit	# Units	Unit Cost	Total Cost
							Resource Total	

EXHIBIT 13.13 *(Continued)*

Services & Consultants

Description	Qty	Source	Cash In-kind	# Cases	Define Unit	# Units	Unit Cost	Total Cost
							Resource Total	

Equipment

Description	Qty	Source	Cash In-kind	# Cases	Define Unit	# Units	Unit Cost	Total Cost
							Resource Total	

Materials & Supplies

Description	Qty	Source	Cash In-kind	# Cases	Define Unit	# Units	Unit Cost	Total Cost
							Resource Total	

Facilities

Description	Qty	Source	Cash In-kind	# Cases	Define Unit	# Units	Unit Cost	Total Cost
							Resource Total	
							Activity Total	

5. Compute total cost of each needed resource. The formula is (Quantity) × (Unit Cost) = Total.

6. Sum the totals of needed resources to give the total budget for that activity.

7. Repeat steps 1 through 6 until you run out of activities.

8. Sum the totals of all the activities. This gives you the budget for the set of activities you analyzed. Note that the budget includes both cash needed and in-kind contributions, so if you want the grant request only you must extract the cash-needed figures.

As with many processes, the actually doing is easier than the explanation. We have included the forms in Exhibit 13.13 to show how the process works. In this case we are working on budgeting the evaluation plan, so the forms show that. Reflection on the steps we have already taken will show where to get the basic information about quantities and personnel. Other information has to be researched as you proceed. This form is on the disk as file 1313.doc.

Wise Guy

Evaluation still seems awfully complicated.

Wise Lady

It is work, but it's not really complicated if you follow the step-by-step process we've outlined. It's important to follow some systematic plan and capture the right amount of information to show fully what your project has achieved and what problems you have encountered. After all, the grantor awarded you funds because it believed you had a viable project that might provide at least part of a solution to a problem in which you are both interested. The grantor wants to know what worked and what didn't. You should want to know too. "Just for the sake of it" is not much of a reason to do anything. It reminds me of the 3-year-old who just emptied five boxes of cereal on the kitchen floor. When asked why, invariably the answer is, "just because." Well, "just because" isn't good enough when you're impacting real people.

Conclusion

Following this step-by-step procedure allows you to create an evaluation plan. Using the summary matrix allows you to display or publish the information you have gathered. Using the budget development tool allows you to create a budget for the evaluation process. Taken together, these three pieces provide the information that a grantor needs to see in an evaluation plan. This process, or one similar, should have been done before a proposal was submitted, but late is better than never. In Chapter 14 we discuss data collection as an activity. We discuss the various ways to collect data, and we discuss the tools that are used during the collection activities. We briefly discuss data analysis.

Evaluation: Performing the Data Collection and Analysis

When people come to inspect . . . farmsteads, it is not to see collections of pictures . . . but collections of fruit.

On Agriculture, Marcus Varro, 116–27 B.C.

Introduction

The data collection and analysis of the data is considered by many to be the evaluation. It is not. It is just part of a long and involved process that begins during development of the project's goals and objectives and continues until the final report is on the desks of all appropriate stakeholders. The data collection may seem more important than other parts of the evaluation, but it is not. If the evaluation questions are not formulated well, the data collected will not tell us what we need to know. If we have not taken into consideration the needs of stakeholders, the reports we publish will not accomplish what we intend. If any link in the long chain of evaluation is broken or missing, the entire evaluation is at risk.

This chapter discusses the nitty-gritty of getting together the necessary facts on which we will base our conclusions about our project. The process can be long and costly or it can be simple and economical. The process can take many people to complete, or it can be done by one person. It all depends on what information is needed and how it will be collected. Data analysis can be complicated or simple, based on evaluation design decisions. What follows is not intended to be complete, but rather an introduction to the concepts of data collection and data analysis.

Data Collection Principles

The prime consideration is to minimize interference with the functioning of the project. Make as few demands as possible on project personnel and participants. Avoid procedures that could be perceived as threatening or critical. Obtain the necessary clearances and permissions. Consider the needs and sensitivities of the participants. Guarantee privacy, or obtain informed consent to release information that can be identified with a particular participant.

Data Collection Activities

We said in Chapter 13 that collection activities could be sorted into five categories: surveys, focus groups, test scores, observation, and review of records. Another way to visualize or think about data collection is to organize it by the methods used to collect the data along with the sources of the information. If we think of data collection from the viewpoint of the collection methods and the sources of the material, we could devise a scheme that looks like this:

I. Data collected directly from individuals
    A. Products & Instruments
        1. Diaries
        2. Anecdotal accounts
        3. Checklists or inventories
        4. Rating scales
        5. Semantic differentials
        6. Questionnaires
        7. Interviews
        8. Written responses to requests for information
        9. Sociometric devices
        10. Projective techniques
        11. Sample of work
    B. Tests
        1. Supplied answer
        2. Essay
        3. Completion
        4. Short response

5. Problem-solving

6. Multiple choice

7. True-false

8. Matching

9. Ranking

II. Data collected by an independent observer

A. Written accounts

B. Observation forms

1. Observation schedules

2. Rating scales

3. Checklists and inventories

III. Data collected by the use of technology

A. Audio tape

B. Video tape

C. Photographs

D. Computers

IV. Data collected from existing information resources

A. Public documents

B. Organization documents

C. Personal documents

D. Databases

Returning to our five basic categories of collection methods—surveys, focus groups, test scores, observation, and review of records—we discuss each briefly, giving the advantages and disadvantages of each data collection method.

Surveys

Surveys are administered by either interview or having an individual complete the survey herself, called self-administered. Surveys are often called questionnaires. Surveys ask people to tell about their attitudes, beliefs, feelings, perceptions, reactions, and opinions. Surveys are less expensive to create and administer than other methods, but the kind of information you can obtain is limited, usually providing wider ranging but less detailed data. Also, some data may be biased if respondents are not truthful.

Self-Administered Questionnaire. This is the least expensive method of administering a survey. It can be done in person, by mail, by fax, or e-mail, whichever is most appropriate for your group. In person it can be done individually, or it can quickly and efficiently be administered when a group is assembled. Disadvantages are that there is no control for misunderstood questions, missing data, or untruthful responses. Also, this method is not suited for the investigation of complex issues.

Interviewer-Administered Questionnaire by Telephone. This method of administering a survey is relatively inexpensive. This method avoids the time, expense, and possible risks of interviewers traveling to respondent's location. It is best suited for relatively short and nonsensitive topics. A disadvantage is that there may be many people in your target population who do not have telephones. Another disadvantage is that this method usually is not considered to be suitable for children, the elderly, and non-English-speaking people. It is not suitable for lengthy questionnaires. And finally, this method is not suitable for sensitive topics because respondents may lack privacy.

Interviewer-Administered Questionnaire in Person. Administering a questionnaire in person has the advantage that the interviewer controls the situation and can probe irrelevant or evasive answers. With good rapport, an interviewer may obtain useful open-ended comments. The disadvantages are that this method of data collection is expensive. It may present logistical problems of time, place, privacy, access, and safety. The time required to perform all the interviews can be lengthy unless the project uses many interviewers.

Open-Ended Interviews in Person. This method can yield the richest data including new insights and detail. This method is the best to employ if in-depth information is required. The disadvantages are the same as in the previous method, interviewer-administered questionnaire in person. Also, the information gathered may be hard to analyze.

Focus Groups

An important use of focus groups is in the design of survey instruments. Before the survey instrument is created, a group of people are brought together. These people can be from the target population, or they can be from the group that will administer the project, or they can be representatives of stakeholders. A leader or moderator helps the group discuss the topics relevant to the evaluation that should be included in the questionnaire. Problems may arise about the meaning of terms and the comprehension of certain concepts. These problems must be kept in mind during the creation of the survey instrument. Clarity about terms and concepts is the main use of focus groups in the summative parts of an evaluation. However, in the formative parts of an evaluation focus, groups can provide good qualitative data. The usefulness of focus groups depends heavily on the skills of the leader or moderator. Also, evaluators must understand that focus groups are in essence an exercise in group dynamics and are no substitute for more quantitative methods.

Test Scores

The tendency to rely heavily on test scores whenever a project has an academic element is understandable. After all, test scores are considered "hard" evidence, impartial, objective, fair, and more accurate than other measures such as opinions, attitudes, or grades earned by students. The problem is that a substantial number of people are poor test takers, and a test can be poorly designed and measure the knowledge and skill of some groups well while failing to measure other groups properly.

Most achievement tests are either norm-referenced or criterion-referenced. This is educationalese that many of us as parents have heard before and perhaps wondered about. A norm-referenced test measures how a person (usually a student) performs compared to a previously tested group of people (students). This type of test measures the relative performance of an individual or a group by comparing their performance to the performance of other individuals and groups that have taken the same test. A criterion-referenced test measures if a person has mastered specific instructional objectives and thereby acquired specific knowledge and skills. This type of test measures the performance of an individual or group against an established set of standards, not performance relative to others.

Another type of testing, called performance assessment or performance testing, is being used in many places, although its acceptance is not universal. Performance testing is intended to measure problem-solving knowledge and skills rather than factual knowledge. Testing may appear more like a project than a traditional test.

It is tempting to create your own test. This urge should probably be ignored. There is much more to creating a test than writing down a set of questions. Strict standards exist. If at all possible, use an established test that has been tested for reliability and validity.

Observations

Surveys and tests provide good measurement of an individual's opinions, attitudes, knowledge, and skills. Surveys can also provide good information on an individual's behavior. However, when it comes to measuring group behavior, observation is the best method for obtaining good data. Subject-specific instruments must be created by the evaluator to fit the specific evaluation question(s). The method of observation can yield quantifiable data when proper instruments have been created.

The main disadvantage of observation is that behavior can change when observed. The presence of the observer can change the behavior of a group. Another problem with observation is that more than any other data collection method, it relies on the training and skills of the data collectors.

Review of Records

Review of records is one place that the importance of project documentation becomes evident and concrete. The project should have complete documentation on all participants, staff, partners, volunteers, activities, and results. Documentation is a prime source of information for evaluators. Other sources of records for review are statistical databases such as are maintained by the Bureau of the Census, or test score results on a state or national basis, or your organization's records, or publicly available research and documentation.

Creating or Obtaining Data Collection Instruments

Tests

Achievement tests are obtained from vendors or may be possessed by your organization or a partner's. Whatever type of test is used, two questions are critical. Is there a match between what the test measures and what the project teaches? And, has the project been in place long enough for there to be an impact on test scores?

Questionnaires

A questionnaire is a set of questions. The answers to the questions can require *free response,* which is a short written or spoken answer. The answers to the questions can require *forced response,* which is a choice between several prechosen answers (multiple choice). We are all quite familiar with questionnaires. We get them in the mail and over the telephone all the time. Questionnaires come from advocacy groups, from political parties, from market researchers, from groups conducting studies, from companies with which we have done business, and many, many other sources. Once every 10 years we get a questionnaire from the Census Bureau that asks questions about our household and that provides information to the federal government about the size and condition of the population of our country. Questionnaires are ubiquitous in our poll-crazed society, because questionnaires form the basis of all the polls, the results of which we see

EXHIBIT 14.1

Free Response Questions and Forced Response Questions

Free Response Questions

1. What is the main reason that you have a computer at home?
   (If you need additional space use the back of the page.)

   _____

   _____

   _____

   _____

   _____

   _____

2. What is the most important thing that you have learned in "Life Skills Training?"
   (If you need additional space use the back of the page.)

   _____

   _____

   _____

   _____

   _____

   _____

Forced Response Questions

1. What is the main reason that you have a computer at home?
   (Choose only one.)

   _____ a. Writing

   _____ b. Finances

   _____ c. Games

   _____ d. Internet and/or E-mail

2. What is the most important thing that you have learned in "Skills for Life?"
   (Choose only one.)

   _____ a. How to get a job

   _____ b. How to handle money

   _____ c. How to deal with people

   _____ d. How to get answers

every day on television and in newspapers and magazines. Exhibit 14.1 shows examples of both free response and forced response questions that might be found on a questionnaire.

Checklists or Inventories

A checklist or inventory is made up of a list of items under a topic statement or question. Respondents are asked to check all the items on the list that they believe to be true or apply to them or fit some other qualification. Most of us have direct experience with this type of data collection instrument through answering market research questions and filling out mail-in warranty cards for purchases. Market research uses this type of data collection instrument to determine how to direct and aim their marketing strategies. Warranty cards are obtaining the information for the same reason. We often find ourselves on mailing lists because of our responses to this type of question from a market research questionnaire, an interview, or from returning a completed warranty card. Exhibit 14.2 is an example of a checklist type of data collection instrument.

Rating Scales

Rating scales consist of a series of statements or questions that the respondent is asked to rate based on a scale, usually numbered. The scale may be from 1 to 5 with 1 being "disagree completely" and 5 being "agree completely." The numbers in between 1 and 5 indicate conditions between the extremes. We have all seen this type of data collection instrument. Often we encounter rating scales in questionnaires about the quality of service that we have received from a recent purchase or repair. If you have attended one of our Polaris grants workshops or almost any other professional development session, you probably have completed an evaluation form that includes rating scales. Exhibit 14.3 is an example of a rating scale that is being used to gather data on the quality of a training session as perceived by the participants.

Ranking Scales

A ranking scale involves putting a set of items into a hierarchy according to value or preference. For example, respondents may be given five foods and asked to rank them from the one they like the most to the one they like the least. Ranking scales generate quantitative data. They are easy to complete if the number of items to rank is kept small. Ranking a large number of items becomes tedious and can cause respondent's attention and interest to wane. Exhibit 14.4 is an example of a ranking scale in which we are trying to ascertain the opinion of respondents about the relative importance to them of various skills they may have obtained during a training course.

EXHIBIT 14.2

Example of Data Collection Checklist

1. For what do you use your HOME computer?
(Check all that apply.)

_____ Federal tax returns   _____ Address list

_____ State tax returns   _____ Birthday list

_____ Checkbook   _____ Drawing (black & white)

_____ Diary or journal   _____ Drawing (color)

_____ Letters   _____ Video

_____ Recipes   _____ Digital photography

_____ Internet user groups   _____ Arcade type games

_____ Internet research   _____ Strategy type games

_____ E-mail   _____ Adventure type games

2. Your "Skills for Life" training has made you more confident with which of the following?
(Check all that apply.)

_____ Filling out forms   _____ Budgeting money

_____ Answering questions   _____ Dealing with creditors

_____ Taking tests   _____ Being able to ask for help

_____ Being interviewed   _____ Knowing who to ask for help

_____ Comparison shopping   _____ Asking the "right" questions

_____ Keeping a checking account   _____ Dealing with government agencies

EXHIBIT 14.3

Example of Rating Scale

	Excellent		Above Average		Average		Below Average		Poor	
	10	9	8	7	6	5	4	3	2	1
1. Content										
2. Expectations Met										
3. Quality of Materials										
4. Worth Cost										
5. Recommend										

EXHIBIT 14.4

Example of Ranking Scale

The list on the left below contains skills taught during the "Skills for Life" course you just completed. In your opinion, and for you personally, rank the skills in the list below from the most important to the least important. (Place the letter that corresponds to each skill in the appropriate rank order in the column on the far right below.)

List of Skills	Ranking		Skill
a. Filling out forms	Most Important	1	
b. Budgeting money		2	
c. Answering questions		3	
d. Dealing with creditors		4	
e. Taking tests		5	
f. Being able to ask for help		6	
g. Being interviewed		7	
h. Knowing who to ask for help		8	
i. Comparison shopping		9	
j. Asking the "right" questions		10	
k. Keeping a checking account		11	
l. Dealing with government agencies	Least Important	12	

Semantic Differentials

Semantic differentials are used to measure attitudes by relying on the indirect meanings of words. Respondents are asked to rate something by placing their attitude or belief on a scale between two words with opposite meaning. A semantic differential is easy for respondents to complete, and often returns results freer of "political correctness" than an ordinary rating scale. In Exhibit 14.5, an example of a semantic differential, we are attempting to ascertain people's opinions about several aspects of health care in the community.

In-Depth Interview Guide

An interview guide is a script that guides the interviewer through a set of questions. The interview guide also includes notes to the interviewer that are not read to the respondent. It is beyond the scope of this book to attempt to provide guidance on preparation of interview guides. Consultation with a

EXHIBIT 14.5

Example of Semantic Differential

Health Care in Our Community	
Available	Unavailable
Excellent	Poor
Fast	Slow
Caring	Uncaring
Comprehensive	Incomplete
Affordable	Costly

person trained in evaluation techniques might be the best way to obtain needed expertise.

Observation Protocol

An observation protocol is a set of questions (both free response and forced response), ratings, and checklists that the observer completes about the group and the activity being observed. The following information must be collected: description of setting, description and identity of participants, description of activities, interactions between project staff and participants, assessment of quality of delivery, and description of unanticipated events that might require the observation protocol to be modified.

Focus Group Topic Guide

A focus group topic guide is the script that the moderator follows during a particular focus group. Typical topic guides have the following sections in this order: an explanation of the focus group process, an explanation of the purpose of the discussion, introduction of participants, rapport building, the group interview questions, and the conclusion or closure.

Data Collectors

Selection

Just anybody will not do as a data collector. The temptation is to use whoever is at hand, such as volunteers, or students, or project staff, or even participants. Although these people may work out just fine for one type of data collection or another, it is unlikely that they are right for all a data collector's jobs. Data collection duties can be divided into three categories: clerical tasks, interviewing and test administration, and observation and recording. Clerical tasks can include compiling data from documentation, data entry, database management, extracting data from records, and tracking self-administered questionnaires. Interviewing can be in person or on the telephone, questionnaire or in-depth.

All people who make good data collectors have a few things in common. They are able to understand a project and its methods. They are thorough, paying careful attention to detail, and they are disciplined enough to follow directions exactly and consistently. They do not let bias or personal interest influence their work.

Interviewers need additional special skills. A good interviewer needs a positive and tactful manner and a pleasant voice. The best interviewers are those who easily establish rapport with respondents. Special skills or qualifications may be needed for interviewers of some target populations. Fluency in a language other than English is one example. Observers are the most highly skilled and qualified data collectors. They should ideally be former practitioners of the type of interactions they are to observe. For all of these reasons, it is not usually acceptable to use project staff or volunteers as data collectors.

Training

Allotting the time necessary to properly train data collectors is essential to the success of the evaluation. Training must be more than a discussion of what the data collector is to do. Training sessions should include practice at performing the actual task, extracting data from documentation, interviews, or observation. Role-playing can be used in the case of interviews. A technique for sharpening observation skills is to have two data collectors observe the same training session, perhaps a videotape, and compare observations afterward. This training is one of the critical jobs accomplished by your outside evaluator. Continued training can be necessary when a project enters a new phase.

Supervision

Constant, ongoing supervision is the only real way to maintain quality control. Data collectors usually do not purposefully begin to do poorer work, but the repetitive and boring nature of much of data collection can lead to let-downs, which can lead to errors in transcription, interpretation, missing data, less follow-up, less probing, and fewer open-ended questions during interviews. Only regular diligent checking of the results of data collection can ensure no drop-off in quality of product. Therefore, on a weekly basis, all results of data collections must be reviewed carefully and any problems dealt with quickly and forthrightly.

Pretest Instruments

Pretesting data collection instruments, almost certainly, is the most neglected step in all of evaluation. "A time and money waster" is how many busy people view pretesting. The result of failing to pretest is that we do not find the problems with our instruments until we actually begin to use them to gather data. The time to find problems is not when we are gathering valuable evaluation data, but rather when we pretest with a set of respondents from whom the data is not important, but only serves as a check of the instrument itself. Problems as simple as the wording of a question or the way a direction is given can cause respondents trouble. Pretesting with a group of respondents similar to the project's target population can save tremendous time and money later. Pretesting falls into the category of things meant in the old saying: "Why is it that we never have enough time to do things right the first time, but we always have time to do them over again?"

Archive and Store Data

This topic falls into the "self-evident" category. However, it is simply amazing how often we have worked with organizations on project evaluations and been told one variation or another of "we did that, and we have the results, but we cannot put our hands on it right now." To effectively store and archive data means that all (ALL) the data collected goes to one central location. If nothing other than that is done, yearly evaluations will be simpler. More should be done, of course. Papers should be bundled, labeled, and preferably filed in some logical sequence. The sequence can be alphabetical or chronological, or some other method that may be more appropriate. The method is not particularly important, just that there is one and that more than one person knows what the method is. Remember from Chapter 7 that the data stored can be in many formats. Prepare to store computer files. Keeping them on hard drives is not archiving them. Computer files must, absolutely must, be pulled off onto movable media and stored with the rest of the project documentation. Also, remember about security issues. Only authorized personnel may have access to certain personal information about project participants. Keep this in mind when archiving data. Do not use security as an excuse for not keeping copies of all data collected (archived) in one place, simply work it our with a locked cabinet or another appropriate measure.

Data Analysis

It is not our purpose and is beyond the scope of this book to teach data analysis. For data analysis you need the help of an expert, a person trained and experienced in the handling of statistical concepts, measurements, and calculations. Be forewarned however, experts are the ones who formulated *The Iron Law of Evaluation Studies*. The Iron Law is that "The better an evaluation study is technically, the less likely it is to show positive program results" (Rossi and Freeman, *The Iron Law of Evaluation Studies*, Crest, 1993, p. 458). This is the sort of Alice in Wonderland statement that makes people who toil in the trenches blanch at the idea of turning over their beloved project to the tender mercies of statistical analysis. After all, some projects do succeed and make a difference. The Iron Law would have us believe that we can never tell if we have been successful. This is clearly nonsense and is the sort of academic pettifoggery up with which Winston Churchill would not have put.

A great deal can be learned from the application of a few very basic principles that a person does not need expertise in statistical analysis to be able to use. For example, one method is simply comparing pretest results to posttest results and averaging the improvement, perhaps developing different averages for different subgroups within the project participants. Another example is what statisticians call frequency distribution, but which we easily recognize as how many participants did "this" as opposed to how many did "that." A concrete example could be how many participants improved their skills 50 percent. Another example is what statisticians call measures of central tendency, which means the average. A concrete example is that our average increase in skills of all participants was 18 percent. This does not take higher math to figure out, but the simplicity can be obscured by the technical terms with which statisticians cloak their handiwork. Subscribe to the philosophy of one of the world's greatest mathematicians:

> The theory of probabilities is at bottom nothing but common sense reduced to calculus.
>
> *Pierre Simon de LaPlace, 1812–20,*
> Theorie Analytiques des Probabilities

Of course, anyone who has been subjected to using M. Laplace's differential equations may differ with the Monsieur about common sense having anything to do with it.

Wise Guy

Can somebody tell me the purpose of this chapter? I don't want to know this stuff. I put money in the budget for an outside evaluator, grantors love it, and I let her worry about it.

Wise Lady

You may not need to know all this if you have a good evaluator, but as Project Director you are the ultimate quality check. You are ultimately responsible. As I said before, this isn't difficult, it's just complex. It would be a good idea to know the basics of evaluation so that you can keep tabs on the process and so you aren't blindsided by the results. You are liable, if you will (and especially if you won't).

Conclusion

This chapter has presented a cursory overview of data collection and data analysis. These two topics can be relatively simple or devilishly complex. The final decision is yours as Project Director. "But," you might protest, "we must follow the advice of our evaluation consultant. After all, she is the expert." Well, yes and no. It is much like the relation between a doctor and patient. A doctor knows vastly more about medicine than you do, but all decisions about treatment, except in emergencies, are made by you or your appointed representative. A doctor can tell you that surgery is an option, but you must make the decision about going under the knife, yes or no. It is up to you.

In the same way, an evaluation specialist will know vastly more than you do about evaluation, but it will be up to you as Project Director to make the final decisions about what will and will not be done during the evaluation. You cannot abdicate your responsibility to another. You probably are the only one who can keep things simple. Yes, you want a complete and thorough evaluation, but a needlessly complex evaluation only makes your job that much harder. Now we have finished data collection and data analysis. We have our results in factual and statistical form. What remains to do is to put that information into a form that others can understand. Chapter 15 discusses this topic, the evaluation report.

## Chapter 15

Evaluation:
How to Create
an Evaluation Report

Report me and my cause aright.
William Shakespeare, *Hamlet*

Introduction

Looking back into Chapter 12 at our outline of the evaluation process shows that we have arrived at the last major part of an evaluation, providing information to interested parties. This is the product culmination of the work that has gone into an evaluation. Creating a report or several reports is not the ultimate purpose of evaluation, but rather one of the necessary steps. Interested parties, what we have called stakeholders, need information on which to base decisions. These decisions differ for different stakeholders. A grantor may decide that the approach taken and evaluated is worthy of additional study, and therefore the grantor may allocate funds in the next funding cycle to make more grants to other organizations to continue analysis of the approach. Or, a grantor may decide that this approach is flawed and new approaches need to be tried. Either way, the outcome of a project evaluation is used by the grantor to make decisions about future funding efforts.

Other stakeholders have different decisions to make. Some of those decisions regard continuation. When success at remedying one of a community's problems is clearly indicated, and when the success can be shown to be cost effective (deliver a return on investment), the stakeholders in that community often rally round and find ways to continue the solution. Stakeholders will not accept vague assurances of progress, regardless of the good intentions behind them. When it comes to allocating scarce community resources, clear evidence of success backed with full documentation wins out over good intentions and promises every time.

Is all this process we are detailing hard work? Yes, it is. Does it take lots of time to get all this stuff done? Yes, it does. It takes time and hard work to do anything worth doing. Those are the wrong questions, though. One of the right questions is: "How much time and effort is it worth to improve the community in which you live, in which your children and your parents and your grandparents live?" Another right question is: "How much time and effort is it worth to help fellow human beings to a better life?" Another right question is: "How else will you know for certain that you are part of the solution and not part of the problem?"

We should not be doing all this work to save our job as Project Director. We should not be doing all this work to create a little fiefdom and a power base all our own. We should not be doing all this work to protect turf. We should not be doing all this work for prestige or glory or renown. We should be doing all this work because we care about our fellow human beings, because we have a passion to help, to solve problems. Seek and find and perfect a solution that works to one of society's problems and you will have a job, you will have a fiefdom and a power base, you will have turf, and you will receive prestige, glory, and renown, more than you can imagine. But be sure to seek the solution first and above all else. Seeking the trappings of success instead of the success itself is a guaranteed formula for disappointment in both.

Once we settle on our stakeholders and their needs, we are ready to create the report or reports. The parts of an evaluation report are background information about the project, the evaluation questions, the evaluation procedures, the data analysis procedures, the findings, the conclusions and maybe recommendations, and perhaps an abstract, an executive summary, and an appendix. In this chapter we discuss each of these parts of an evaluation report, what belongs in each section, and how one might look.

Stakeholders

Stakeholders are those individuals or organizations that have an interest in the outcomes of your project and that may make decisions based on those outcomes. The decisions can vary widely and therefore the information that stakeholders need and in which they are interested will differ from one to the other. The table in Exhibit 15.1 gives an idea of the range of decisions that stakeholders can make and the information they may need. We have included a worksheet to help you with determining your stakeholders needs, 1501.doc.

With this variety of needs and interests, a single evaluation report probably will not succeed with all stakeholders. A three-tiered approach may be best. For those stakeholders interested mainly in the results of the

EXHIBIT 15.1

1501.DOC

Stakeholders' Decision-Making Table

Stakeholder	Decision(s)	Information Needs
Grantor		
Your Organization or Agency		
Partners in Implementation		
Partners in R & D		
Partners in Donations		
Partners in Data		
Interested Observing Agencies		
Volunteers		
Citizens of Community		
Local Governing Bodies		

project, prepare an executive summary that concisely delivers the summative findings and conclusions, and perhaps recommendations. For those stakeholders interested in all aspects of the project, both process and outcome, prepare a full-fledged evaluation report. For those stakeholders with specialized needs and interests, prepare and conduct customized briefings with handouts. If at any time a stakeholder wants additional information, you can give them a copy of the executive summary or the full evaluation report. Burdening stakeholders with more information than they need can lead to pertinent project results being ignored simply because they are so hard to dig out of the mass of information in the full evaluation report.

Background

The background section begins with information contained in the pro-posal. It sets the stage by explaining what you planned to do once the project was funded. Stay focused on the original plan in this section. Later we discuss how things may have changed as the project progressed, but for now keep the information in this section focused on the original intent and plan. The following list shows the information that goes in the Background section:

1. Problem(s) addressed by project (sometimes called need)
2. Target population (expected participants)
3. Partners and expected roles
4. Mission
5. Goals and objectives
6. Principles, strategies, activities, or components that will help clarify understanding
7. Staff of project with roles, including volunteers and partner's staff
8. Location(s)
9. Length of project
10. Resources needed to implement
11. Expected outcomes

This is sectional narrative, although you may want to use charts (boxes) to display the goals and objectives in an easy-to-grasp style. Another use-ful chart might be the partners and their roles, if there are a number of them. Be sure to put headings at the start of each new part of this section. Make it as easy as possible for a reader to know what to expect at all times.

Evaluation Questions

Delineate all the evaluation questions that you decided to use. A simple and straightforward way to organize the evaluation questions is by using the goals and objectives as the outline. The reader has already seen the goals and objectives in full in the background section, so this second time around, the organizational scheme will be familiar. Include the standard or criteria by which each question is to be judged. It is very important to include the benchmarks against which each question is evaluated, or the rest of the report lacks substance and clear measurability.

You may want to list questions that could have been asked but were not included for reasons of time, money, or lack of a means of measurement. This information can be used as the setup for one or more recommendations later. A recommendation, for example, might be to continue the formal evaluation for another year or two, incorporating one or more of the neglected questions the answers to which have, with experience, become very important.

Evaluation Procedures

The Evaluation Procedures section should have two main parts. The first part is a narrative discussion of the steps that were taken in the implementation of the evaluation. The narrative can be organized around the various pieces of evaluation procedure as shown in the various charts in Chapter 13. Each of the following procedural points should be discussed fully. In the preceding section the reader has seen the evaluation questions and the standards, so this section builds on that information, explaining how we gathered the information we needed to make our judgment about each question. It is not necessary to discuss every incident in the evaluation procedures, just representative ones. A complete summary follows this narrative.

1. Name, describe, and give roles of the individuals and groups that performed the evaluation.
2. Describe the participant population that participated in the evaluation.
3. Sources of data.
4. Types of data collected.
5. Methods of collecting data.
6. Data collection instruments or tools.
7. Number of times data collected.
8. When data collected (schedule).
9. Sampling strategies, selection, number, representation.
10. If comparison or control groups were used, explain how they were selected.
11. Data collection instruments or tools.
12. When the grantor requires, point out use of both formative and summative evaluation.
13. When the grantor requires, point out use of both quantitative and qualitative evaluation measures.

14. Schedule.

15. Personnel assignments.

16. Discuss selection, training, and supervision of data collectors.

The second main part of this section should be a matrix that summarizes the following information: evaluation questions, sources of data, data collection methods, sampling plan, schedule, and number of times data is collected.

Data Analysis Procedures

The Data Analysis Procedures section describes the techniques used in the analysis of the information gathered by the data collection discussed in the previous section. Explain who performed the analysis. Describe any stages in the analysis. Were various iterations of analysis necessary? If so, what and why? Describe the checks that were implemented to ensure the integrity of the data. Name and describe the software packages used in the analysis, and discuss the appropriateness of your choice of packages. Name and briefly explain the analysis techniques that were chosen and why those techniques are appropriate. A combination of a narrative followed by a summary matrix is a good way to organize this section.

Findings

The Findings section presents the results of the data analysis. Use the evaluation questions for the organizational scheme. Include the preestablished standard for each question. Provide the results for each evaluation question, good, bad, or indifferent (inconclusive). Presentation of dry summative statistics can be brought to life and made interesting by including quotations gleaned from qualitative evaluation measures. A three-part approach to this section works well. First, use narrative to describe findings. Include charts and graphs to illustrate important or interesting or difficult points. Next, use a summary matrix in which every evaluation question is given full and equal treatment. Finish with a summary narrative section in which you explain what was learned about specific project activities or components. You might call this "Lessons Learned." This Findings section stays focused on individual evaluation questions. Broader statements come later in the conclusion section.

Remember that you need to present two equally important sets of findings, formative as well as summative. The formative evaluation measures provide information about the processes and the internal workings of the project. This information is extremely important to the grantor and to other organizations that might want to replicate your solution. Be sure to label the formative measures clearly and give them the importance they deserve. You probably used both quantitative and qualitative measures. Scatter quotations from the qualitative data throughout the Findings section to enliven what can be dull statistics and provide visual relief from large blocks of text.

Conclusions (Perhaps with Recommendations)

In the Conclusion section we move away from findings about individual evaluation questions and make statements that apply to broader aspects of the project. Here we comment on the success or failure of entire goals and objectives and explain why one failed and why another succeeded. For example, we might comment on a mentoring component (goal). We would discuss individual issues, such as recruitment, training, retention, and matching mentors to mentees. Then we would describe how these issues impacted the expected outcomes of the mentoring component from the viewpoint of project management as well as participant results.

If recommendations are appropriate, meaning that it is OK to include them, they should only be made when there are substantial findings to support the recommendations. If you do not know whether it is appropriate to include recommendations, do what you always do, or rather always should do, when faced with a question for which you do not have the answer. Ask the grantor. Grantors are the one and only true authority on what is necessary to make them happy. Not you, not us, not any consultant can substitute for getting information directly from the grantor. When in doubt, ask.

Other Sections

Abstract

An abstract is a summary of the project, the findings, and conclusions, all jammed into one-half page. This size limit is important. Your abstract has multiple uses, one of which is for publication in clearinghouse databases and Internet sites where space is at a premium. Another use is as an informational handout. You might use this piece to determine if the publisher of a newsletter or magazine has interest in an article about your project. In short, a carefully crafted abstract serves as the introduction to your project for almost any interested inquirer.

Executive Summary

An executive summary is a summary of your project that includes a non-technical overview of the evaluation, its findings, and its conclusions. The executive summary can be up to four pages long. The keys to a good executive summary are to include only conclusive findings, present them in a nontechnical manner, and relate the findings and conclusions to practical matters with human proportions and meanings.

Appendix

An appendix is where you put stuff that is informative, helpful, and perhaps even necessary, but that would break up the flow of the narrative if inserted. There is one ironclad rule about an appendix. The rule that may not be broken is this. When you do not refer directly to an item in the narrative, that item has no business in the appendix, leave it out. The following list contains a number of items that are appropriate to include in the appendix of an evaluation report unless you are directed otherwise:

1. Examples of data collection instruments
2. Complete results of surveys when only part is used in report
3. Complete test results when only part is used in report
4. Complete data analysis calculations
5. Compilations of qualitative data, of which only representative items are used in report
6. An accounting of expenditures
7. Footnotes
8. Bibliography

Publishing

The following list is no substitute for the expertise of a person knowledgeable and experienced in layout and design. It will, however, keep you from committing a few of the mistakes commonly made when publishing a document such as an evaluation report.

1. The purpose of a cover is to convey information, not to be cute. Anyone picking up your document should be able to tell what it is, where it came from, and the audience for whom it is intended. In addition, be sure to include the full and correct names of the grantor, the funding program, and the project.

2. Include a title page immediately behind the cover. The cover may be repeated on the front of the title page, or additional and/or different information can be given. On the back of the title page give the date of publication, author(s) name, names of other contributors (contributions such as data entry, graphics or page layout and design), name, address, and contact information of sponsoring organization.

3. The next page can be a reproduction (copy) of a signed letter from the person in charge of the evaluation. This page is a formal letter of transmittal of the report to the grantor. The back of this page should be blank. Be sure that the letter is on appropriate letterhead.

4. A detailed contents page is absolutely necessary. All sections and parts of sections must be referenced in the contents, including all material in the appendix. The reverse side of the contents is left blank, unless the contents extends that far.

5. Number the pages of the document consecutively, with no breaks and no repeated numbers.

6. Page 1 is the first page of the first section.

7. All right-hand pages are odd numbered.

8. All left-hand pages are even numbered.

9. Number and name the sections.

10. All sections begin on odd-numbered pages (right facing), even if you must insert a blank page to make it come out correctly.

11. Create a section title page to begin each section.

12. Begin the content of each section on the reverse side of the section title page.

13. In a header on each page beginning with page 1, put the title of the document and the section name and number in which that page falls.

14. In the footer on each page beginning with page 1, put the page number. An appropriate place for the page number in a publication printed double-sided is in the middle of the page.

15. Use frequent headings and subheadings. Break the text into small blocks at every opportunity.

16. Use healthy margins, at least one inch on all four sides.

17. Use a proportional text font that does not look like a typewriter for all narrative.

18. Use a type size that is easy to read but presents a professional appearance.

19. Avoid full justification. Use "rag right" (left justified).

20. Avoid underlining for emphasis. Use bold face instead.

21. Unless told otherwise, use 1.5 line spacing instead of double-spacing. It improves readability, but does not make a page look as empty as double-spacing.

22. Do not allow orphans. An orphan is a heading either alone or with only one or two lines of text with it at the bottom of a page. Force orphans to the top of the next page.

23. If directed by the grantor to publish differently than any item on this list, follow the grantor's directions.

Wise Guy

Who in the world has time to cater to all these so-called stakeholders? Not me, that's for sure. It's my neck on the line, not theirs. I signed on the dotted line, so I answer to the grantor. Everybody else can take a long hike off a short pier.

Wise Lady

Stakeholders ensure that your project is successful and continues. They are the ones that you serve—your target population. They're why you have a job in the first place. Everyone in every job in every part of the world deals with stakeholders. In retail, it's the general public and your managers and supervisors, as well as the corporate folks who make overall decisions. In education it's the students, parents, board members, community, administration. In farming, it's consumers, regulators, and government officials. And on it goes. We are an interdependent society. You cannot do anything in a vacuum. Yes, you are ultimately responsible to the grantor, but if you don't keep your stakeholders happy and informed, you won't have anything positive to report to the grantor. You can't do it alone.

Conclusion

One of the key things said in this chapter is that one evaluation report probably is not appropriate for all stakeholders. Each category or type of stakeholder deserves its own customized evaluation report. We suggest that the full evaluation report go the grantor and only such other stakeholders as can understand and have a use for such voluminous data. The executive summary is distributed to those stakeholders who need summative evaluation information on which to make decisions. A third category of stakeholder has special narrow needs. These stakeholders can be best served with customized presentations accompanied by a matching handout. Of course, we must be ready to provide full documentation if it is requested. The purpose of the differing approaches is not to hide information, but to better serve stakeholders by bringing forward the data, findings, and conclusions they need, not letting it get buried in the mass of detail in the full report.

An evaluation report is no different than any other report or document. Understand the needs of your audience and meet them. Present the information in a way that is easy to understand. Explain your organization, leaving nothing to the imagination of the reader. Use the old teacher's maxim. "Tell 'em what you are going to tell 'em. Tell 'em. Then tell 'em what you told them." It sounds extreme, but it works.

We sincerely hope that we have explained things, not hidden them. Our intention has been to clear away the distractions and complications that attend the topic of evaluation, to simplify, to make the process understandable. If we have oversimplified certain topics, it has been with good intentions. One thing you always can count on. Somebody knows. Whatever it is that you need to know, somebody knows. Search out the expertise and ask for help.

## PART IV

Dissemination
and Continuation

## Chapter 16

Dissemination

The codfish lays ten thousand eggs,
The homely hen lays one.
The codfish never cackles
To tell you what she's done.
And so we scorn the codfish,
While the humble hen we prize.
Which only goes to show you
That it pays to advertise.

Anonymous

Introduction

In general usage, as in a dictionary, disseminate means "promulgate widely." Promulgate means "make widespread." Putting the two definitions together, it seems as though disseminate really means "make widespread widely," or perhaps "make widely widespread." The latter one sounds like Captain Blowhard on the capital ship Walloping Window Blind telling Ensign Widespread to do one of those nautical things like come abaft or haul braces. "Sharply now! Make widely, Widespread."

The grantor does not think that dissemination is a laughing matter, however. Read this quotation from a grantor. You will see how serious dissemination is. You will also see how integral a part of a project the grantor expects dissemination to be.

6. Follow-up and Dissemination

Describe follow-up activities. These may include curricular projects, workshops with colleagues, in-service presentations and other means. Where pertinent, show how materials produced by a project, or other results of broad significance, would be made accessible nationwide, particularly to people who would most benefit from their use. For example, indicate why the format or formats chosen for a final product (printed volume, CD-ROM, Internet distribution) represent the most effective means of dissemination to the intended audience. Indicate what publication arrangements have been made and whether an agreement to publish has been reached, and append any pertinent correspondence. Provide the expected price of the product and the plans for publicity, including announcements in professional journals, electronic discussion groups, or newsletters, the preparation and distribution of demonstration versions, and participation in conferences or exhibits.

Grant Application and Forms,
Education Development and Demonstration
National Endowment for the Humanities (NEH)

Dissemination is getting the word out, letting other people know what is going on, spreading the news, and passing the word. In our case, "the word" and "what is going on" and "the news" is information about our grant project. Dissemination, when applied to grant projects, has two purposes. One purpose is to encourage others to use your work, to aid replication. The other purpose is to convince local individuals and groups that your project is worthy of their support, to aid continuation. Four questions leap immediately to mind. To whom do we disseminate? What do we disseminate? When do we disseminate? How do we disseminate?"

The answers to these questions should have been answered during project development while you were preparing to write the proposal. A dissemination plan is a required part of most proposals. As Project Director, all you should have to do is find the dissemination plan in the proposal that won the grant that is funding your project, and then manage the plan. The dissemination plan that you find may be sketchy, incomplete, or even nonexistent, so we discuss the process. The main topics of the chapter are the four questions we asked at the end of the previous paragraph.

Before beginning the meat of this chapter, one more important message is appropriate. The time for which this message is appropriate is when we are fully developing our project and completing the proposal to send to our potential grantor. Dissemination is one of the most commonly overlooked parts of a project, and therefore the treatment of dissemination in the proposal is often given short shrift. This is a terrible mistake. Neglecting dissemination sends a clear message that we do not understand the great importance to the grantor of this aspect of a grant project.

To Whom Do We Disseminate?

Who we disseminate to depends on the purpose of our dissemination. Remember the two purposes of dissemination, to aid replication and to aid continuation. When our purpose is to aid continuation, our target audience is the stakeholders that can help us with continuation. When our purpose is to aid replication, our target audience is the people and organizations who would be likely to use our solution to solve a problem of their own. The following list can help define to whom we should disseminate information, what to disseminate, and how to disseminate. To help with this activity we have included Exhibit 16.1 on the disk as file 1601.doc.

1. Identify your target audience(s): Who are potential users of the information?

2. Identify the information needs, interests, and desires of your target audience(s): This knowledge determines what information you disseminate.

3. Identify how the target audience acquires information: This knowledge determines the method of dissemination and the media used.

4. Identify any special characteristics of the target audience that will influence the message, the method, or the media (for example, children, elderly, visually impaired, etc.)

What Do We Disseminate?

The flippant answer is: "What do you have?" Actually that answer is not completely flippant; it contains the core of the issue. What we disseminate is information that we have collected about our grant project. The common theme of all disseminated information is that it should be useful to those who wish to learn from the experience of the project. This information can include any or all of the items in the following list:

- Project status
  - Announcement of grant award
  - Announcement of project start
  - Progress updates (continuously)
  - Process outcomes (results of formative evaluation measures)
  - Meetings of boards and advisors
  - Event announcements
  - Event invitations
  - Public service announcements
  - Announcements of availability of products

EXHIBIT 16.1

1601.DOC

Project Dissemination: Target Audience Worksheet

Target audience (To whom to disseminate)	Information needs, interests, and desires of target audience (What to disseminate)	How target audience acquires information (Method of dissemination)	Special characteristics of target audience (How to cast message)

- Usable results
  - Procedures
  - Products
  - Materials
  - Evaluation tools
  - Evaluation report
  - Web pages with information
  - Curricula or training materials
- Project outcomes (probably from summative evaluation measures)
  - Changes in knowledge and skills
  - Changes in behavior
  - Changes in health
  - Changes in economic status
  - Changes in attitude
  - Changes in process or procedure

When Do We Disseminate?

We must, we absolutely must, tell people about our project from the very beginning. We must let people know that we won the grant. We must let people know when we start the project. We must let people know what is going on continuously throughout the life of the project. And, we must let people know the results, outcomes, and impact of the project, not just at the end, but at every milestone along the way. Dissemination is a continuous process. It begins before we get the grant, continues after the grant is gone, and goes on at all points in between.

How Do We Disseminate?

Basic Principles

The many and varied dissemination techniques can be categorized in four major ways or methods: oral, audiovisual, written, or online. Oral dissemination techniques include conversations, interviews, formal presentations, and manned exhibits. Audiovisual dissemination techniques include video, audio, slides, overheads, and films. Written dissemination techniques include brochures, manuals, reports, press releases, and print media articles. Computer dissemination techniques include both audiovisual and written methods in such forms as web pages, links to and from web pages, a question and answer bulletin board, postings to clearinghouses, postings to appropriate user groups, postings to appropriate bulletin boards, and use of e-mail.

Other Considerations

Choosing a Dissemination Technique. We need to consider three major issues when selecting a dissemination technique: the content of the message, the use to which the target audience will put the information, and effective use of project resources. First, we need to ensure that the dissemination technique is appropriate for the content of the message. Complex descriptions with statistics and charts and graphs do not belong in a brochure, but rather in a report to a professional journal. Guidelines and basic information alone do not belong in an article for a professional journal but rather in a brochure.

Second we need to match the dissemination technique to the use to which a target population would put the information. Consider how, where, why, and who could use the information so a practical and useful dissemination technique is chosen. For example, if replication material will be used outside in a hostile environment, it may need to be printed on plastic or laminated. If, for example, spreadsheets make illustrating a procedure much simpler, a computer disk may need to be provided. The users of certain information may have hearing, vision, or other physical factors to take into consideration.

Finally, we need to be cognizant of the use of project resources including especially staff time and project funds. Constraints on available staff time as well as lack of expertise may make it necessary to bring a consultant on board for certain aspects of dissemination. It may be necessary to contract with a service provider in the areas of public relations, graphics, and video and audio production. Enough time for all the phases of dissemination must be scheduled. Material production can be more time consuming than originally planned. Printing, reproduction, video production, audio production, and packaging consistently take more time than scheduled. The amount of money available can be a controlling factor in which dissemination technique is chosen. A good guideline with respect to money and resources is that it is better to use a simple inexpensive technique done perfectly and with style than to use a more expensive technique that is poorly executed because of lack of resources.

Legal Issues. Your organization may have copyrights or patent rights to material, processes, and inventions created during a grant project. Your grantor can tell you. If you do have such rights you will want to use the services of an appropriate lawyer to protect your intellectual property.

Worth noting is that if your grant is from a federal source, the federal government has the right to reprint anything produced by the project even if it is copyrighted. Music, recordings, motion pictures, video recordings, and computer software can all be copyrighted.

In the same way that you do not want others to infringe on your rights to your own intellectual property, you must be sure not to break copyright law yourself. In this age of multimedia computer presentations it is easy to use pictures, animation, video, graphics, music, and sounds that are actually copyrighted material.

When you produce a video or audio presentation that uses staff or participants, you must obtain a *talent release* from everybody appearing in the production, so you can legally use the images and voices. This same talent release can be necessary for still photographs as well.

The key to all this information is to consult your lawyer. Always start with the lawyer with whom your organization has an established relation. While that lawyer may not have specific expertise with copyrights and patent rights, she or he will be able to bring in the necessary expertise, and your general-purpose counsel is kept apprised of developments in the process. Of course, nothing we have said here should be construed to constitute legal advice. We are not lawyers.

Dissemination Techniques

Personal Communication

Personal communication means conversations, speeches, and presentations before individuals, small groups, and large audiences. This technique can be the most expensive dissemination technique in terms of cost per contact because of the travel and personnel time expenses. Expenses can be cut by using existing opportunities such as speaking at meetings that you must attend anyway, using the telephone, sharing costs with other nonprofits that also want an opportunity for personal communication time. A time saver is to develop standard presentations. You will need a variety of lengths. An hour is usually the most time you will be allotted. The complete presentation needs to be pared down to create a 30-minute and a 15-minute presentation. The great temptation here is to create only the hour presentation and assume you can cut it on-the-fly during a shorter time frame. It will be apparent to your listeners that you are doing just that. Take the time to create the shorter presentations. You also need a standard one-sentence explanation of your project. This needs to be interesting and leave the listener wanting to ask a question, which allows you to converse about your project at someone else's request.

One more essential action to take at every personal communication opportunity is to invite response. Tell people that they are welcome to get in touch to get questions answered or obtain more information. Tell them that you have lots more information if they are interested. Point out that all the ways to get in touch with your project are on each page of the handout. Also, be ready to give out business cards at every opportunity. Be sure that an email address and website URL (if you have a website) are on your business card. Exhibit 16.2 (1602.doc) provides a checklist for personal communication dissemination.

Formal Presentation

By formal presentation we mean the type of presentation made at a professional conference or symposium or any other venue in which you speak before peers, people with similar backgrounds and professions. These presentations are often scheduled up to a year in advance. Travel costs can be substantial. Of prime importance is to be prepared. Your audience will be more discriminating than a group of local citizens. Write the presentation carefully, but do write it. Do not assume you can wing it. Create custom handouts that carefully match the presentation. Take a portable clock to sit on the podium. Visit the room in which you will speak before the actual speech. Attend someone else's speech in the same room for example. See how the room "works." Every room is different. You need to be prepared.

Use handouts effectively. Reference the paragraph about handouts in the Personal Communication section. You want to fulfill the expectations of your audience, so you may need to distribute handouts before or during your presentation. Our suggestion, however, is that you not give the audience something to read and fiddle with during your presentation. We suggest that you create a take-home handout that the audience can pick up at the exit at the end of the session. To make this work you will need an assistant, something we suggest strongly. An assistant can handle audiovisual aids, handouts, and logistics, freeing you to concentrate on your presentation. Another important task an assistant can perform is to gauge audience response and reaction. Be sure to hold a debriefing session with the assistant to get her observations.

A feature of many professional presentations is time set aside for questions from the audience. How you handle this session is as important as the presentation itself, so prepare carefully. Anticipate questions and prepare answers. Always restate questions from the audience so everyone will understand the question. Take quick notes as questions are being asked. Use these notes during the last minute or two of your time to summarize all that has just happened and to announce your take-home handout that is available at the exit. Be sure to close the session by telling them that

EXHIBIT 16.2   1602.DOC

Project Dissemination: Personal Communication Checklist

		Description
		Consider every personal communication an opportunity to disseminate information (singly or groups).
		Develop a one-hour presentation on project.
		Develop a thirty-minute presentation on project.
		Develop a fifteen-minute presentation on project.
		Develop a standard one-sentence reply to the question, "What do you do?"
		When presenting before a group, use a handout.
		Handout must match the presentation; add to it, not simply repeat it. Do not use print-out of overheads.
		Every page of every handout must have project identification information.
		Contact person's name
		Voice number
		Fax number
		E-mail address
		Website URL
		Include copyright notice on every page of every handout.
		For presentations before groups, use visual aids whenever possible.
		Always invite response, point out contact information on handout.
		Tell listeners that you have more information and will be glad to share it.
		Be ready to give out business cards, carry at all times.
		Be sure that e-mail address and website URL are on your business card.
		When you give a business card, get a business card.
		Carry blank three-by-five cards for those people who do not have business cards.
		Note interest of individual on back of their card.
		Respond quickly to all obtained names and addresses.
		Enter obtained names and addresses in project dissemination database.
		Train all staff to view personal communication as dissemination opportunities.
		Create standardized presentation kits for staff use.

you want to hear from them and that the access code to your chosen method of communication is on the handout. We think e-mail is best, but you need to use the mode with which you are most comfortable.

You may have the option, or you may be requested, to use a panel during your presentation. If you have control of the makeup of the panel, select credible experts who are also good speakers. Be sure to coordinate the approach to the topic among the panelists. You want no surprises. Also, be sure to produce all handouts and visual aids yourself. Seldom will a panelist turn down an offer to produce their handouts. This gives you quality control over what the audience receives. One last thing—meet with the panel in advance of the session to establish personal rapport. Get names down pat. Exhibit 16.3 (1603.doc) provides a checklist for formal presentations.

Exhibits

An exhibit is a booth or table or both in the exhibit area of a conference. You display what you have to offer and are available for conversation. This can be expensive, but can allow exposure to a large and varied audience. The display can be costly, and travel and personnel time can be a large expense. If you create an exhibit, be sure that it will attract attention. Keep the basic message simple and large. Exhibit design may be a place that professional assistance is appropriate. Staff the exhibit at all times when the exhibit hall is open, creating as many opportunities for personal interaction as possible. The people manning the booth must stand, not sit. They need to be open to conversation but not pounce on passers by. This is hard work, so rotate staff. Expenses can be cut by attending conferences that are local or in your state. Production of a tabletop exhibit rather than a booth saves money. Another way to minimize cost is to ship the exhibit early. Ground delivery is always much cheaper than next day or second day delivery.

One way to attract visitors is with giveaway items. Giveaways can be information handouts, brochures, or items with the name and access information imprinted on them. Several well-produced information handouts on different aspects of your problem and solution make excellent giveaways. Another way to attract visitors is with a drawing for a big-ticket giveaway. Put a fishbowl on the table for business cards. The drawing can be held at the final assembly at the conclusion of the conference. This provides additional publicity.

One purpose of an exhibit is to provide a means to add to your project mailing list. When a visitor expresses interest, request a business card. Note on the back of the card their interest. Respond quickly after returning from the conference. Send them something, even if as little as an e-mail message, thanking them for their interest. Then enter all your new names into your database. Exhibit 16.4 (1604.doc) provides a checklist for exhibits.

EXHIBIT 16.3

Project Dissemination: Formal Presentation Checklist

	Description
	Research opportunities early—programs can be set up to a year in advance.
	Research expectations of audience (handouts, visual aids, questions, panel, etc.) (See File 1610.doc)
	Write presentation carefully. (Do not attempt to "wing it," you are speaking before professionals).
	Create visual aids as appropriate.
	Create custom handout, do not simply repeat presentation. No print-outs of overheads
	Take a portable clock to sit on podium or table.
	Visit the room in which you will present before presentation, stand at podium or sit at table.
	Practice the presentation, practice, practice, practice.
	Memorize the opening and the closing of your presentation.
	Eliminate vocal mannerisms.
	Eliminate physical mannerisms.
	Do not wear or take a watch, use the portable clock you place on the podium or table.
	Use an assistant to handle audiovisual aids, handouts, and logistics.
	Use your handout as a "take-home" to be picked up by listeners on the way out of the room.
	Put complete contact information on every page of handout (see File 1602.doc).
	Debrief assistant after presentation to gauge response and guide improvements for future.
	Anticipate questions and have answers ready.
	Always restate questions from audience so every one will understand the question.
	Take notes during questions and in last two minutes of time summarize Q&A session.
	Final comment to audience is to invite response, point out contact information in handout.
	Get off the stage and "work" the room as it is emptying, give and get business cards (see File 1602.doc).
	If you have control, pick members of your panel to be credible experts who are also good speakers.
	Coordinate topic and point of view among panelists before presentation.
	Volunteer to produce all handouts and visual aids, ensuring quality and consistency.
	Meet with panel before presentation, establish personal rapport, and get names down pat.

EXHIBIT 16.4

1604.DOC

Project Dissemination: Exhibit Checklist

	Description
	Research profile of target audience (see File 1601.doc).
	Keep message of exhibit simple, colorful, and large.
	Obtain professional help with design of exhibit if necessary.
	Use large pictures, graphics, and physical items to get message across.
	Plan ahead and save money by shipping exhibit and material by ground.
	Staff exhibit at all times that exhibit space is open.
	People staffing exhibit must stand, not sit.
	People staffing exhibit must be open to conversation, but not pounce on passers by.
	Rotate staff to maintain energy and positive attitude.
	Staff must wear professionally made name tags (their name and organization and/or project name).
	Staff must be prepared with business cards and blank three-by-five cards.
	Attract visitors with interactive experiences (models, computer, video, telecommunication, etc.).
	Attract visitors with giveaway items.
	Brochures
	Series of single-page information sheets on different aspects of project.
	Items with name and access information imprinted on them, such as pens, coffee mugs, etc.
	Attract visitors with a drawing for a "big-ticket" giveaway.
	Create large sign announcing drawing.
	The item should relate to your project—software, manual, database, etc.
	Provide fishbowl for business cards.
	Hold drawing at final assembly at the conclusion of conference.
	Place live plants or flowers on table or in exhibit, then give them away (or make them part of drawing).
	Give a business card, get a business card.
	Note interest of visitor on back of their business card or three-by-five card.
	Respond quickly after conference; send them something.
	Add names and addresses to project dissemination database.

Video and Audio

This topic is about the production of a video or an audio presentation to be distributed, probably by tape, but CD-ROM and the Internet are growing possibilities. Production of video or audio is a time-consuming and expensive process. Unless your organization possesses the facilities and equipment for production, it is best to use professionals. Top quality picture and sound are essential. Poor quality in these two areas distracts viewers and listeners from your message. Professional facilities and professional personnel can ensure that the quality of your production is what it should be.

Define the audience for the production and target the message appropriately. If the target audience is children, the message will be different than if the target audience is their parents. Settle on the script and storyboard before beginning production and do not change them once production is under way. Changes in midstream of production are very expensive. At least think about using professional actors. Professionals can actually save money in the long run by conserving production facility time. Get the appropriate legal advice about the production, especially about talent release statements. Also, music is a copyrighted intellectual property that cannot be indiscriminately used. Your professional production people can help you with this, as well as your legal advisor. Exhibit 16.5 (1605.doc) is a checklist for video and audio productions.

Brochures

A brochure is a short printed piece, usually smaller than a standard page. Brochures are used to provide short, simple, and targeted messages. Brochures work best when communicating broad general ideas. The best brochures incorporate graphics integrated with simple, uncomplicated text. A typical approach to brochures is to create one overview brochure and a number of topic-specific brochures. The brochures should be differentiated by color or graphic design, while at the same time appear to be one of a coherent series. When designing a brochure, be sure to create a mock-up early on. A mock-up is made to look just like the final brochure including folds. A mock-up will allow you to see if the flow and appearance of the brochure are working. Exhibit 16.6 (1606.doc) is a checklist for brochure production.

Manuals

A manual is a collection of facts and instructions that provide a guide or direction. Manuals are used as guides to accomplish a task or activity. A manual could be produced about installation, process, operations, project implementation, project organization, procedures, trouble-shooting,

EXHIBIT 16.5   1605.DOC

Project Dissemination: Video and Audio Production Checklist

	Description
	Research profile of target audience (see File 1601.doc).
	Target message to audience.
	Choose media based on target audience (tape, CD-ROM, Internet, etc.).
	Unless you possess top quality production facilities, use professional facilities.
	Unless you possess top quality production expertise, use professionals.
	Allow nothing other than top quality sound and picture.
	Write script and create storyboard before production begins.
	Do not make major changes in script or storyboard once production begins (very expensive).
	Use professional actors and voices.
	Obtain legal advice about people appearing in production (especially children & note privacy issues).
	Obtain legal advice about pictures, graphics, video and audio clips, and music used in production.

Exhibit 16.6

Project Dissemination: Brochure Checklist

	Description
	Research profile of target audience (see File 1601.doc).
	Attempt to communicate only broad general concepts or ideas.
	Incorporate graphics, charts, graphs, and pictures.
	Keep text simple.
	Create a "flow" through the brochure, from start to finish.
	Create a series of brochures.
	One overview brochure
	Several brochures on specific project topics
	Brochures must be united by a consistent "look" and consistency of language and design.
	Brochures must be differentiated by color or design of cover.
	Create a mock-up as early as possible, including the folds.
	Ensure that flow of information is correct in mock-up.
	Ensure that appearance of brochure is correct in mock-up.
	Edit text painstakingly (illiteracies send a powerful message, but not the message you want to send).
	Proof text and captions painstakingly (misspellings and typos send a powerful message).
	Proof graphics, charts, graphs, and pictures painstakingly (mistakes send a powerful message).
	Ensure that all names, titles, addresses, phone numbers, URLs, etc. are exactly correct.
	Use outside people to edit and proof, people who did not create the brochure content.
	All brochures must include complete and correct contact information (phone, fax, e-mail, etc.).
	All brochures must include copyright information.
	If brochure is to a "mailer" or has a return mail part, check appropriate Postal Service regulations.
	Size and weight
	Method of securing folded material
	Positioning of address and return address
	Bulk mail regulations
	Prepaid return mail regulations
	Use mock-up when dealing with printer, obtain written bid with delivery date and penalties for lateness.

repair, and basically anything you can imagine including curriculum and lesson plans. Define the target audience, the end user of the manual, and produce accordingly. A curriculum guide is produced differently from an operations manual for a computer network. In the case of curriculum, two manuals may be appropriate, one for the instructor or teacher, another for the student. Exhibit 16.7 (1607.doc) is a checklist for manual production.

Reports

A report is an accounting or information about a happening. In the case of grant projects, reports usually are documents that provide information to stakeholders about the progress or outcomes of the project. Reports are used extensively in continuation activities. The document that delivers the final evaluation result is a report. The key to a good report is to carefully define the target audience. Define the needs of that audience in relation to what you are trying to accomplish with the report and tailor the style, content, and design of the report to fulfill those needs. A report should be no longer than necessary. Padding for the sake of making large impressive documents is not appreciated by anyone who receives reports and is expected to digest them. Exhibit 16.8 (1608.doc) is a checklist for report production.

Print Media Articles

Media articles are pieces that are published in magazines, newspapers, and newsletters. Take every opportunity to get articles published. You may write them, or they may be written about you. If you do the writing, pay attention to the audience of the publication. Get copies of the publication and carefully review the style and composition of articles. Yours must match. The normal way that articles are published is to first approach a publisher with an idea for an article. This approach can be in writing or by voice. The publisher will want to see your "treatment." This short piece tells what you intend to do in the article. It summarizes the main points and gives the viewpoint or position or slant that you will be taking. The purpose of the treatment is to let the publisher know what the article is going to be about and what your approach will be. When a publisher accepts your article idea, you will receive instructions about the length of the article, any sidebars the publisher wants, along with requests for biographical information, and possibly a "head shot" picture to include in the byline. Exhibit 16.9 (1609.doc) is a checklist for print media article production.

Press Releases

A press release is sent to newspapers and other media outlets announcing an event or happening, such as the grant award, or program startup, or a

EXHIBIT 16.7   1607.DOC

Project Dissemination: Manual Checklist

	Description
	Research profile of target audience (see File 1601.doc).
	Make decision about what the manual is and maintain consistency of effort, stay focused.
	Decide on appropriate media (print or computer based or a combination).
	If print media, decide on:
	Binding (perfect, hardback, GBC, Velo, three-ring, etc.)
	Size (8.5 x 11 or 7 x 10 or 4.25 x 7, etc.)
	Type of paper
	Type of cover
	If computer media, decide on:
	Platform (Windows, Mac, Unix, etc.)
	File format (MS Word, Word Perfect, Page Maker, etc.)
	Delivery media (flex disc, CD-ROM, ZIP, Internet, etc.)
	Manuals are generally structured like this:
	Cover, title page, and dedications
	Table of contents
	Preface or introduction
	Acknowledgments
	Manual content in a series of parts, chapters, topics, subtopics, etc.
	Appendix or appendices
	Index
	Keep content clear, organized, and consistent.
	Use drawings, pictures, charts, and graphs for explanation and clarity.
	Use an outside reader to check for clarity, flow, and consistency.
	Edit and proof for zero errors.
	Create mock-up.
	Use mock-up when dealing with printer. Obtain written bid with delivery date and penalties for lateness.

Exhibit 16.8

1608.DOC

Project Dissemination: Report Checklist

	Description
	Research profile of target audience (see File 1601.doc)
	Decide on purpose of report and
	Tailor content of report to the needs, interests, and desires of the target audience
	Tailor style, tone, and viewpoint of report to the type of target population
	Remember that the purpose of the report is not simply to inform but to convince and persuade
	A report, regardless of how short, will generally contain these parts (see Chapter 15 for full discussion)
	Front matter (cover, title page, and table of contents)
	Background information
	The questions to be answered in the report
	The procedures used to answer the questions
	The answers to the questions (findings)
	Conclusions based on findings
	Optional: recommendations, abstract, executive summary, and appendix
	Include complete contact information (phone, fax, e-mail, Website URL, etc.).
	Make the report no longer than necessary.
	Establish a "look" for your reports and maintain consistency (project logo is part of this).
	Use many clear and descriptive headings and break up large blocks of text.
	Use drawings, pictures, graphics, charts, and graphs to explain and clarify only, not for decoration.
	"Tell 'em what you're gonna tell 'em—tell 'em—then tell 'em what you told 'em."
	Introduce, explain, and summarize.
	This applies to each part, chapter, and topic.
	Do not use double spacing; no one likes double spacing except editors.
	For narrative use an attractive text font in an easy-to-read size.
	Create an attractive, self-explanatory, heavy-stock cover.
	Bind in a practical easy-to-use manner (for example, will the report need to lie flat?).
	Avoid expensive production items such as the use of four-color graphics or pictures.
	Give an impression of frugal professionalism. Do not be cheap but do not be extravagant, be prudent.

EXHIBIT 16.9   1609.DOC

Project Dissemination: Print Media (Periodical) Article Checklist

	Description
	Research profile of target audience, readers of periodical (see File 1601.doc).
	Obtain published issues of periodical.
	Match style and composition of your article to those published by periodical.
	In the "treatment" sent to the publisher be sure to:
	Toot your own horn (explain why you are the best person to write such an article).
	Summarize the content of the article.
	Explain the importance of the subject (material on this should be in the funded proposal).
	Explain how readers of the periodical will be interested in and benefit from the article.
	Give publisher a clear "hook;" a hook is a novel slant or point of view or opinion or comparison.
	When treatment is accepted, follow exactly the directions given to you by publisher.
	Send the proper length narrative, usually measured by number of words, not pages.
	Meet the publisher's deadlines, consider them absolute.
	If drawings, graphics, charts, or graphs used in article, provide "camera ready copy".
	If computer files are delivery method, ensure compatibility of versions of software.
	Get it done early, expect glitches, allow time to work them out.
	Write the article described in the treatment; do not unilaterally change any significant aspect.
	Avoid jargon and technical language unless you are *absolutely positive* it is OK (it normally is not).
	Use short paragraphs, no more than four short sentences (normally, but be guided by periodical style).
	Keep sentences short, avoid complex construction (normally, but be guided by periodical style).
	Articles for newspapers and newsletters are normally cut from the end forward, write accordingly.
	Write in active voice and use action verbs.
	If you raise questions, provide possible answers.

EXHIBIT 16.9 *(Continued)*

	Description
	Get article read by outside reader before submission; if reader is confused, so will be periodical readers.
	Edit and proof painstakingly; do not expect periodical staff to catch your mistakes.
	Proof numbers, dates, calculations, names, addresses, etc. with extraordinary care.
	Proof painstakingly the galley received from publisher (this is your last chance).
	Obtain "tear sheets" (copies of published article). This is part of project documentation.

major project event. The initial intent is to have the press release printed in the media outlet to which you send it. Therefore, a press release contains an actual newspaper or other media article that can be published "as is," perhaps along with other information. The format is standardized. You can find the format in most basic books about marketing. The key to an effective press release is to target the press release to the target audience of a media outlet. The secondary purpose of a press release is to get a media outlet interested enough in your event or project that they cover it in their publication using their own writers. Exhibit 16.10 (1610.doc) is a checklist for press release production.

E-mail

The use of e-mail as a communication tool should not be neglected. We know that many of you are reluctant to take the leap into cyberspace, but you must "screw your courage to the sticking-place," and get on with it. You may have to take the leap on faith, but please, please trust us, e-mail is the best communication tool since conversation, and we mean face-to-face communication. The telephone is handy, but it is rude. Who among us has not experienced this scenario? You are standing at the counter of some government agency. You have taken time off from work, battled traffic, won a parking place in a fierce contest of wills, explored a labyrinth of government hallways, and now stand triumphant at the right place before the right person. That person says, "Hello, can I help you?" You open your mouth to respond, and the telephone rings. What happens next? Your "right person" leaves you, abandons you, and ignores you, to answer the telephone. That is the definition of rude. E-mail, on the other hand, would have deposited a message in the person's electronic mailbox to be opened and responded to at a more appropriate

Exhibit 16.10

1610.DOC

Project Dissemination: Press Release Checklist

	Description
	Research profile of target audience, the readers of the target periodical (see File 1601.doc).
	Obtain published issues of periodical.
	Match style and composition of your press release to those published by periodical.
	Follow the format publishers expect, available in basic marketing texts and style handbooks.
	Be creative with content but NOT with format.
	Submit press release early enough for publication at appropriate time.
	To make your press release noticed among the many received:
	Make the subject clearly of interest to readers of the periodical.
	Provide information that is useful to and/or needed by readers.
	Solve a problem for readers.
	Create a catchy heading (headline). They probably will not use it, but they might.
	Create an intriguing first line that grabs reader's attention.
	Establish personal relation with publisher.
	Press releases get cut from the end forward to fit available space, write accordingly.
	If announcing an event open to the public be sure to:
	Describe the event fully.
	If a fundraising event, describe fully how the funds raised will be used.
	Include times and locations.
	Include discussion of any costs, or say clearly that the event is free.
	Include information about transportation and parking.
	Include any needed advice concerning environment or weather (bugs, no chairs, etc.).
	Be sure to give credit to grantor, partners, volunteers, and project participants.
	When mentioning a partner, have the partner read and approve the release before sending.
	Obtain tear sheets and distribute copies to grantor, partners, volunteers, and appropriate stakeholders.
	Keep and file copies of all published releases. This is project documentation.
	For help, consult books or a professional.

EXHIBIT 16.11

1611.DOC

Project Dissemination: E-mail Checklist

		Description
		Ensure that a correct active e-mail address is on every communication of any kind from the project
		Brochures
		Handouts, giveaways, business cards, and faxes
		Manuals and reports
		Video and audio productions (both on labels and in actual production)
		Articles and press releases
		Direct mail pieces
		E-mail and website
		Check and respond to e-mail faithfully. It is not a toy, it is a powerful communication tool.
		Responding on a schedule will "train" correspondents to trust e-mail as a communication method.
		Print and file important messages; most e-mail systems save messages for only so long.
		Diligently collect e-mail addresses from all contacts.
		Create personal e-mail "address book"—most e-mail programs have one. It saves time and mistakes.
		Put field in dissemination database for e-mail addresses.
		Integrate dissemination database with e-mail program for large scale e-mailing.
		Use e-mail for normal communications among project staff.
		Use e-mail for normal communications among project partners.
		Use e-mail for normal communications with service providers and consultants.
		Use filter (screening) program to block unwanted e-mail.
		Craft carefully any e-mail message sent for other than individual business purposes
		Write as carefully as a printed piece.
		Edit for grammar.
		Proof for misspellings and typos.
		Avoid large number of addresses (cc) in one transmission. Make the e-mail as personal as possible.
		Never download files from people you do not know (they can contain viruses).
		Shop for the right e-mail service (we prefer AOL, but then we have a site there, so we are biased).
		If in doubt about implementation, hardware, software, etc., obtain professional guidance.

time. Why do you think that everybody at work hides behind voice mail these days? It is because the telephone is a rude way of conducting business. Exhibit 16.11 (1611.doc) is a checklist for the use of e-mail in dissemination.

Direct Mail

Direct mail is sending a marketing piece that advertises your product or service through the mail. For some projects this can be an appropriate technique of information dissemination. If your project produces a product, it can also be a method of marketing the product and producing revenue for the project. Direct mail marketing is completely beyond the scope of this book. Many good books on the subject can be found in the business section of any well-stocked bookstore. Exhibit 16.12 (1612.doc) is a checklist for the use of direct mail in dissemination.

Internet and Website

Dissemination of project information via the Internet is fast growing into major importance. Creating a project web page and working to establish links to and from other appropriate websites is an excellent way to broadcast information about your project. If done thoroughly and well, your site can become an authoritative source of information for organizations around the world. Exhibit 16.13 (1613.doc) is a checklist for the use of the Internet and a website in dissemination.

Dissemination Database

A powerful tool for dissemination of project information is a database of interested or possibly interested people and groups. Such a database is the foundation of any direct mail campaign. The database should be constantly expanded with contacts made through dissemination efforts. A computer database is not absolutely necessary. With three-by-five cards and enough time you can do almost everything a computer database can. However, a computer database integrated with a word processor capable of mail merge allows "form" letters to be customized to individual readers. The database software chosen should be capable of easy modification and manipulation and have the capacity to handle the number of contacts you expect to gather. The amount of information that can be stored in a properly constructed database is enormous and can be extremely useful if managed properly. One properly constructed database can serve for both stakeholders and more casual contacts. This means that for key

Exhibit 16.12

1612.DOC

Project Dissemination: Direct Mail Checklist

	Description
	Collect names and addresses diligently at all opportunities.
	Personal communications
	Formal presentations
	Exhibits
	From partners
	Project events
	Information inquiries
	Direct mail can be used for:
	Fundraising
	Project information dissemination
	Marketing project services
	Marketing project products
	Take advantage of nonprofit bulk mail rates.
	Obtain and comply with all Postal Service regulations.
	Research profile of target audience (see File 1601.doc).
	Research successful direct mail strategies.
	Craft carefully all aspects of a direct mail piece.
	Appearance of mailing envelope
	Appearance of inside pieces
	Content and style of message
	Content and style of response piece
	Include a clear call to action: Tell the recipient exactly what you want them to do.
	Give complete contact information in all direct mail pieces, including e-mail and website.
	Code each mailing for tracking purposes.
	Track response rate of direct mail pieces.
	Test mail a limited number of a new piece before investing in a mass mailing.
	If in doubt, obtain professional guidance.

EXHIBIT 16.13

Project Dissemination: Internet and Website Checklist

	Description
	Shop for an appropriate provider of Internet access and website server, consider:
	Cost
	Speed and number of access lines
	Storage capacity for website and cost as size of site expands
	Reliability
	Full featured e-mail service
	Website should be useful, professional, information packed, and easy to use, not flashy and gaudy.
	When building website, above all make it "load" fast. Not everyone will have a high-speed modem.
	Avoid complicated backgrounds.
	Use graphic and colors, but keep it simple and uncluttered.
	Avoid "frames," which slows loading time.
	Use all the gimmicks you need, but only what you need. Do not use just because it looks "cool."
	Give away lots of information, and update regularly. Make it worthwhile for visitors to return.
	Ensure that the HTML (hypertext markup language) web builder that you use is compatible with most web browsers.
	Establish links to other related websites.
	Actively pursue the establishment of links from other related websites to yours.
	Actively pursue becoming registered on as many search engines as possible.
	Construct your website for maximum exposure to web searchers.
	Put an automatic counter on the site so you know how many "hits" are occurring.
	Solicit e-mail from interested visitors.
	Provide "smart forms" to:
	Gather information about visitors
	Get requests for information
	Collect comments and suggestions
	Take orders for products
	Seek professional guidance if necessary.

EXHIBIT 16.14

1614.DOC

Project Dissemination: Database Checklist

	Description
	Create data fields to capture the following information:
	Category of entry (key stakeholder, stakeholder, target audience, information contact, etc.)
	Source of entry (personal communication, exhibit, website, etc.)
	Date database entry initiated
	Name (first, middle, and last)
	Job title (President, Mail Clerk, Director of Development, etc.)
	Courtesy title (Mr., Ms., Mrs., etc.)
	Professional title (MD, PhD, EdD, MSW, etc.)
	Name of business, organization, or agency
	Street address of business, organization, or agency (allow three lines for government addresses)
	City, State, Zip Code (nine digits and dash, 12345-1234)
	Country (if applicable)
	Main organization voice line
	Direct voice line or extension to main number
	Fax line
	Cell phone
	Pager number
	E-mail address—work
	Home address
	Home phone
	Home fax
	Home e-mail address
	Birthday (year not usually necessary)
	Appropriate personal information such as:
	Spouse's name and birthday, anniversary date (may be "significant other")
	Children's names and birthday
	Interests, needs, and desires in relation to project (scrollable field)
	Contact history (parallel linked scrollable fields)

EXHIBIT 16.14 *(Continued)*

		Description
		Date
		Type (phone, fax, mail, e-mail, meeting, report delivered, etc.)
		Content or purpose of contact
		Outcome of contact
		Action item resulting from contact
		Any special "flag" field(s) needed for sorting (partner, volunteer, stakeholder, etc.)
	The database should be capable of:	
		Handling, at speed, the number and size of records contemplated
		Creating multiple display screens
		Finding and sorting on any field or group of fields
		Integrating with work processor for mail merge, or performing mail merge on its own
		Integrating with e-mail program for large scale e-mailing
		Notification of special events (birthdays, anniversaries, action items, etc.)
		Printing labels of various size
		Creating and printing customized reports
		Flagging duplicates even if spellings are not perfect matches
		Spell checking entries, and adding words to spell checker dictionary
		Being password protected (information may be confidential)
		Creating scroll boxes that can hold large amounts of data
		Intelligent data entry (finishes entry for common words, cities, states, etc.)
	Continually purge and screen to keep database "clean."	
	Backup every day (as with all computer matters, it is not a matter of "if" a crash will occur, only "when")	
	For mission critical files, transport backup off site each day (in case of fire, flood, etc.)	
	Obtain professional help when necessary	

stakeholders many fields will be used, while for simple information contacts, relatively few fields will be used. Creating different display screens for different purposes effectively hides unused data fields. Exhibit 16.14 (1614.doc) provides a checklist of information to capture as well as pointers in setting up and managing a dissemination database.

Project Objective with Budget

It should be manifestly obvious by now that dissemination takes time and money to accomplish. The grantor knows and expects this. One way to ensure that a grantor sees your commitment to dissemination is to make the dissemination a project objective, probably under the Manage and Communicate goal. As a project objective, it has its own set of activities, people assigned responsibility for activities, resources allocated for the activities, and money in the budget. Money may need to be allocated for such things as consultants, printing, production facilities, and technicians. A grantor expects your dissemination to cost something. In fact, budgeting no money for dissemination activities raises a red flag with most grantors.

Wise Guy

Oh, I'm good at tootin' my own horn. This'll be fun. As my daddy always said, "It ain't bragging if it's true." And, I've wanted to be a movie producer since I was a kid. Seriously, I really didn't know that dissemination was so important to the grantor. It seems like such a throwaway part of a proposal, at least I always treated it like that.

Wise Lady

Actually it is fun. Yes, it is important to the grantor. Remember that making a grant award is not charity. It's an investment in starting up something or seeding something that will grow and prosper. It's a way of impacting change and advancement toward solving a problem. If no one knows about it, then how can others benefit? Once I talked to a grantor who was grumbling about the reticence of awardees to share information. He said, "I'm tired of funding projects for four kids in a closet." Your dissemination plan is very important to the funder.

Conclusion

Dissemination of project implementation serves two purposes. One is to keep key stakeholders informed so they will help with continuation. The other purpose is to encourage replication, to give other people and organizations the information they need to know if your solution is right for them, and how to implement the solution if they choose to do so. There is one other use of dissemination, but it actually falls under a whole other discussion that we are not having in this book. Some grant projects are intended to produce a product, and the expectation is that the product will then be marketed and sold. Still, the underlying reason for the project is to solve a problem. The product is seen as a solution that other people or organizations can purchase and apply. This means that a business plan becomes part of the project plan. In any business plan, marketing is a prime consideration. Publicity and advertising are key elements in marketing. Dissemination bears close resemblance to publicity and advertising, as you no doubt have noticed.

That first purpose of dissemination, to help with continuation, is the subject of Chapter 17. Continuing the project, the solution, after the grantor's money runs out is one of the most misunderstood topics in the field of grants. We hope to clear up a lot of misunderstanding and clarify what is, in reality, simple. We also hope to give you a step-by-step approach to continuation, something we doubt that you have seen elsewhere.

Managing Continuation

**Great is the art of beginning, but
greater is the art of ending.**
Henry Wadsworth Longfellow,
Elegiac Verse

Introduction

Continuation seems impossible for almost every beginner seeking grants and managing grant projects. Knowing that is probably small consolation. You want answers. You want to know what to do. With that in mind, we will work very hard to make continuation a conceivable, believable process by the end of this chapter.

Continuation is only one of several terms used to mean "continuing a project after the term of the grant." Another term used in the place of continuation is sustainment or sustainability. At times you might be asked how you intend to institutionalize your project or solution. In this case, institutionalize means continue, as in make the project a normal operating part of your institution. And, you might even be asked about the survivability of your project. How will your project survive after the grantor's funds run out? Multiple names for the same thing are common throughout the field of grants. Why should continuation be any different?

Applications will be evaluated against the standard criteria listed below. . . .

5. . . . ; and the feasibility of plans to sustain the project after federal grant support is ended.

*Program Guide FY 1999, Rural Health Outreach Grant Program,
U.S. Department of Health and Human Services*

Sustainability. To be competitive, a project should exhibit economic and organizational viability beyond the grant period. You should

therefore present a credible plan that includes a discussion of antici-
pated ongoing expenses and potential sources of non-federal funds to
sustain the project.

Application Kit for Fiscal Year 1999, Telecommunications and
Information Infrastructure Assistance Program (TIIAP)
U.S. Department of Commerce

(f) Commitment and capacity (10 points)
(1) The Secretary reviews each application to determine whether
the applicant is likely to continue the magnet school activities
after assistance . . . is no longer available.

Selection Criteria 1999, Magnet School Program
U.S. Department of Education

Chat with a Grantor

The way you handle continuation is a direct and open window for the
grantor to get a clear view into your heart, enabling a grantor to gauge
your sincerity or your lack of it. The reasoning follows this imaginary conversation between a grantor and an applicant (grantee).

"About your proposed project," the grantor asks. "That project is a solution to a problem, right?"

"Yes," the grantee responds, "it is."

"Let me ask you then," the grantor queries, "will that problem be
solved and gone at the end of the term of my grant?"

Answering, the grantee says, "We do expect things to have gotten better, we expect to have made a lot of progress, but no, the problem will not
be solved and gone."

"Yes, exactly. Now, let's assume that your proposed solution works,"
says the grantor. "We will know if it does from the results of the evaluation, and we will assume for this discussion that the evaluation results
are great."

"Yes," the grantee responds, "we believe that our evaluation plan is
comprehensive, and we will be able to show conclusively that our project
makes real progress against the problem."

"Yes, exactly. It seems reasonable for me to assume then," the grantor
continues, "that if you are sincere about solving the problem, and if you
are sincere about helping your target population, you must want very
much for the project to continue to apply your proven solution after my
grant runs out."

"Yes, of course we want our project to continue," agrees the grantee,
"but there is just no way that is going to be possible without getting more
grant money."

"You, then," answers the grantor sadly, "are not a good candidate for a grant to start with. The purpose of our grant money is not to fund your solution into perpetuity. The overall purpose of our grant making is twofold. First, we want to see what solutions will work, so we fund a number of projects to attempt to find successful solutions. Second, we see our role as providing 'risk capital,' or 'venture capital,' to help nonprofits start up innovative problem-solving projects. We recognize that the projects we fund have a fair chance of failure. We fund start-up projects that an organization like yours might not take the risk to do on your own. It may seem as though we have huge amounts of money, but in comparison to the work that needs doing, our funds are tiny. We multiply, or leverage, our limited funds by picking and choosing, among nonprofits such as yours, projects in situations that we think have a good chance of success and that have a reasonable chance of going on after our grant funds run out. Yes, we could help you year after year. And that would be one less innovative solution that is given a chance. We are trying to provide the best 'bang for our buck' by continuing the search for solutions that work. It is your job, as the nonprofit on the ground, in the trenches, to do the hard slogging, to find ways to keep successful solutions going. It is hard work. We understand that, but when it proves impossible to get support in a community for a solution that can be shown to work, you need to ask yourself why the community values the solution so little. Is it a lack of understanding? Or is it that among all the competing needs, yours is not a high enough priority? To you, to your organization, it seems very important, critically important. Perhaps to the community at large the problem simply seems only unfortunate. Weighed against other needs, it loses out. Fighting these battles is the job of the nonprofit on the street, not the grantor. Unless, that is, you can show an innovative approach to solve this problem. We might be interested in that. In closing, you may not agree with our approach, but we hope you see now why we do things this way, and we hope you now understand why we will not be funding your proposed project. But maybe you would like to think over this other problem and submit a proposal on that. A workable solution could be used all over the country by hundreds of nonprofits. You could make a real difference."

The Lesson of the Chat

How many of us would love to sit down with a grantor and have such a conversation? Perhaps if we talked long enough, and about enough different subjects, we would begin to see with grantor's eyes. And when we see with grantor's eyes, we observe situations in a new light. What before seemed a perfect example of pettifoggery, now might become clear and reasonable. Successful grant seekers see with grantor's eyes. They see their projects and their proposals as a grantor sees them. To a grantor, this seemingly small issue of continuation is gigantically important. How you treat continuation goes to the heart of your passion, your sincerity, and your commitment.

When we are passionate, sincere, and committed to solving a problem, we work and plan and organize until we find a way for our successful solution to continue solving the problem. When we are passionate, sincere, and committed to helping our target population, we scratch and claw and fight until we find a way for our solution to continue to help them. Grantors are looking for grantees that are passionate about their cause, grantees that have strong feelings that are ardent, intense, and vehement. Grantors are looking for grantees that are sincere about their cause, grantees that are truthful, honest, genuine, and real. Grantors are looking for grantees that are committed to their cause, grantees that bind themselves to their cause, that pledge themselves, that promise and produce action.

When we ignore continuation activities we send a clear and direct message to the grantor that we are not passionate, we are not sincere, and we are not committed to solving the problem. We just want to take the money and run.

This simple truth gives to the continuation plan in your grant proposal and to your continuation activities in your project much more importance than is evident at first glance. The continuation plan in a proposal is a short section, and the temptation to give it short shrift is hard to withstand. The result of shortchanging the continuation section is usually an unfunded proposal. The continuation activities of a project are few and relatively simple. The temptation is to put them off until the last possible moment. This is a recipe for disaster. It is the formula for watching your beloved project wither and die.

Projects That Should Not Continue

Another truth about continuation is that all grant projects do not need to continue. Some projects are carried out with a single, achievable goal in mind, and when that goal is accomplished, the need for the project is over. An example of this is the planning grant. The purpose of the grant is to fund a planning project. The purpose of the planning project is to do the research, writing, and other work necessary to create a realistic plan of action for the solution of a problem. Usually we already know what the broad problem is. What we don't know is what to do about it, how to go about solving it. A planning grant for a planning project gives us the time and money to put together a plan that has a good chance of succeeding. We would like to make just one simple point about planning projects, however. The end point of the planning project is not, or rather should not, be to create a plan. Rather, the end point of a planning project is the starting point for implementing the plan, your solution to your problem. The purpose of planning is not to create a plan. The purpose of planning is to create progress, change, innovation, action.

There is a second category of project that does not need to continue. This is the project that does not work. All the good intentions in the world cannot change the fact that some projects fail. It is not to anyone's benefit to expend time, money, and resources on a solution that is not working. It breaks the hearts of those who tried hard to make the solution work. Those people are often incapable of seeing that the solution simply isn't working. They will ask and beg to be able to continue. They believe fervently that if they just work harder, or smarter, or faster, or use more computers, or get new software, or hire more trainers, or do any of the hundreds of things attempted when trying to prevent failure, they can make the solution work. Sometimes they are right, and sometimes they are wrong. But it still remains that there is no reason, except perhaps for an employee of the project to stay employed, to continue a project when it has demonstrated that it does not work. Organizations and agencies cannot stand the drain on time, money, and resources. Simply put, there is too much that needs doing, too much demand for limited resources, to continue to do things that are not working. Listen to what B.F. Skinner has to say about a similar situation:

> I remember the rage I used to feel when a prediction went awry. I could have shouted at the subjects of my experiments, "Behave, damn you, behave as you ought!" Eventually I realized that the subjects were always right. It was I who was wrong. I had made a bad prediction."
>
> *B. F. Skinner,* Walden Two

The outcomes of projects are predictions also, and sometimes we make "a bad prediction." When we do, admit it, learn from it, and move on. As Einstein told us, "Continuing to do the same thing while expecting different outcomes is a definition of insanity."

In summary, two types of projects are not candidates for continuing: (1) the project that can achieve its purpose during the term of the grant and (2) the project that is not succeeding. For the sake of this chapter, however, we assume that your project is the type of problem-solving project that needs to continue. We also assume that your project is successful. You can demonstrate that your solution works and indeed is working. Therefore, from this point on, we talk no more about not continuing projects, but we focus on the thought, management, and activities that go into continuing a project after the grantor's money runs out.

Introduction to Rest of Chapter

We make several major points in this chapter. We discuss the proposal killer aspect of continuation. The next point is that the key to continuation, as to so much in grant project management, is in the project design and development. So, once more, we come back to a point we've made time and again. The simplest way to avoid problems is to design them out of the project to start with. Our next major point is to explain the philosophy of continuation. Who might be interested in helping you and why? Finally we discuss the activities involved in continuation.

The Proposal Killer

We have already agreed that two types of projects do not need to continue—those that do not work and those that complete their purpose during the term of the grant. The viewpoint of this proposal killer section is that you are creating your proposal, getting ready to submit. In that case we can eliminate projects that do not work from our discussion, since we assume that our project, if funded, will work. We have not started the project yet so optimism runs rampant. We also eliminate from our discussion the type of project that will fulfill its purpose during the term of the grant. Our project is not going to be like that. What we have is a project with the potential to solve a serious problem in our community, our state, our region, and in our country. That is how we present the situation to the grantor.

We show our community need. We show that this same problem exists in many places. The widespread nature of our problem means that if our solution works, it can have a real impact on the problem, perhaps even nationwide. Our problem is an ongoing one. A new generation or a new population is always growing or moving into the problem, so even once we demonstrate a solution that works, the solution needs to be applied continuously to have long-term impact.

We develop our project carefully, with detail and thoroughness. Our goals and objectives fairly sing. We understand how to evaluate both our processes and our outcomes, and we detail a good evaluation plan. Everything is falling into place. And then we come to create the continuation plan. We think, we scheme, we brainstorm, and we cannot find a realistic way to continue the project beyond the term of the grant. So, we put into the continuation plan that 25 percent of the effort of the full-time, grant-funded Project Director will be spent seeking grants to continue the project. Surely this commitment will impress the grantor.

As did Frankenstein, we have created a monster, in our case a proposal killer—a cancer eating away at our chance of being awarded the grant. The simple truth is embodied in this blunt statement. If you cannot see a way to continue your project after the term of the grant, do not bother to apply. Grantors are not stupid. They are not slow. Grantors have read thousands of proposals over the years. They have funded hundreds of programs over the same years. From experience it becomes obvious to them which continuation plans are realistic and which are dreams. They have experience.

Do not make this mistake. Many grantees, when they speak with representatives from a grantor, find the person to be deferential to the grantee's knowledge and expertise in the area of the proposed project. This can mislead the grantee into believing that the grantor does not truly know its business. Nothing could be further from the truth. Grantors may not understand your subject matter area, but they understand grant making. They understand what they have asked for in a proposal, and they recognize when they do not get it.

Another mistake is to look at little statements such as, "show how you will continue the project after the term of the grant," as just throwaway items. Surely those 13 words do not have much weight and meaning when stacked against all the verbiage in the application package. Why, they spent three times more words telling me how to fill out block 24a on form 56-3H than they did talking about continuation. You have fallen into a major trap. The importance of a thing in grant seeking has no relation to the amount of space the thing occupies. In fact, one of the parts of a proposal that takes up the most space is often one of the least important, and that is the project narrative. Yes, the narrative provides detail, but the heart of the project is in the problem statement and the goals and objectives. The money is in the budget. Evaluation, dissemination, project management, continuation, and documentation usually have their own sections. Key personnel are explained elsewhere. The time lines give the project schedule. The fact is that the longest part of a proposal may well be the least important part. Never judge the importance of a thing in grant seeking by its size.

Project Design and Development

The Worker Bee Problem

Never use grant funds to hire worker bees. Worker bees are those indispensable people in every organization who get things done. The people who do the daily chores, who file and sort and data enter, who research and carry and stack, who collate, staple, and bind, who teach, organize, and clean, who travel and meet and sell, and who generally do the work that makes the place tick. Worker bees—no organization survives without them. And, you should never hire worker bees with grant funds.

When you hire worker bees with grant funds, what happens when the grant runs out? The work stops. Yes, yes, the temptation is great, especially for those of you in direct services. Your lament is, "the only way we increase our impact is with more staff." Once we sat next to a sincere, dedicated director of a community service nonprofit at a proposer's conference held by a federal grantor. As the grant program director discussed continuation, she made it clear that if proposed projects intended to hire staff with grant funds, that applicants would need to show concretely that they would continue to fund those staff positions after the term of the grant. The director of the nonprofit sitting next to us hurriedly and disgustedly dashed a note onto a three-by-five card and flipped it over to us. The note said, "More staff is the only thing I need, and I can't get it here." He packed his briefcase and left. Was he being unreasonable? No, he was being realistic. When your needs and the grantor's agenda do not align, there is no reason to apply. Find another program, one that makes the match between you and your project and the grantor and its needs.

By this time you might be ready to ask this question. "If we can't hire worker bees with a grant, just what can we do with it?" That is an excellent question and one that gets right to one of the core issues about the purpose of grants and the process of continuation. We are supposed to use the grant money to increase institutional capacity and intellectual capital. We have just been invaded by jargon. We hope that this book has a wide audience, so we avoided the jargon in any particular field to try our best to make it easier to read and understand. We suspect you do not believe us about not using jargon when it comes to the chapters on evaluation. We tried, but now let's get back to our topic. What is institutional capacity, and what does it mean to increase it? Also, what is intellectual capital, and what does it mean to increase it?

Institutional capacity is the sum total of your organization's capabilities to serve its target population. To get an idea of what that means, do the following. List all the target populations you serve. List all the services you provide. Figure out how many of each target population there are to whom you can provide services at any given time. This is one way to look at institutional capacity. The basic idea is simple—how much can we do for how many? Increasing institutional capacity is increasing the number of services, or increasing the capacity of services, or increasing the quality of services, or increasing the target populations that can be served. "That's all well and good," you might say, "but what does increasing institutional capacity look like in concrete terms?"

Assume your organization teaches job skills to females who are head of household and who have children. You provide day care while the mothers are in training. You upgrade the day care to include child development activities, and you expand your training into the computer skills of word processing and database management. You have just increased your institutional capacity. You did this by purchasing the necessary materials and training the existing day care providers on child development activities, and partnering with the necessary agencies and professionals to monitor the quality. You did this by upgrading your computers and software and training several job trainers on the new curriculum.

Intellectual capital is the sum total of the knowledge held by your organization. Most, if not all, of this knowledge is in the heads of your staff. Increasing intellectual capital is done with training and education. A serious problem is that job turnover depletes intellectual capital. Whenever a grant project has a professional development component, that component increases the intellectual capital of your organization, but job turnover can undo the professional development in a short time. What is the answer? Use a "train the trainer" model when developing a professional development component of a grant project. Trainers can do two things. They can train, of course, but they can also clone themselves, that is, train more trainers. If you spend grant money on training trainers, then when job turnover depletes the training, you simply hold more training sessions. If one of your cadre of trainers leaves, you have an existing trainer train in another one. This process institutionalizes the intellectual capital so it remains part of your organization as long as trainers are vigilant to see that everyone remains trained.

This all relates to a grant project like this. Use grant money to increase institutional capacity by purchasing equipment, materials, renovations, upgrades, wiring, and services that after the term of the grant will remain in place. Use grant money to increase intellectual capacity by using a train the trainer model and thereby institutionalizing the new knowledge in your organization.

You may hire a person if you hire expertise. The person you hire must be an expert and must know that the contract is for a limited time. Often a service provider or a consultant will work out better than an employee. When the person works for your organization, the purpose of this person is NOT to get day-to-day work done, but rather to increase institutional capacity and intellectual capital. You spend the time they have with you getting everything they know into the brains of your staff and onto paper in the form of manuals and procedures, and trouble-shooting guides and instructions and training curriculum. This, grantors love. And this knowledge enables you to continue the project much more easily after the term of the grant has been completed.

The Money Problem

A common lament among grant seekers is that continuation is impossible, because there is no way to come up with that much money after the grant runs out. The thinking is that it takes the same amount of money to continue a project as it did to get it going during the term of the grant. But, if we developed our project as we suggested under the worker bee topic above, will it then cost as much to continue the project as it did to get it started? The answer is, of course, no.

Yes, if your project is heavy with staff, then the continuation costs remain high, but if you stay away as much as possible from staff, continuation costs will go down dramatically. One concrete way to show to a grantor that this is happening is to decrease the amount of money you request each year for any multiyear project. The largest expenditures should be the first two or three years, then spending should taper down dramatically. This shows in concrete terms what is going on, where you are headed with respect to cost of continuation, and therefore your chances of continuation.

Continuation Philosophy

Make two assumptions. Number one, you have not loaded up on staff positions that you cannot fund after the term of the grant. Number two, you do not need as much money to continue the project as it took to get it up and running. As you now know, these assumptions will be true only if you designed and developed your project properly from the very beginning. With these two assumptions in place we can move to the two pieces of continuation philosophy that allow you to continue your project after the grantor's money runs out. The first point is that your stakeholders are the source of continuation resources. And the second point is to break up continuation needs into small chunks and spread them around.

Stakeholders

Stakeholders, as you know, are people or organizations that have an interest in the operation or outcome(s) of your project. You are looking for stakeholders that will benefit from the success of your project. If a stakeholder benefits when your project succeeds, you have leverage, something in common that is of interest to you both. You can make the case that it is in the best interest of the stakeholder to see that the project continues so the benefit can continue.

At times your search for stakeholders will lead you to list such groups as community members, shoppers, citizens, drivers, or other general labels for large segments of your local population. When this happens, and it will, think of what organization exerts power or influence because of this group. This logic will lead you to elected entities such as county council and city, town, or village council. The names of such governing entities vary from place to place. You may have alderpersons or an assembly, but the principle remains the same.

Three key stakeholders often get left off the stakeholder list: project participants, community citizens, and the grantee organization. Do not forget that your own organization is always a key stakeholder. Do not make the hasty assumption that your organization or agency would never take on continuation costs. If your project is successful, and if your project has the backing of large portions of the community (through stakeholders), then your organization might well be forced by public opinion to continue the project. Keep in mind, though, that you are competing for possibly scarce resources, and if you are the winner, it is possible that someone else loses. As an aid to keep track of your stakeholders and their interests, we have included Exhibit 17.1 (1701.doc).

Keep Stakeholders Informed. Keep stakeholders informed from the beginning of the project. Keep stakeholders informed about the aspects of the project that interest them and in which they have a stake in the success. Report to stakeholders regularly and formally. This generally means in writing. Telephone calls are useful as a personal touch, but the written, regular reporting shows professionalism of the highest order. There are, of course, many other ways to communicate information to stakeholders such as television, radio, newsletter, newspaper articles, and many more. Refer to Chapter 16 for a discussion of all the ways that information can be distributed. This subtopic, "Keep stakeholders informed," actually refers back to the topic of Chapter 16. One of the main purposes of dissemination of information is to create support among stakeholders so that your project can continue, and one of the main ways continuation is ensured is to keep stakeholders informed. Project information dissemination and project continuation go hand-in-hand. Both need each other.

When completing the information required in Exhibit 17.1 (1701.doc) from the previous subtopic, you will have listed matching goals and objectives along with matching evaluation questions. The information pointed to by these items provides ongoing information collected by your formative evaluation measures that make up a large part of what you communicate to stakeholders. Properly documenting all aspects of your project progress makes keeping stakeholders informed much easier. Documentation is discussed in Chapter 7 and plays a key part here in continuation.

The tool provided in Exhibit 17.2 (1702.doc) is intended for tracking the information provided to a single stakeholder (target population).

EXHIBIT 17.1

Continuation Plan: Stakeholder Information

Stakeholder	Key Interests	Matching Goals & Objectives	Matching Evaluation Question
1. Grantee Organization			
2. Target Population			
3. Community Citizens			
4. Partner Organization			
5. Partner Organization			
6.			
7.			
8.			
9.			
10.			

EXHIBIT 17.2 1702.DOC

Continuation Plan: Keeping Stakeholders Informed Worksheet

Project Year _____

Stakeholder Name	
Address	
Contact Person	
Phone	
Fax	
E-mail	

Information to report*	When	Method of distribution
Announcement of grant award	On award	
Announcement of project start	On project start	
Progress update	End of PM 3	
Progress update	End of PM 6	
Progress update	End of PM 9	
Progress update	End of PY (PM 12)	
Event announcement/invitation		
Event announcement/invitation		
Event announcement/invitation		
Event announcement/invitation		
Availability/sample of product		
Availability/sample of product		
Availability/sample of product		
Availability/sample of product		
Availability/sample of product		

*See Chapter Sixteen, topic "What do we disseminate?" for additional items.

Therefore, you need to print this worksheet as many times as necessary so each stakeholder has its own tracking tool. If a group of stakeholders have similar profiles, then they can all be tracked using one copy of the tool. To identify the needs of stakeholders and the appropriate method of delivery for each stakeholder, use Exhibit 16.1 (1601.doc). Note from the content of Exhibit 17.2 (1702.doc) that we suggest reporting to stakeholders no less than quarterly (every three months). You may report more often, but you may not report less. If you want continuation help from your stakeholders, you must keep them informed and keep them interested. Regular, consistent reporting is essential.

Revenue Generation. Revenue generation is an excellent method of cutting the amount of continuation funding needed. If a project can be made self-supporting by revenue generation, then that solves the entire continuation problem. Generating revenue is a foreign concept for many in the nonprofit world, and certain types of service providers have difficulty generating any revenue at all. That does not mean that all nonprofit organizations and agencies cannot make money from projects, it just means that it might take a bit of creativity. The most obvious place to look for revenue is the worst, the target population. Although it is at times possible to raise revenue from a target population, many, if not most, nonprofits provide free services precisely because a target population is unable to pay for them in the marketplace. This means that we need to look elsewhere for our revenue. In general, revenue generation divides into two basic types: sale of product and events. The types of products that can be produced by a grant project are many and varied. Examples of products are: curriculum, software, procedure manuals, evaluation instruments, video productions, products produced by the target population, and consultations. Events can be anything from arts festivals to tractor pulls, from ballet performances to mud wrestling, from opera to rap, from elegant dining to hot dogs on the sidewalk. Chapters 6 and 10 contain information useful in the pursuit of revenue generation. The form provided in Exhibit 17.3 (1703.doc) will help you think through the revenue generation possibilities of your project.

Generating revenue from products and events calls for additional skills that are beyond the scope of this book. You will need a marketing plan. An assortment of good books containing instructions on creating a marketing plan can be found in the business section of any well-stocked bookstore. One thing to note is that our continuation plan is itself a marketing plan, in this case for the grant project itself. The philosophy of a marketing plan is simple. There is, of course, much more, but these are the basic steps.

EXHIBIT 17.3

1703.DOC

Continuation Plan: Revenue Generation Worksheet

Revenue Generation from Products					
Identify Possible Products	**Identify Target Market for Product**	**Size of Target Market**	**Cost of Product**	**Estimate Number Sold**	**Revenue from Product**
Procedure manual					
Curriculum or training course					
Curriculum/training material					
Book or other literature					
Software					
Video production					
Audio production					
Product of target population					
	Total Product Revenue for Year				

1. Identify your market (individuals or organizations with an interest in purchasing your product or service).
2. Set price of your goods or services based on production costs and market price range.
3. Identify ways to get your message to your target market.
4. Produce targeted marketing materials.
5. Deliver marketing material to target market.

Pieces

A major stumbling block to many continuation philosophies is thinking that the resources needed for continuation should come from one source. Break your continuation needs down into smaller, manageable pieces. To do this you will need a budget for the first year of project operation after the term of the grant, the first year of continuation. Compute the needed resources of the following types: (1) personnel and fringe, (2) travel, (3) stipends, (4) services and consultants, (5) real property, (6) equipment, (7) materials and supplies, and (8) facilities. Look at each small piece and decide if cash is needed or a donation (in-kind) will work just as well. Assign the appropriate stakeholder to approach for each small piece of the continuation budget. Exhibit 17.4 (1704.doc) will help you with this activity.

Not Only Cash

Another major stumbling block for project continuation is to think only in terms of cash. Think deeply about each different continuation resource need. Are there ways that in-kind contributions can substitute for cash? When there are, go for the in-kind. It is easier to get than cash. A column in Exhibit 17.4 (1704.doc) allows you to record which resources can be in-kind and which must be cash.

Make Concrete

When approaching a stakeholder for continuation resources, if at all possible, make your case in terms of return on investment, not in terms of statistics, good will, or public relations. Do not talk of reducing juvenile crime by 20 percent. Rather, make the case that an investment of $10,000 in your program will return $100,000 to the community because of reduced use of police, court, social, and incarceration services; because of reduced damage due to vandalism; and because of reduced time lost by community citizens. Remember that the investment can be in-kind as well as cash. The return on investment will not be in the form of cash, but in the form of unused resources by stakeholders. This frees up these resources to attack other community problems.

EXHIBIT 17.4

1704.DOC

Continuation Plan Project Budget Worksheet: One Year of Continuation Costs

Budget Item Description	Line Total	Amount Covered by Revenue	Amount Needed	Cash or In-kind	Stakeholder
1. Personnel & Fringe					
2. Travel					
3. Stipends					
4. Services & Consultants					
5. Real Property					
6. Equipment					
7. Materials & Supplies					
Totals					

    Translating the outcomes of your project into terms of return on investment can be a challenging task. It will take imagination, and it will force you to think like a stakeholder, not a bad thing at all. Exhibit 17.5 (1705.doc) provides guidance in this challenging but extremely important task. Keep in mind that the basis for calculating a return on investment

EXHIBIT 17.5

Continuation Plan: Return on Investment Worksheet

Stakeholder Name	
Address	
Contact Person	
Phone	
Fax	
E-mail	

#	Evaluation Question	Criteria	Benefit to Stakeholder if Criteria Met	Dollar Value of Benefit Per Person/ Event	Qty Person/ Event	Total Dollar Value of Benefit (return on investment)	Investment Amount (continuation request)
Total Return on Investment Compared to Investment							

will change for each stakeholder. What a stakeholder considers important is based on that stakeholder's needs, which you identified with Exhibit 17.1 (1701.doc). The matching evaluation question (from Exhibit 17.1 (1701.doc)) paired with its measurement criteria (from Exhibit 13.5 (1305.doc)) provides the basis from which the return on investment is calculated using Exhibit 17.5 (1705.doc).

Continuation Activities

For the following set of continuation activities to work effectively, two assumptions must be true. The first assumption is that the project is developed such that continuation does not need funding for salaries and wages. The second assumption is that the project needs substantially less money to continue than it did during the grant term. With those two assumptions in mind, the following list contains the step-by-step procedure for implementing continuation activities:

1. Identify stakeholders capable of providing continuation resources.
2. Identify key interests of each stakeholder.
3. Match key interests of stakeholders with specific goals and objectives.
4. Ask evaluation question(s) about each stakeholder's key interests, both formative and summative.
5. Keep key stakeholders informed about their key interests from the start of the project and on a regular basis, the more personal the contact the better, but make it official, in writing.
6. Identify methods and calculate amount of revenue generation.
7. Create a project budget for the first year of continuation.
8. Determine what parts of the project budget could be provided by in-kind contributions.
9. Identify a part or portion of the needed continuation resources appropriate for each stakeholder, cash or in-kind.
10. Several months before the term of the grant expires, translate project outcomes into return on investment statements for each stakeholder.
11. Approach each stakeholder separately, no big meetings. Show project results, explain return on investment, ask for their share of continuation resources.

Exhibit 17.6 (1706.doc) is a checklist format tool, the purpose of which is to keep the steps in continuation before you in a simple one-page

EXHIBIT 17.6   1706.DOC

Continuation Plan: Activities Checklist

	Description of Activity	Exhibit to Use
	1. Identify stakeholders capable of providing continuation resources.	17.1
	2. Identify key interests of each stakeholder.	17.1
	3. Match key interests of stakeholders with specific goals and objectives.	17.1
	4. Ask evaluation questions(s) about each stakeholder's key interests, both formative and summative.	17.1
	5. Keep key stakeholders informed.	17.2
	6. Identify methods and calculate amount of revenue generation.	17.3
	7. Create a project budget for the first year of continuation.	17.4
	8. Determine what parts of the project budget could be provided by in-kind contributions.	17.4
	9. Identify a part or portion of the needed continuation resources appropriate for each stakeholder, cash or in-kind.	17.4
	10. Translate project outcomes into return on investment statements for each stakeholder.	17.5
	11. Approach each stakeholder, explain return on investment, and request continuation resource, cash or in-kind.	

format. This checklist refers to other tools that are needed to accomplish the continuation activities.

Project Objective with Budget

Continuation is a small but very important part of any project. Continuation should be a project objective, falling under the Manage and Communicate goal, and just as any other project component, the continuation objective needs its own budget. You need money to spend on continuation activities. Remember, though, that some of the money spent on documentation, evaluation, and dissemination also contributes to continuation activities. We do not try to break out all continuation costs from those other project components, but be sure to include any funds necessary for

EXHIBIT 17.7

1707.DOC

Continuation Plan: Budget Worksheet

Continuation Activities Cost							
Personnel & Fringe (project staff, partner staff, volunteers)							
Position	**Qty**	**Source**	**Cash or In-kind**	**Define Unit hr, wk, mnth**	**# Units**	**Unit Cost**	**Total Cost**
						Resource Total	

Travel								
Trip Description	**Qty**	**Source**	**Cash or In-kind**	**Air Cost**	**Ground Cost**	**Meals Cost**	**Lodge Cost**	**Total Cost**
							Resource Total	

Stipends & Honorarium							
Description	**Qty**	**Source**	**Cash or In-kind**	**Define Unit**	**# Units**	**Unit Cost**	**Total Cost**
						Resource Total	

Services & Consultants							
Description	**Qty**	**Source**	**Cash or In-kind**	**Define Unit**	**# Units**	**Unit Cost**	**Total Cost**
						Resource Total	

EXHIBIT 17.7 *(Continued)*

Equipment							
Description	**Qty**	**Source**	**Cash or In-kind**	**Define Unit**	**# Units**	**Unit Cost**	**Total Cost**
					Resource Total		

Materials & Supplies							
Description	**Qty**	**Source**	**Cash or In-kind**	**Define Unit**	**# Units**	**Unit Cost**	**Total Cost**
					Resource Total		

Facilities							
Description	**Qty**	**Source**	**Cash or In-kind**	**Define Unit**	**# Units**	**Unit Cost**	**Total Cost**
					Resource Total		
					Continuation Activities Total		

continuation in your project budget. As usual with budget discussions, you should have computed your continuation budget needs before completing the project budget that you sent to the grantor. If, however, that was not done, Exhibit 17.7 (1707.doc) will help you collect the costs of continuation.

Wise Guy

Well, I am forced to admit that I liked this chapter. Continuation for me is always an exercise in begging my board to come through just this once. I've never actually seen a continuation process before, didn't know one existed, and this one looks like it has at least a chance of success. However, I don't like not getting staff. That's how I get a lot of my work done, with grant-funded go-fers. I'll keep slipping them in. There's got to be something in it for me. That's only fair, isn't it?

Wise Lady

There are many other ways to tackle the "getting work done" aspect of any project. You just have to be more creative. Don't look at grant funding as a way to build a bureaucracy. It's not and it shouldn't be. How can you work smarter? Look at the work you already do and the work you intend to do in the project and think of other ways to get manpower. Can you get some from volunteers? What about your participants and partners? Can you make fewer people more productive by providing the right organization, support structure, and resources? It seems that we always want to throw money or people at a problem when a little creative thinking would provide a better solution. That's why we emphasize planning and thinking before doing. That's why we insist that folks think things through. Too many inefficient process and work situations exist because when some problem arises, those in charge have just said, "hire someone." That's not usually the best way to affect a solution. A well-thought-out grant project can grow and prosper and attract more funding for improvements and advancements. It can really solve problems for us all.

Conclusion

We come to the end of a long journey. Not many other fields in which you can work can be so demanding but so rewarding. Just think, you recognize a problem in your community, among your neighbors and fellow citizens. You design a solution to the problem. You find a funding source. You fully develop the project. You write the proposal. You get the money. You run the project. It works, and lives are changed. You have made a difference. You have contributed to the betterment of humankind. You have become a leader and an innovator.

About the Disk

Contents

Title	Exhibit File Name
Evaluation Process Checklist	1201.DOC
Goals and Mission Worksheet	1302.DOC
Identifying Stakeholders and Their Interests	1303.DOC
Evaluative Question Worksheet	1304.DOC
Worksheet to Develop Criteria	1305.DOC
Evaluation Strategy Worksheet	1306.DOC
Determining Source of Data Collection	1307.DOC
Form to Determine Sampling Plan and Timing	1308.DOC
Final Data Collection Plan	1309.DOC
Data Collection Tools Log	1310.DOC
Determination of Data Analysis Technique	1311.DOC
Evaluation Matrix	1312.DOC
Development of Evaluation Budget	1313.DOC
Stakeholders' Decision Making Table	1501.DOC
Project Dissemination: Target Audience Worksheet	1601.DOC
Project Dissemination: Personal Communication Checklist	1602.DOC
Project Dissemination: Formal Presentation Checklist	1603.DOC
Project Dissemination: Exhibit Checklist	1604.DOC
Project Dissemination: Video and Audio Production Checklist	1605.DOC
Project Dissemination: Brochure Checklist	1606.DOC
Project Dissemination: Manual Checklist	1607.DOC
Project Dissemination: Report Checklist	1608.DOC
Project Dissemination: Print Media (Periodical) Article Checklist	1609.DOC
Project Dissemination: Press Release Checklist	1610.DOC
Project Dissemination: E-mail Checklist	1611.DOC
Project Dissemination: Direct Mail Checklist	1612.DOC
Project Dissemination: Internet and Website Checklist	1613.DOC
Project Dissemination: Database Checklist	1614.DOC
Continuation Plan: Stakeholder Information	1701.DOC
Continuation Plan: Keeping Stakeholders Informed Worksheet	1702.DOC
Continuation Plan: Revenue Generation Worksheet	1703.DOC
Continuation Plan Project Budget Worksheet: One Year of Continuation Costs	1704.DOC
Continuation Plan: Return on Investment Worksheet	1705.DOC
Continuation Plan: Activities Checklist	1706.DOC
Continuation Plan: Budget Worksheet	1707.DOC

Introduction

The forms on the enclosed disk are saved in Microsoft Word for Windows version 7.0. In order to use the forms, you need to have word processing software capable of reading Microsoft Word for Windows version 7.0 files.

System Requirements

- IBM PC or compatible computer
- 3.5″ floppy disk drive
- Windows 95 or later
- Microsoft Word for Windows version 7.0 (including the Microsoft converter*) or later or other word processing software capable of reading Microsoft Word for Windows 7.0 files.

  NOTE: Many popular word processing programs are capable of reading Microsoft Word for Windows 7.0 files. However, users should be aware that a slight amount of formatting might be lost when using a program other than Microsoft Word. If your word processor cannot read Microsoft Word for Windows 7.0 files, unformatted text files have been provided in the TXT directory on the floppy disk.

How to Install the Files onto Your Computer

To install the files, follow these instructions:

1. Insert the enclosed disk into the floppy disk drive of your computer.
2. From the Start Menu, choose **Run.**
3. Type **A:\SETUP** and press **OK.**
4. The opening screen of the installation program will appear. Press **OK** to continue.

---

*Word 7.0 needs the Microsoft converter file installed in order to view and edit all enclosed files. If you have trouble viewing the files, download the free converter from the Microsoft website. The URL for the converter is:
http://officeupdate.microsoft.com/downloadDetails/wd97cnv.htm

Microsoft also has a viewer that can be downloaded, which allows you to view, but not edit documents. This viewer can be downloaded at:
http://officeupdate.microsoft.com/downloadDetails/wd97vwr32.htm

5. The default destination directory is C:\QUICK. If you wish to change the default destination, you may do so now.

6. Press **OK** to continue. The installation program will copy all files to your hard drive in the C:\QUICK or user-designated directory.

Using the Files

Loading Files

To use the word processing files, launch your word processing program. Select **File, Open** from the pull-down menu. Select the appropriate drive and directory. If you installed the files to the default directory, the files will be located in the C:\QUICK directory. A list of files should appear. If you do not see a list of files in the directory, you need to select **WORD DOCUMENT (*.DOC)** under **Files of Type.** Double click on the file you want to open. Edit the file according to your needs.

Printing Files

If you want to print the files, select **File, Print** from the pull-down menu.

Saving Files

When you have finished editing a file, you should save it under a new file name by selecting **File, Save As** from the pull-down menu.

User Assistance

If you need assistance with installation or if you have a damaged disk, please contact Wiley Technical Support at:

Phone: (212) 850-6753
Fax: (212) 850-6800 (Attention: Wiley Technical Support)
E-mail: techhelp@wiley.com

To place additional orders or to request information about other Wiley products, please call (800) 225-5945.

Index

Visit us on the World Wide Web

NONPROFIT
Resource Center

www.wiley.com/nonprofit

Our nonprofit website features:

• **A nonprofit catalogue** where you can order and search for titles online. View book and author information about our management, law/tax, fund-raising, accounting, and finance titles.

• **A threaded discussion forum**, which will provide you and your colleagues with the chance to ask questions, share knowledge, and debate issues important to your organization and the sector.

• **Over 500 free forms and worksheets** to help run any nonprofit organization more efficiently and effectively. Forms are updated monthly to cover a new key area of nonprofit management.

• **Useful links** to many nonprofit resources online.

The Wiley Nonprofit Series brings together an extraordinary team of experts in the fields of nonprofit management, fund raising, law, accounting, and finance. This website highlights our new books, which present the best, most innovative practices being used in the nonprofit sector today. It also highlights our established works, which through their use in the day-to-day operations of thousands of nonprofits, have proven themselves to be invaluable to any nonprofit looking to raise more money or improve their operations, while still remaining in compliance with all rules and regulations.

For nearly 200 years, Wiley has prided itself on being a publisher of books known for thoroughness, rigor, and readability. Please browse the website. You are sure to find valued titles that you need to navigate the new world of nonprofit action.

Wiley Nonprofit Series

For information about the disk see the **About the Disk** section on pages 361–364.